A CHRISTIAN APPROACH TO MUSLIMS
REFLECTIONS FROM WEST AFRICA

A CHRISTIAN APPROACH TO MUSLIMS
REFLECTIONS FROM WEST AFRICA

james p. dretke

William Carey Library

1705 N. SIERRA BONITA
PASADENA, CA 91104

Library of Congress Cataloging in Publication Data

Dretke, James Paul, 1931-
    A Christian approach to Muslims.

    Bibliography: p.
    Includes index.
    1. Islam--Relations--Christianity. 2. Christianity
and other religions--Islam. 3. Islam--Africa, West.
I. Title.
BP172.D73   261.2   79-11912
ISBN 0-87808-432-0

Published by the William Carey Library
1705 N. Sierra Bonita Avenue
Pasadena, California 91104
Telephone (213) 798-0819

In accord with some of the most recent thinking of the aca-
demic press, the William Carey Library is pleased to present
this scholarly book which has been prepared from an author-
edited and author-prepared camera ready copy.

PRINTED IN THE UNITED STATES OF AMERICA

To
BARBARA
whose self-sacrificing love
is an inspiration to all
and to
MOTHER and DAD
who brought me to Christ
and nurtured me in His love

Contents

Foreword

The Christian approach to the Muslim is a theme that is a
constantly recurring one. It *should* recur again and again
among those charged with the task of effectively conveying
the good news of God's reconciling love. It should so not
only because of the magnitude of the Church's task in communicating the Gospel to Muslims. It recurs because the
eternal Gospel itself is set in a changing world, and both
the bearers and receivers of the Gospel are participants
in change. It recurs because, given the natural human and
cultural diversity of both Christians and Muslims, there
is no single approach that can be judged to be the final
one. It recurs because the Holy Spirit endlessly continues
His ever-surprising work among His people.

Thus, in going back to this theme again and again, the
Church does not vacillate in purpose. Rather it renews itself and prepares itself for its task. In fact, perhaps
we should hope for and rejoice over a variety of approaches,
each constituting a facet of the mission mosaic. That variety will be a sign of life. It will also reflect realities, for there are great differences among Muslims and the
corresponding mission situations in various areas of the
globe. In dealing with this subject, there is, therefore,
an important place for specific regional studies. These
may seldom uncover approaches so particular as to be unique,
for there is a genuine commonness in Muslim faith and culture in the world. But they will detect indigenous aspects
of Muslim experience that will in turn be reflected in the
development of approaches relevant to the particular milieu,
and in similar situations elsewhere.

It is against this background that we welcome the appearance of James Dretke's *A Christian Approach to Muslims:
Reflections from West Africa.* With his long experience in
that area of the Muslim world, and especially in Ghana, he
is well able to reflect creatively on the theme of *Christian approach.* His contribution will undoubtedly be wel-
comed everywhere, and especially by those engaged in the
sharing of the Gospel with Muslims on the African continent.
The William Carey Library is pleased to make available this
interesting and lively study by the current director of the
Islam in Africa project.

Roland E. Miller
*Editor, William Carey Library
Series on Islamic Studies*

Preface

A joyful adventure and great blessing await those Christian
and Muslim men and women of faith who are courageous enough
to seek to cross the communication barriers that separate
Christians and Muslims. The author, for the past fifteen
years, has been engaged in just that kind of an enterprise
as part of a team of consultants connected to an interdeno-
minational effort called the Islam-in-Africa Project. The
target area of concern is Africa South of the Sahara and the
goal is to help the churches in their understanding of Islam,
and in a faithful obedience to their being the "sent ones"
of Jesus' High Priestly Prayer (John 17). This undertaking
is called a "Project" because it is openended -- waiting upon God to act when Christian and Muslim people face each
other in honesty and integrity, witnessing to that which is
most sacred to each.

I am grateful for the guidance received at Fuller Seminary
(Pasadena, California) in the development of this book, especially for the help received from Arthur F. Glasser, Charles
H. Kraft, and Donald A. McGavran. I also owe a debt of grat-
itude to past and present co-workers in the I.A.P., especially
Willem Bijlefeld, Lamin Sanneh, Jeremy Hinds, Emmanuel Oyelade,
and many others, too numerous to mention. Besides these who
deserve special thanks, there are my former colleagues of the
Christian Council of Ghana staff and the Evangelical Lutheran
Church of Ghana, and the many hundreds of people from many
areas of West Africa along with whom I participated in various
Bible study programmes on the subject of Christian Witness
Among Muslims. Appreciation is also extended to *The Muslim*

World for permission to reprint "The Name Isa" from the
July, 1911 issue.

The perspectives which are here offered for wider consideration, development, and application grew out of these
associations and have been tested in various kinds of inter-
actions with Muslim friends and acquaintances. They, too,
have made their own unique contribution to my personal spiritual growth and understanding of Christian witness, which
contribution is reflected also in the pages of this book.
To one and all, I say thanks with the prayer that what has
been here produced will redound to the glory of God and to
the eternal peace and salvation of many souls.

I am grateful to Art Glasser, Chuck Kraft, and Donald
McGavran of Fuller Seminary (Pasadena, California) for
guidance in the development of this book. I owe a debt of
gratitude to past and present IAP co-workers, among them
Coby van der Steen, Wim Bijlefeld, Jeremy Hinds, E.O. Oyelade,
Roelf Kuitse, John Crossley, Emory van Gerpen, and Lamin
Sanneh. Besides these, there are my former colleagues in
Ghana -- members of the Christian Council and the Evangelical Lutheran Church, along with the many hundreds of people
from all over West Africa who participated with me in various Bibly study programmes around the theme of Christian
witness among Muslims. While thankful for their help, I
alone am responsible for what has been said. Appreciation
is also extended to *The Muslim*.

James P. Dretke
Nairobi, Kenya

Introduction

Daily millions of Christians and Muslims rub elbows with
each other during a variety of encounters. The door to a
healthy dialogue on spiritual matters is always open, but
seldom entered. Both Christians and Muslims have experienced frustration and discomfort in initiating a mutually
fruitful dialogue because of communication difficulties.

This study endeavours to isolate some of the communication problems that beset Christians and Muslims. Our primary concern is not, however, upon how and what Muslims
must do to alleviate these problems, but upon what Chris
tians can do. As God in Christ took the initiative in dealing with man's problem of sin, so the disciples of Jesus --
commissioned as God's ambassadors -- are to take the initiative in proclaiming this message of reconciliation to others.

The great gift which the Christian has to offer is the
gift of Christ Himself. As our story unfolds, we may be
surprised to learn how much Islam knows of Jesus and the
high honour and reverence He is accorded in Islamic thought
and worship. At the same time, we shall discover that for
all the Muslim knows about Jesus, he has never met Him as
He really is -- Lord and Master, Saviour of the world,
Resurrected, Ascended, and Returning.

Our story is told by a Christian named Yakubu. To begin
with, Yakubu introduces us to his neighbours, each of whom
is like him a fictitious character. Chapter by chapter
Yakubu and his neighbours interrelate with each other in

typical everyday life situations in present-day urban Africa.
The scene is set in Ghana, West Africa, the former Gold
Coast, but the life situations are common to other parts of
Africa and the world.

The conversations between these different characters give
testimony to varying religious convictions, prejudices, and
motivations. Together they represent a spectrum of religious belief running from orthodox through nominal Muslim
to members of a Muslim sect; the Christians, an equally wide
spectrum. Their interaction with each other illustrates the
kind of tensions and difficulties people confront as they
try to relate to each other across the barriers that grow
out of differing religious orientations. Yakubu, for instance, stereotypes each of his neighbours -- a natural human tendency, but as he tries to understand his neighbours
and live among them in faithful discipleship to Christ, he
discovers how inadequate and misleading such stereotyping
can be. People do change as they interact with each other
and influence one another over a period of time. Herein
lies hope for paving a new way in Christian-Muslim relations.

After the opening narrative in each chapter (which is set
apart by italic script), various of the issues raised are
examined from a biblical perspective. No effort is made to
answer all the questions that arise. The aim, rather, is to
present a study in the dynamics of Christian witness -- in
particular, as these dynamics relate to Christian witness
among Muslims. It is our prayer that Christian people will
be helped to a more loving and practical concern for Muslims
while being motivated to a more faithful witness to the
risen Lord Christ. For those who are interested in pursuing
some of these questions to a greater depth, the footnotes
and references should be of special value. Two useful ap-
pendices are also included -- the first, a discussion of
whether Christians and Muslims worship the same God; the
second, a related theme, Loewenthal's 1860 article thoroughly
exploring the question of Christians using the name *Isa* in
talking with Muslims.

As to methodology, we have attempted to combine a study
of the biblical substance of witness with an accurate assessment of where many Christians and Muslims are in their
relationships with each other, and in their understanding of
their relationship with God. We have endeavoured to analyze
some of the communication difficulties between Christians
and Muslims by way of a critical look at certain common mis-
understandings, misleading generalizations and faulty as-

sumptions. This procedure has helped to point out avenues
that are open for the pursuit of a potentially fruitful dialogue which, under the Holy Spirit, yields promise of mutual
edification in matters that affect present relations and
eternal destinies.

The fact is that Christians and Muslims are in some kind
of dialogue with each other whenever they meet. Their interaction may be stimulating and edifying, or it may be extremely negative. Whatever happens, there is always some
kind of communication in progress. Even when a Southern
Ghanaian Christian roughly crowds his way into a post office
queue ahead of someone he assumes to be an ignorant, illiterate Northern Muslim, he is in dialogue with that person
and communicating a message to him -- however negative and
demeaning his message. It is the conviction of this author
that Christians and Muslims have more to offer each other
than constantly fanning flames of superiority, suspicion,
distrust and antagonism.

Our thesis is that Christians, having been incorporated
into the Body of Christ, have a distinctive message of salvation to share with their Muslim neighbours, that this message has as its objective introducing Muslims to the living
and real Christ and incorporating them, too, into His Body,
and that the proclamation of this message can be presented
in such a way that Muslims are not alienated from understanding it before they have properly heard it.

Our most profound finding is that which sets forth the
primary distinction between Christianity and Islam as resting in the attitude of each towards the Law of God and the
practice which grows out of this understanding. For Islam,
the Law (*Shari'a*) is central: for Christianity, it is the
Gospel. Through God's gracious revelation in Jesus, the
Christ, the Christian has come to understand that "Christ
is the end of the Law" (Rom. 10:4). Man who is found wanting under the Law receives a new stature of dignity before
God and man through Christ's having become a curse for us.
His fulfilling of the Law for us gives us a new freedom to
love and to serve our fellow man.

Whenever this important and essential distinction between
the Law and the Gospel is minimized, Christianity's message
to mankind appears no different from Islam's. As Satan
works among men, he keeps pushing the Law into prominence
in such a way that the Gospel is often overshadowed. When
that happens, Christianity loses its distinctive message

and preaches the same message of reliance upon self and the
Law as does Islam. Because the potential for lapsing from
a dependence upon God's grace to a dependence upon our own
feeble efforts is always with us, we come to realize that
Christians are as continually and absolutely dependent upon
the grace of God as are the people they are inviting to
share in that grace.

Herein, we discover, rests an unexpected power in the
Christian's witness to the Muslim. Looking to the resurrected Lord Jesus for new strength each day, he demonstrates
in his daily living, conversation, and example what it is
to live the forgiven life. Standing as a visible testimony
to God's redeeming, sanctifying, and sustaining work in the
midst of men -- not upon his own merit, but upon Christ's
and under the power of the Holy Spirit -- he invites men to
become part of God's fellowship by way of repentance and
faith in Christ. Moved by this creative dynamic, and carrying the highest credentials in the world, people like this
-- their pride first broken by God's Law, their honour then
restored by God's forgiveness -- are called to build bridges
between God who loves and man who desperately needs assurances of that love. Having personally experienced that
love, they are anointed the King's ambassadors. With Yakubu
they mean it when they say, "Muhammadu, God loves you ...
Muhammadu, we love you, too." In this spirit a born-again
Christian approaches his Muslim neighbour.

1

Akwaba — Meet Me and My Neighbours[1]

SUNANA YAKUBU

When speaking Hausa, I introduce myself by saying "Sunana Yakubu" (My name is Yakubu). Although I am called Yakubu, I am a Christian.[2] While this may not strike some of you as strange, it will strike others as being quite unusual. Anyone whose name is Yakubu ought to be a Muslim.

The argument over whether or not I should be a Muslim because my name is Yakubu is typical of the mystery and the tension I feel at many different points in my life. There is the question of our neighbourhood -- some of us Christian, some of us Muslim, and how we are to relate to each other. There is not only the question of how I should interact with Muslims and they with me, but how we as Christians are to interact with one another. Then, there are other questions I wonder about: Were I to have been a Muslim and given a choice of being a Christian or a Muslim, would I now be a Muslim and not a Christian? If I had been a Muslim, would I be a different kind of Christian than I am now? Being a Christian, am I like a Muslim in any way, or is it all a matter of differences? Is being a Christian really that different from being a Muslim? What does it mean that I am a Christian and not a Muslim? Is it possible for me, a Christian, to understand what being a Muslim is like? If people call me Yakubu, why am I supposed to be a Muslim?

MY NEIGHBOURHOOD

Alihu

Alihu, my next door neighbour to the right, is a Muslim.
He finds it odd that I am called Yakubu and that I am not a
Muslim. Our children play together, but there is a growing
barrier between them. You see, my children are going to
school while Alihu's children have stopped. He is afraid
that while his children are learning English, they are going to be weaned away from their religion. It is better
they continue only in the Arabic school. Alihu feels that
when they finish the Quran, they will have learned all that
is important to know in life.

All the same, Alihu is a good neighbour. He is hardwork-
ing and honest. He says his prayers regularly -- at least
five times in the day, and takes his religion very seriously.
If I had a big trouble, I would go to Alihu for help. If he
needs help, even if he needs a loan, I will try to assist.
I know I can trust Alihu, which is more than I can say for
some of my Christian neighbours.

Muhammadu

My neighbour across the road is also a Muslim. His name
is Muhammadu, and he is quite a different Muslim from Alihu.
He doesn't go to the mosque on Fridays, and he isn't regular
with his prayers. In fact, he doesn't see why they have to
be said that often, or for that matter, why they have to be
said in Arabic at all. Arabic is not his language, he says.
He thinks most of the malams are out of touch with the times,
as is Alihu, whom Muhammadu regards as ignorant and backward.
That's one of the reasons why there's a growing animosity
between Alihu and Muhammadu.

My children have a lot of fun with Muhammadu's kids. They
go to school together, and it seems they have a lot in common with each other. All of them are planning to go on to
college after finishing high school.

Matthew

Matthew, the neighbour to our left, is a Christian. Unfortunately, we don't get along very well. He lets his goats
run around all over the neighbourhood, and they've caused
problems for everybody. It wouldn't be so bad if Matthew
would think of compensating us for what his goats ruin. In

the village he could never get away with this kind of management, but it's different in the town. Another thing,
Matthew has a telephone while the rest of us do not. He's
quite open about the fact that he gave a bribe to get it,
but he says he had no way out -- he can't get along without
a phone in his business. Now that Matthew's children are
old enough to make their own decisions, they don't have to
go to Sunday School or church unless they want to. They
usually go on Easter and Christmas, but the rest of the time
their father keeps them busy on Sundays washing the car or
his clothes, or sometimes he sends them to the farm.

When you hear Matthew talk, he seems to feel that he's
made it pretty good without God. He saw a lot of people in
America and England who got along good without church, and
he feels that if he wants to, he can do the same. In fact,
one day when I hinted to him that we had missed him at
church, he seemed provoked and told me that if I wanted to
take religion seriously that was fine with him. He took
God seriously all right, but as for church and all that,
everyone is free to serve God in his own way.

Oh, I forgot to tell you about Muhammadu's oldest daughter. It was she who was recently married to Matthew's
oldest son. You can imagine the stir which that created,
both close to home, and in the whole community!

Abdullahi

In order that you get the neighbourhood picture straight,
I should also say something about a few other people. One
is Muhammadu's nightwatch, Abdullahi.[4] Abdullahi is typical
of a lot of people who are settling in the city today. He
comes from somewhere in the North, but he's only become a
Muslim since moving into Alihu's boys' quarters.[5] When he
came south about a year ago, he didn't have any place to
stay, and a friend of Alihu's, also from the North, made the
arrangements.

Abdullahi came south without his wife. Last year, during
the rainy season, he went home to see her and to help with
the farming, but this year he says he's only going home when
he has leave -- that will be two weeks during the harvest
season.

I still don't know how much of a Muslim Abdullahi is. A
malam gave him the name Abdullahi when he was born, but he
really never knew what Islam was all about until he began to

see Alihu at prayer. Alihu told him he could stay with him
as long as he wanted to, but that he ought to start saying
his prayers, too. When Abdullahi hinted that he didn't
know the prayers, Alihu said he would teach him. Now
Abdullahi knows the motions and the words, and he does them
regularly, but I'm not sure he knows what they mean since
everything is done in Arabic. It seems he does them because
he feels it offers him the kind of protection he needs when
in the city.

The Ghana Muslim Mission and the Muslim Community[6]

I know Abdullahi is in some turmoil as to just what he's
going to do. He likes staying in Alihu's quarters, and he
likes working for Muhammadu, but the tensions between Alihu
and Muhammadu are starting to bother Abdullahi. As I said
earlier, Alihu takes his Islam very seriously. He is pious,
honest, and a man of considerable integrity. He is, however, a Hausa. He was born in Ghana, as was his father before him, and yet, to most Ghanaians, he is still a Hausa.

Muhammadu says it is time for native-born Ghanaian Muslims to throw off the yoke of the old Hausa, Yoruba, and
Wangara dominated leadership, and guide their own destinies.
That's why Muhammadu has become active in a group that calls
itself the Ghana Muslim Mission. The leadership of the
group is made up of young, educated Ga, Akan, Gonja, Dagomba,
and Wala leaders who say that the Islam of the old foreign
leaders is too much tradition-orientated, and out of touch
with the times. As one of the Ghana Muslim Mission leaders
told me, "Some of the old malams think that all you have to
do to be a Muslim is to wear a long robe, sit on a prayer-
skin, and chew kola nut, but that's not what Islam is all
about."

The people of Hausa, Yoruba and Wangara descent -- formerly, the three largest groupings of Muslims in Ghana--
have not been sitting idly by while the Ghana Muslim Mission
has been raising this challenge. They, too, have organized
themselves -- more so than was previously the case. They
call themselves simply, "The Muslim Community." Perhaps
you know that one of the troublesome questions among Muslims
is that of choosing an imam. When it comes to choosing an
imam, the Muslim Community says the most important question
is not whether the man is a Hausa, a Wangara, or a native
Ghanaian, but is he the most learned and the most pious man
in the whole community? They say that in Islam there is no
tribe, or nationality, but that all men are equal before God.

Abdullahi's problem came to a head a few weeks ago when there was some trouble because of a disagreement between the Muslim Community and the Muslim Mission. Even though Abdullahi's basic sympathies rest with the Muslim Community, he had to go down to the mosque and join hands with some Muslim Mission people who were trying to stir up a riot. He had to do this because he's working for Muhammadu. Abdullahi has, however, the greatest respect for Alihu because he knows him to be such a picus and such a good man. At the same time, he can't overlook the fact that he himself is a Ghanaian, and that's where his problem comes in. He doesn't really know whether he should side with Alihu in whose house he lives, or with Muhammadu, who is not only his master, but also a fellow Ghanaian.

Kwesi and Ama

Then, there is Matthew's cook and steward. Most of our neighbours have relatives from the village who stay with them and do the housework and cooking, but Matthew's wife attended school and now works in a government office. She and Matthew are trying to keep down the number of relatives who move in on them in the town. This means they don't want any relatives coming and working for them in exchange for room, board and spending money. They finally found Kwesi. He's from the same village, but is not related to them. After about a year, Kwesi wrote back home for a wife and Ama came to join him.

Kwesi and Ama have been married now for several years, but they don't have any children. Perhaps this explains why they have been so excited about the new spiritual church which meets in the house just down the road.[7] We thought we were through with those people when the City Council told them they couldn't use the school block for services any more, but that didn't stop them. They're carrying on all the same in a private compound, and it seems they are getting more people all the time. They gather every night from about six until midnight -- beating drums, shouting and singing praises to God, and sometimes even, throwing themselves on the ground. To me it's a strange kind of Christianity, and to our Muslim neighbours it's even more than that -- it's a perversion of the true worship of God. As you know, Muslim worship is solemn and dignified, and I can see why they are puzzled by the form of the spiritual church worship. As I said before, I'm a Christian, and their worship is something I can't understand or get used to either.

Kwesi and Ama are all excited because the prophet at the spiritual church has told them he can help them have a child. I think that's the main reason why Ama is there almost every time the group meets. Even Kwesi goes down every night after he finishes work, although he isn't anywhere near as zealous about the church as Ama is. In fact, he still thinks of himself and Ama as being Presbyterians.

I don't know what will happen if Ama doesn't become pregnant soon. Kwesi was talking with Abdullahi the other day, and Abdullahi thinks they ought to go to a certain Fulani Alhaji who lives in the next town.[8] This Alhaji has a wide reputation for working miracles. Abdullahi has never seen him himself, but he has heard that it does not cost much, and he has also heard that a lot of Christians go there, too. The Alhaji has gone on pilgrimage several times, and according to Abdullahi, he's had more "power" after each return from Mecca. Kwesi said that if this other doesn't work out, they would maybe visit the Alhaji. He asked Abdullahi to find out more about the man.

Abdullahi also said he thought Kwesi ought to think about getting a second wife. In fact, he was thinking about the same for himself, but for a different reason because his wife already has two children. He feels he needs a wife in the South while his other wife is working on the farm in the North. The only problem facing him is money, although he's sure his father will help him out whenever he's ready to marry another. If all goes well, he says, he might just come back from leave with another wife.

Jonathan and Pius

Each of Muhammadu's and Matthew's next door neighbours are also Christians. Even though they live right across the road from one another, they really don't have anything to do with each other. The one neighbour is called Jonathan; the other, Pius. As you might guess, Pius is a Roman Catholic, and this seems to be the whole problem as far as Jonathan is concerned. He says that Catholics are worse than pagans, and that any Christian who associates with a Catholic is endangering his own faith and giving a negative witness to the world. When I tried to defend Pius' good name to Jonathan (after Jonathan had questioned my friendship with Pius), Jonathan asked me if anything had really changed with Catholics. The Pope is still in Rome and Catholics still worship the Virgin Mary. Besides, they keep their people in ignorance by worshipping in Latin, and much of their worship

is nothing more than dressed-up idolatry. When I told him
that I thought other Christians ought to be excited about
the kind of renewal going on in the Catholic church, and in
fact, that they had stopped worshipping in Latin long ago,
he wasn't ready to listen to me at all.

Jonathan is a riddle to me in more ways than one. He
talks a very good Christianity, and makes me a little uncomfortable, because as you know, talk is cheap. In many
ways he is a likable person. He knows the Bible better
than I do, but he seems so inconsistent with how he uses
the Bible. He thinks more of obeying the rules his church
has set up about smoking and drinking than he does about
trying to understand what kind of a person Pius is and how
to love and befriend him even though they come from quite
different religious backgrounds. Jonathan doesn't have much
to do with our Muslim neighbours either, but I think he
might feel closer to them than he does to Pius. Even my own
relationship with Jonathan has been strained because I am
friendly with Pius.

Another inconsistency which troubles me about Jonathan is
that he accuses the Catholics of being subject to the Pope
in Rome, when as a matter of fact, he and his church are in
a kind of subjugation all their own. I don't think Jonathan
would be anywhere near as hostile to Pius if it were not for
the fact that the overseas church which is supporting his
church is so strong in its denunciation of Catholicism. I
can almost understand the position of the overseas church
better than I can that of the local church. The overseas
church can at least defend its position because of its historical experience, but I'm not sure that the animosities
and bitterness of something that took place elsewhere and
long ago should dictate our relationships in this neighbourhood right here. It's strange to me how we all come to be
so intimately wrapped up in controversies which come to us
from outside.

I haven't even mentioned something else that's strange.
It's purely an historical accident that Pius is a Roman
Catholic and that Jonathan is a Protestant. If Pius had
grown up in Jonathan's village and Jonathan in Pius', the
situation would have been just reversed. It just happens
that the Catholic church came to Pius' village and the Protestant church to Jonathan's.

The Two Ahmadis

Before we go on to other things, we ought to say just a word about the two young fellows who recently moved in down the road. They're Fanti, and they say they are Muslim -- Ahmadiyya Muslims. They've already antagonized our other Muslim neighbours because they say the Ahmadiyya are the true Islam. I saw one of them preaching on a street corner the other night, and I listened to what he said. Actually, it was quite a good sermon, I thought. The topic was the love of God and he preached with the Quran in one hand and the Bible in the other. As a matter of fact, he seemed to know his Bible a lot better than many Christians know theirs. Both of our Muslim neighbours, however, in spite of their differences, agree in their attitudes toward the Ahmadiyya. They say they are only a troublemaking sect, and that they have perverted the teaching of the Quran. Among other things, they accuse the Ahmadiyya of saying that Jesus was not taken to heaven, but that he died somewhere in India. After hearing Muhammadu and Alihu talk, it sounded to me as if the Ahmadiyya are to Islam something like the Jehovah Witnesses are to Christianity.

Animism

The rest of our neighbourhood is made up mostly of Christians, who represent somewhat the whole spectrum of the Church in Ghana. Most of them are Presbyterians, Catholics, Methodists and Anglicans, but then, there are also Apostolics, Assemblies of God, Lutherans and others. I suppose the neighbourhood reflects the National Census averages which show about sixty per cent of the people in town are Christian and seventeen per cent Muslim. The rest are listed under what is called African Traditional Religion, but to us who are Christians and Muslims, these are just pagans. In some educated circles, they call traditional religion animism, but in common everday language, you never hear that word. In fact, some of us wonder if this thing called animism is a religion at all. It's more just a part of our culture -- just how people live. In fact, none of our languages has even got a word for it -- it's just part of life.

The fact is that hardly anybody will admit to being a pagan anymore -- especially anybody in the town. When you are living in the town, it simply isn't very acceptable to say you are something else besides a Christian or a Muslim. This doesn't mean there still aren't a lot of pagans around. There are -- in the town as in the country, and many of them

are even right in the church, or they're a part of Islam.
Although they call themselves Christian or Muslim, they
really at heart and in practice are still animists. Under
a veneer of Islam or Christianity, they still follow the
religious practices of their ancestors.[9]

Yakubu

Sunana Yakubu, and these are my neighbours. As I said
before, the questions that trouble me are these: Where do
we go from here? How do I as a Christian relate to each of
them? I should repeat, perhaps, I am not a Muslim even
though I have chosen to be called by the name Yakubu. Actually, Yakubu is the equivalent of James in Hausa. I've been
trying to learn Hausa because it's an important language to
my neighbours, I mean, especially my Muslim neighbours. Even
more so than English, it's the language of the Muslim community in Ghana. This is just one of the many indicators of
the influence of the Hausa upon Islam in this part of the
world. As you know, many thousands of them settled here
along the kola trade routes established by their ancestors
centuries ago. As they came, they carried their religion
with them, and often, through intermarriage, or magic, introduced it to various people among whom they came to live.

My trying to learn Hausa (along with Arabic) is just a
little effort on my part to discover for myself the meaning
of a faithful witness of the Gospel to Muslims. Unless you
can communicate with someone and he with you in a language
you can each understand, it's hard to know each other well
at all. I'm somewhat disturbed that a lot of people have
misunderstood my intentions. Some Christians, unfortunately,
are so sensitive to the kind of separation they think ought
to exist between Christians and Muslims that as soon as you
show an interest in Islam, or a sympathy for Muslims, they
begin to hold your Christian faith as suspect. Even some
Muslims wonder why I, a Christian, would want to learn Arabic and Hausa.

Although you can see there are many differences between
us in the neighbourhood, the fact is that I have some things
in common with each of my neighbours. To some of us --
Alihu, Ama, our Ahmadi neighbours, and me -- our religion --
same, or different -- is something very important in our
lives. I'm not sure that religion isn't equally important
to Matthew, Abdullahi, and Kwesi even though the attitude
they express is only a very practical one. You use religion
if and when you need it. The rest of the time you just carry
on yourself because God helps those who help themselves.

*In many ways, I feel the closest to Alihu. Even though
he is a Muslim and I am a Christian, we feel a common bond
between us because we take our convictions seriously, and
each respects the other for it. So far, we have avoided disturbing our relationship by trying to pressure our beliefs
upon each other. I wonder if Alihu is bothered by this ques-
as much as I am. Sometimes my conscience bothers me that I
am not courageous enough to try to convert Alihu. Or sometimes, I wonder, is God pleased with Alihu's life as he is?
Certainly, he's much more of a godly man than is Matthew or
Muhammadu.*

*Muhammadu and I get along well together as long as we're
talking about government and crops and business. He's somewhat progressive in his thinking, and while he doesn't take
his religion very seriously, he's interested that everybody
has an equal chance, and everybody -- regardless of who they
are -- should work together. It's funny -- on a local neighbourhood level Muhammadu is even quite civil to Alihu, although he doesn't have any use at all for the Hausa on a
community or national level. I was surprised about another
thing also. When Matthew asked Muhammadu to contribute something to our Church Building Harvest, he actually sent over
a donation. In some ways, Muhammadu is a good man to have
in our neighbourhood. When he wants to, he has a way of getting people to work together in spite of their differences --
like when he helped to organize the campaign to get the
Government to establish a secondary school in this area.*

*You'd think that Matthew and I would be really close be-
cause we're both Christians, but sometimes I think this bond
is more imaginary than real -- especially when I question
whether or not Matthew is really a Christian. Time and time
again I'm disappointed over the kind of witness Matthew gives
to our neighbours. But, I don't know that it is for me to
say that he is or is not a Christian. The simple fact is
that to our Muslim neighbours, whether Matthew is a good
Christian or a bad Christian, he is still a Christian, and
in a sense, I'm judged as much by what Matthew does, or does
not do, as much as he is. In a way, it doesn't really matter
how I'm judged, but what concerns me more is that Christ is
judged by the judgments our neighbours put upon each of us.
Whether I'm happy over this fact, or not, the situation still
stands that all of us -- Matthew and I, Ama and Kwesi,
Jonathan and Pius -- are in this thing of Christian witness
together. When a Muslim or any other outsider looks at any
one of us, he doesn't see us as Catholics or Protestants,
Presbyterians or Pentecostals. He sees only Christians, and
he judges us all by what he sees.*

I often have a feeling there are things which I ought to
be saying to my neighbours, but I don't quite know how or
what or when. Some people say that it doesn't matter what
you believe as long as you believe. Then there are others
who say that a man's religion is his own private business.
Matthew's opinion is that we're all serving the same God
anyway, so there's no reason to bother too much about the
different ways we serve Him. Muhammadu echoes this same
sentiment. He says there are quite a few ways to get to
Kumasi from Accra, and that's the same way it is between
man and God. It's all a matter of following your conscience
and being faithful to what your fathers have taught you.

As for Kwesi and Abdullahi, they think there are certain
things we have to do to keep in tune with the world about us.
When they say this, they're talking about something a lot of
people would agree with. We're all surrounded by spiritual
forces -- like the Bible says, "principalities and powers."
The only way to survive is to keep these spiritual forces in
balance. You do this by giving attention to a set of prescribed ways at prescribed times according to particular
situations. When everything is done exactly right, it tends
to keep the precarious balance between man and the spiritual
forces of the universe in some kind of equilibrium. You
have to always be on your guard not to upset this balance.
If you take the necessary precautions so that no one else
upsets the balance either -- either unconsciously or mali-
ciously -- then everything will usually be all right.

Now Ama isn't like that at all. In fact, I probably have
more in common with her than with anyone else, even though
our forms of worship are so different. We had a talk just
yesterday. Jesus told us that we are His witnesses and that
we are to go and make disciples of all nations. Ama asked
me if I thought what Jesus said had anything to do with Muslims -- if they're a part of "all nations," or not. I told
her that I had wondered about that very question, and especially more so after I thought about some of the other things
the Bible says. There's the place in John 14:6 where Jesus
said, "I am the Way, the Truth, and the Life; no man comes to
the Father but by Me." Then, there's the place where Peter
said, "There's none other name under heaven whereby we can be
saved" (Acts 4:12). Finally, there's what Paul said in
I Cor. 3:11, "Other foundation can no man lay than that is
laid, which is Jesus Christ." The more I thought about it,
the more I concluded that if these words are true, there's
a special something about Jesus that can't be found anywhere
else -- a special something that everybody ought to know
about.

*Ama said she'd been wondering a lot lately about what
the truth really is, especially after overhearing an argument between the two Ahmadis and Alihu. The two Ahmadis
were trying to convince Alihu that Muslims should be more
active in trying to convert their Christian and pagan neighbours to Islam. If they don't do this, then they're not
good witnesses for Islam, but God will hold them accountable.
Alihu thought this was all a matter of God's will. If it's
God's will that you become a Muslim, you become a Muslim; if
it's His will that you die a kafir, you remain a kafir. The
Ahmadis agreed with Alihu, but they said that such a conclusion doesn't mean that when you are a part of Islam and follow the truth, you don't have to try to show the way of
truth to others. This matter about the truth had come to
bother Ama. She said, "I never thought of Muslims as having
the truth. How do we know who is following the truth? Do
they have the truth, or do we?"*

I didn't quite know how to answer Ama. How would you?

RELIGIOUS PLURALISM -- A NEW KIND OF CHALLENGE[10]

The preceding description of an urban community in
present-day Ghana is typical of the kind of community in
which a growing number of people are living -- not only in
modern Africa, but elsewhere in the world. The normal pattern in Ghana is still one of Muslims living in separate
quarters called *Zongos*.[11] More and more, however, the kind
of religious pluralism depicted in the foregoing is becoming
a fact of every day living for urban man.

If you were part of the community described in the preceding pages, where would you fit into the religious spectrum there pictured? Are you Yakubu, or Muhammadu, or Kwesi?
Or, are you Abdullahi, or Ama, or Matthew? Are you Alihu,
or one of the Amadis? Or are you a combination of some of
them, or different from all of them? Have you thought at
all about what is involved when people of different backgrounds interact with each other? Have you felt any tensions yourself in any such interaction?

History is filled with stories of the bitterness and ran-
cour which often accompany religious conviction. People
have died and people have killed for what they were convinced
was right. There have been overstatements and unfair generalizations which have distorted historical facts and shaped
prejudices which disappear from the minds and hearts of men
only slowly once they have taken a feeble root. To insist,

for example, that Islam spread across North Africa and into
Europe by peaceful means alone is to try to convert a half
truth into the whole truth. Similarly, to defend the Christian Crusades as a well-deserved punishment of God upon the
heathen Turk is to inject an interpretation into history
which is difficult to prove.

We do not, however, have to go so far back into history
to find evidences of religious conflict and the results of
such tension. We need only look on our own doorsteps, and
the problem is there. Alihu refuses to allow his children
to go to "English" school for fear that they'll lose their
religion. His position is strengthened by what he saw happen between Matthew's son and Muhammadu's daughter. To
marry a Christian is the same as becoming one, and the proper thing is to cut such a one off from the family altogether.
Muhammadu, in spite of his seeming laxity with his daughter,
forces Abdullahi -- against Abdullahi's own will -- to be
part of a riot-inciting group at the central mosque. Everybody, it seems -- except Kwesi and Ama -- has some resentment
against the noisy, handclapping, spiritual church at the corner. Then, there's the friction which arises because of the
relationships between Jonathan, Yakubu, and Pius. They are
all Christians, but Jonathan has trouble relating to Yakubu
because Yakubu and Pius are friends.

The foregoing personalities are -- like all of us --
complex individuals with a wide range of preferences and
allegiances. They are people with individual roles to play
in society -- some assigned and some achieved. Most of
their behavioral patterns have been borrowed from their
parents, or thrust upon them by their peculiar life situations -- among these are religious biases, tribal prejudices,
ethnocentric loyalties. As each of these people are now
hurled into the arena of life in the modern city, their basic convictions are daily threatened by a wide array of
challengers -- including the very people who live up and
down the streets of their own immediate neighbourhoods. Turmoil and heartache, misunderstanding and suspicion, distrust,
and distortion, fear and apprehension -- these, in varying
degrees, more often than not becloud the human relationship
horizon when time and circumstance hurl people of one religious background into the pathway of people of another religious orientation. Instead of bringing out the potential
best in people, these encounters tend frequently to bring
out the worst -- all sadly, in the name of God, and on the
authority of conscience and self-proclaimed religious conviction.

This study is concerned with the problem of religious pluralism. In approaching this problem we shall not investigate the complicated question of how much each individual is moved by his own conviction and how much he is just a puppet of his society -- his thoughts molded by its collective will, his actions dictated by its despotic stranglehold on individual personality and behaviour. We shall rather concern ourselves with the very practical stuff of everyday living -- how a Christian relates to a non-Christian in a way that gives glory to God, respects his neighbour of whatever persuasion, and yet, faithfully witnesses to the Christ he loves and serves.

Specifically, this study is an effort to explore and define new and meaningful relationships between Christians and Muslims. While the target area of concern is primarily relations between Christians and Muslims, the general principles outlined here will have a far wider validity and applicability. They should find a usefulness wherever Christians are concerned about approaching people of other faiths in a way that is pleasing to God. In fact, there will be much of value for Christians themselves as they try to relate more perfectly to each other.

The assignment before us is not an easy one, by any means. The situation is much like what Paul described when he said, "A wide door for effective work has opened to me," but in the same breath went on to acknowledge that there were "many adversaries" (I Cor. 16:9). From Perga to Troas God had "opened a door of faith to the Gentiles" (Acts 14:27; 2 Cor. 2:12). In some ways, the response was not as striking as what was first experienced in Jerusalem (Acts 5:14; 6:1), and yet, "the Word of the Lord grew and prevailed mightily" (Acts 19:20). The reputation of the apostles as men who had "turned the world upside down" (Acts 17:6) preceded them as new doors continued to open before them. Surprisingly, Paul's faith and confidence was not crushed even when his adversaries got the upper hand. Even then, under circumstances which many of us would interpret as altogether unpromising -- when in jail -- Paul petitioned his friends to pray that God might "open a door for the Word, to declare the mystery of Christ" (Col. 4:3).

Our circumstances for faithfully proclaiming the Word in our religiously pluralistic communities might appear almost as hopeless as Paul's. Paul met his unfavourable situation with a plea for prayer. Pray, as you begin this study, that God might open new doors before us so that understanding "the mystery of Christ" more fully, we might declare it more faithfully.

2

The Problem of
Where to Begin

A DEBATE ON THE BUS

*The debate was over whether Islam or Christianity is the
superior religion.*

"Yes, but why don't you Christians fast?"

I finally turned around to see who the contestants were.
They had started arguing from the moment we'd boarded the
Benz bus in Kumasi almost two hours previous, and it looked
as if they would continue the argument right on into Accra.
Wow, that would make it a four hour marathon! I admired
their stick-to-itiveness, but it was quite clear from the
beginning that the whole enterprise was more an exercise in
subtly clever insults than an active search for truth.
Simultaneously amused and aggravated -- for I was trying to
catch up on some needed rest -- I had only partially followed the argument in between brief snatches of sleep. All
along I wondered if either party was going to get the upper
hand, and how the battle would end -- whether in friendship,
or bitterness. It finally did end -- quite all of a sudden
-- thanks to the big market mammy who sat just behind me.
She caught everybody by surprise. And ... I mean everybody!
When she'd had enough, she turned around and shouted out
something in a language which I didn't understand. I don't
know if anybody else understood it either, but what she said,
or how she said it, brought a miniature roar of laughter from
everybody on the bus and terminated what had been an interesting, but quite obviously fruitless discussion. Maybe you
would disagree with me, but it seems to me that such debates
rarely get anywhere.

15

As the two men argued back and forth, and as I myself
puzzled over some of the questions they were asking, I wondered more and more if such heated discussions over seemingly insignificant things are necessary before people can
get down to some real substance in talking about their religious concerns. Maybe the normal pattern has to take this
kind of format. When you visit an old friend, you first
have to go through the small talk routine of set greetings
and questions about your trip, your health, and his poverty
before you finally get down to the subject of your visit.
Similarly, in discussing religious matters, maybe you have
to first play around with various surface issues which don't
really have any depth before you can set the stage for matters which have more of the real stuff of life in them. Then
again, maybe some of these preliminary questions have more
depth than is usually indicated by the shallowness of the
arguments about them.

Perhaps you've debated some of these questions yourself
and know what it's like to argue back and forth without
really making any visible progress. This factor didn't seem
to deter the debaters on the bus, for they kept on minute
after minute with each man challenging the other as if they
were in a sparring match. It was like a kind of game, each
trying intellectually to outmanoevre the other. It was evident that they weren't looking for answers as much as they
were trying to set traps for each other. Whether or not the
argument had any possibility of getting anywhere, I don't
know, and of course, will never find out. It all came to
such a sudden halt when the market mammy spoke up and blurted
out her unqualified opposition to the whole proceeding.

I was even a little disappointed when it stopped because
I wondered what the fellow was going to say about Christians
fasting. Before that, they had chewed around on questions
like: Why don't Christians pray? Why don't Christians take
off their shoes when they enter church? Why do Christians
clap their hands and shout when they worship? Why do Christians eat pork? Why do Christians worship three Gods? Why
do Christians call Jesus the Son of God? Why do Muhammadans
marry many wives? Why has Islam always spread by the sword?
Why do Muslims pray in a language they don't understand? Why
do Muslims worship Muhammad instead of Christ?

As the give and take went on, frequent reference was made
to the Bible and the Quran. Each disputant was struggling
with how to convince the other that his source of revelation
was the more authoritative. The Christian argued that the

Bible was the final authority because it had been completed
long before the Quran came into existence. The Muslim, on
the other hand, maintained that this argument supported his
cause all the more. Since the Quran came after the Bible,
it stood as a corrective to the earlier Scriptures and as
God's final Word to man. He said we had to use the Old and
the New Testaments with caution because the Jews had corrupted the Old Testament and Christians had corrupted the
New Testament. This was why nobody could agree on the proper text of the Bible and why Christians were always coming
out with new editions of the Bible. As for the Quran, it
could be verified that there was only one text -- the original given to Muhammad by the Angel Gabriel. This was why
Muslims insisted that Arabic had to be used all over the
world.

In some ways I was glad the woman put a stop to the argument. While I was amused by the wit and resourcefulness of
the debaters, I wondered if the argument was helping either
one understand Islam or Christianity any better. It seems
to me that life in our modern urbanizing society is surrounded with enough uncertainty and uneasiness without add-
ing to it by a lot of useless argument about religious
superiority. If anything, it seems to me that such arguments turn people off rather than on, and make them even
more indifferent to what ought to be some of their primary
concerns.

Do you agree with me, or not? Is anything to be gained
by such argument? Is this the way to begin a Christian witness to Muslims?

THERE MUST BE A BETTER WAY

While we find such unscheduled and unplanned debates on
religious issues amusing, and sometimes informative, there
must be a better way. As such battles of words rage on,
insinuations are made and conclusions are reached which
serve to erect barriers to understanding rather than bridges.
The truth is often distorted, inaccurate quantities are compared, and unfair assessments and judgments are made which
prejudice future attempts at breakthroughs in communication.

There are several problems with the kind of discussion
depicted in the foregoing illustration, two of the most obvious being the timing and the circumstance. Perhaps the
contestants had not intended to make their discussion the
main source of entertainment for the travellers to Accra,

but the fact is that it became that. Pushed into the fore-
front in this way, the debate took on exaggerations which
may not have happened in quieter surroundings. As it was,
each participant came to view himself as the temporary
standard-bearer of his religious tradition, and the various
encouragements -- pro and con -- from fellow passengers
fanned the flames of emotion even more. Another problem
revolves around the kind of questions raised in such debates,
some of which have some substance, but many of which are simply tossed out as thorns to aggravate and upset the opponent.
There is enough distance between Christian and Muslim as is,
without intentionally increasing the distance even more.

Unfortunately, an important communication ingredient is
often missing altogether in such attempts to talk about religious conviction.   There is little effort, if any at all,
to try to understand what the other person is saying. There
turns out to be a lot of talking with very little listening,
and while there is often a rich display of emotion, that
which emerges is little more than a deft intellectualizing
of religious assumptions and propositions.[12] Bereft of love
and compassion, such arguments stir passions, but promise
little in spiritual growth. There must be a better way.
There has to be a better way because the issues involved are
of much more urgency than the flippant arguments and laughter
over them would indicate. They are matters of life and death.

THE URGENCY OF FINDING A BETTER WAY

This subject is of such crucial concern because we are
dealing with matters of permanent importance. In the fast
swirl of life, the element of permanence is an elusive quantity for life moves forward at a frighteningly frantic pace.
Survival concerns, along with change, development, destruction, and decay occupy and usurp our central attention in
such a way that we are constantly engulfed with the sensation that life is a series of fleeting uncertainties. As a
consequence, we live with a gnawing insecurity which keeps
us in a kind of unsettled tension and turmoil. Old values
are questioned and new values take root feebly, slowly and
insecurely. That which injects a measure of stability into
what would otherwise be chaos are our religious convictions.
These dictate our behaviour in crisis situations and order
our actions in many ordinary circumstances.

RELIGIOUS CONVICTIONS AND MISSIONARY DIMENSIONS

For the purposes of this study, we shall define religious convictions as those beliefs and perceptions of reality which commit us to a particular way of life. There is, of course, a close connexion between our religious convictions and our philosophy of life, but there is a distinction. Religious convictions carry with them commitments which consciously, or unconsciously, regulate our behaviour. These commitments may or may not be there, when talking in terms of a philosophy of life.

The religious convictions of Christians and Muslims are similar enough to cause outsiders to wonder what all the arguments are about, and different enough to stir up bitter controversy between Christians and Muslims. This fact has many repercussions. The deeper our religious convictions, the less open we may be to investigate other alternatives for belief and action. The deeper our awareness of the consequences of our beliefs and actions for life and for eternity, the more zealous we may be in the propagation to others of our own patterns of life and ideas. The more we are convinced that our convictions are the only correct ones, the more intolerant we may be of the views and practices of others.

Unlike animism or some of the other great world religions, Islam and Christianity have both looked upon propagation as an important duty. Thus, they are both "witnessing" religions, or you might say, "missionary" religions. This basic orientation has often meant conflict -- like the kind described on the bus between Kumasi and Accra -- but it can also mean opportunity -- as we shall try to prove in the course of this study.

As we investigate this opportunity, we shall try to come to terms with the religious convictions and commitments of both Christians and Muslims. In the process, we shall endeavour to understand and analyze some of the things which combine to give Christians and Muslims their similar, and yet distinctive perceptions of reality. We shall make an effort to probe into the very heart of things as perceived by Christians and Muslims with a view toward isolating the factors which make Christian belief and practice different from Muslim belief and practice. As we shall see, there are significant differences, but we should also note that there are some fundamental agreements, one of them being the anticipation of an end to the world. Not only that, both Christians and Muslims agree that when the end comes, man will meet his ultimate and eternal fate face-to-face.[13] It is this conviction which gives a dimension of cruciality to all that Islam and Christianity have to say to each other and to the world.

If the message of Islam and Christianity were the same, or very similar, our problem would be greatly simplified. In spite of many efforts to harmonize the messages and minimize differences, however, the gulf between what Islam and what Christianity says remains wide and irreconcilable. This does not mean that, as a Christian, I have to stand in opposition to Islam's message being heard. No, on the contrary, I want to hear that message myself, I want to weigh it against my own and test it. In return, I want the Muslim to hear my message -- all in the full confidence that God's truth will triumph, for it is His will that "all men ... come to the knowledge of the truth" (I Tim. 2:3).

What considerably complicates the problem are the distortions and the misrepresentations we ourselves bring into the picture. Our understanding and interpretation of the central message of our faith, and the Muslim's of his, may wander far from the ideal, becoming overlaid with all manner of superfluous and useless cultural baggage. Sorting the situation out, and endeavouring to keep a clear, undistorted and unmuddled perception of reality and witnessing of that to the world is never an easy struggle. It is difficult because "we are not contending against flesh and blood, but against the principalities, against the powers, against the world rulers of this present darkness, against the spiritual hosts of wickedness in the heavenly places" (Eph. 6:12). This struggle of Satan's for the hearts and allegiances of men rages on today as it has throughout history and as it will continue until the end of time. He is the "father of lies" (John 8:44), and both Christians and Muslims must become aware of his subterfuges. He continually seeks to sabotage the truth and to lead men to forget God. This is why -- for Christians and Muslims alike -- these are matters of life and death.

CONFLICT, COEXISTENCE, COMPLACENCY, OR CREATIVITY

Given the kind of background described above, it would seem that the missionary concerns of Islam and Christianity could supplement and complement each other, rather than stand in mutual opposition. We have seen that Christians and Muslims are mutually concerned about the "end of time." They hold in common an understanding of man's accountability

before God. They believe that when the end comes, man will
face God in judgment. But this is where the antagonism
comes in. They also believe that their religions separately
and uniquely have the right answers for man in his unavoidable dilemma.

While similar, the Christian and the Muslim answers for
the human predicament are not the same. This situation
produces a wide number of reactions whenever Christians and
Muslims come into contact with each other. In many cases,
it leads to conflict. In others, it leads to various efforts
at coexistence, sometimes mutually agreed upon, but more often, forcibly controlled by whoever has the balance of power.
In still other instances, especially where there is a widespread nominality, there appears an overall complacency.

You must have observed something of each of these reactions in your own experience, or from your knowledge of history. History shows that the relations between Christianity
and Islam have often been marred with conflict.[14] There was
the victorious sweep of Islam across the north of "Christian"
Africa through the heart of "Christian" Spain to southern
France. There was the armed movement of Islam across the
"Christian" territory of Asia Minor, now Turkey, an area
which had been evangelized by the Apostle Paul himself. Then,
to counteract that offensive, there was the retaliatory move
on the part of Christendom to regain lands lost to the Muslims
via the unhappy route of military crusades.

It isn't only in ancient history, however, that we find
signs of conflict. We see them in our own neighbourhoods as
typified by the urban community described earlier, and we see
them in the bus dispute we just heard about. In addition,
Christians who were Muslims can testify to the conflict which
has accompanied their decision to become Christian -- estrange-
ment from their families, disownment, and sometimes, disin-
heritance. Muslims who were previously Christian can possibly
do the same. The simple truth is that conflict has been very
much a picture of the past, and is still a common picture of
relationships in the present. Conflict is an avenue still
open to us. Unfortunately, it is one which many Christians
and Muslims feel is unavoidable, and even ordained by God.

Other voices today, like those of Matthew and Muhammadu in
the opening chapter, are calling for coexistence. According
to them, each religion has its good points and its bad points,
and since we have no way of passing final judgment, nor any
right to, the best procedure is simply to carry on in our own

cultural traditions. After all, they say, all religions
serve a useful purpose -- although many who argue for this
alternative rarely take the time to define that purpose carefully. In a kind of vaguely conceived and naive spirit of
brotherhood, they conclude that people of all religious per-
suasions should simply bury their differences, or overlook
them. Having done this, they can then work together for the
goal of all mankind. As Muhammadu said, there are many roads
that lead to Kumasi, and so it is with man's pathways to God.
Since we have no way of determining which path is more correct than the other, let us minimize conflict in society by
simply agreeing to disagree. Coexistence is one avenue open
to us. It is an alternative which, like conflict, has a lot
of popular support.

Another alternative, sometimes linked to coexistence, but
actually quite another phenomenon altogether, is that of complacency. Many who argue for coexistence are, unlike those
who are complacent, actually quite honestly concerned about
people's religious convictions. They take for granted that
people have such convictions and that people will seriously
follow them. One of their premises is that as people have
different tastes in food, so people have different tastes in
religion. In some instances, the mentality behind such a
philosophy of coexistence sees God working out something good
for man in every religion.

Complacency, however, has quite another character altogether. Its enthusiasm for religious convictions and practices is little, if any at all. It feels that it has tasted
and tested the religious offerings of man and finds them
wanting. It sees religion as a remnant of man's supersti-
tious past, and is sold on the idea that man is master of
his own destiny. The feeling is that there are more serious
problems which ought to command our attention than the highly
speculative matters which worry Christians and Muslims --
things of heaven and hell and God and His will -- none of
which can be empirically tested, or proved. The idea is that
if somebody wants to go overboard in religion, that's his
privilege, but let's not have him trouble the rest of us. We
have observed how this was pretty much Matthew's philosophy.

Much of the complacency that surrounds us today is linked
to the secularism which continues to spread throughout the
world.[15] Secularism is a way of looking at life almost entirely in terms of its observable, man-controllable aspects.
It seeks to explain all that happens and all that exists in
terms of purely human cause and effect, without reference

to God or other spiritual beings. Secularism is not a new
development as some think. It was afoot already in King
David's time: "The fool says in his heart, 'There is no
God'" (Ps. 14:1). What seems to be new is that secularism
is taking a deep root in places like Africa and Asia.

In recent decades, many Christians and Muslims have come
under the deceptive influence of secularism. In the process,
their religious convictions have been diluted and weakened.
What remains is a bare skeleton of their original faith and
a visible compliance with certain outward requirements. When
secularism takes its full toll, the last spark of faith in
anything supernatural disappears, being replaced either by
a total faith in man or a refusal to trust anybody or anything. There survives only a hollow shell of allegiance to
former loyalties and a cool complacency towards even the
subject of religion.

We suggested above that there must be a better way. There
is -- a possibility as exciting as it is new. It is a possibility which has always been there, but which has, more
often than not, been overlooked. It is the possibility of
something altogether new happening between Christian and
Muslim. It is the challenge of being creative. We observed
earlier how Islam's and Christianity's orientation toward
"witness" is a source of conflict, but we proposed that it
could also be a source of opportunity. That opportunity
lies, in part, in tapping this dynamic of creativity.[16]

Our usage of "creative" in this context is not to put
man into the same category with God who created the world
out of nothing. God stands alone and supreme as the Creator
of all things, including man. Man, in spite of his limitations, however, when he is, as Christians put it, "in Christ,"
stands at the frontier of all kinds of new possibilities.
"He is a new creation. The old has passed away, behold, the
new has come" (2 Cor. 5:17).

Admittedly, we are now starting to look at this matter of
inter-religious relationships through specifically Christian
lenses, but that point of demarcation has to come sooner, or
later. I can fully empathize with a Muslim and seek to understand and define his attitudes, values, faith and practice
only to a point. Beyond that I cannot go because I am a
Christian. Similarly, with the Muslim. No matter how he
tries, he cannot completely enter my world of experience as
a Christian.

Thus, while we can both observe the conflict which has been and is now, while we both can honestly speak of a desire for peaceful coexistence, and at the same time can lament together the creeping spread of a secularistic complacency, the Muslim may not share with me the possibility that God can work creatively through us, His creatures. He may not be open to the possibility that God can speak through us to each other. He may not admit to the possibility of our growing together into a new and closer relationship with God and with each other.

But it is not only the Muslim who shares these apprehensions. Many Christians do as well. Many Christians have strong misgivings about anything good coming out of any kind of a relationship with Muslims. Raising the possibility, for example, that God can speak to Christians through the Quran meets with as much opposition among certain Christians as the suggestion that God can speak to Muslims through the Bible meets with opposition among Muslims. In the minds of many, a potential mutually fruitful relationship with others presupposes a kind of common ground. Unfortunately, Christians who put Muslims under condemnation do not agree to the existence of any such common ground. Because of this problem, it is difficult to appeal to reason, or even a sense of common humanity to bring Christians and Muslims together in a common pursuit of the truth.

Thus, we are right back to the problem with which we started -- the problem of where to begin. I cannot speak for the Muslim -- he may, or may not, be interested in making a beginning.[17] I can speak only for myself, a Christian motivated by the love which Christ taught, gave, and now, through me, shares with the world. That love does not give me a claim to superiority, for it is not "jealous or boastful, arrogant or rude." It does not seek to dominate, for it "does not insist on its own way." Even attacked, it cannot retaliate in kind, for it is "patient ... not irritable or resentful" (I Cor. 13:4f).

At the same time, this love is not a passive love. It is active in a constant ferment. It takes the same initiative among men which God's love has taken among us. "We love because He first loved us" (I John 4:19). It is a love which reaches out and embraces our neighbour, no matter who he is, or what his religious convictions.

If we're serious about being obedient to this love, it means that we meet our neighbour where he's at. We love him where he's at. We try to understand him and relate to him where he's at. It means that we can't set any preconditions on our love -- that he first become a Christian, or that he first adopt a particular kind of life-style, or even that he listen to our message.

The origins of this unusual love are draped in contrary-to-reason mystery. As St. Paul explains,

> While we were yet helpless, at the right time
> Christ died for the ungodly ... God shows his
> love for us in that while we were yet sinners
> Christ died for us (Rom. 5:6-8).

God so reverenced the life He gave us in creation that He spent Himself in death to redeem us.

Our love, patterned after His love, begins with the same great reverence for people. Whether our neighbour is ignorant, illiterate, prejudiced, argumentative, learned, or whatever, Christ died for him, and an immeasurable value has been thereby placed upon his person. We need to look up to him because Christ died for him. This is where Christian witness begins.

3

Same Words —
Different Meanings

"I didn't know you Muslims knew so much about Jesus."[18]

I had been telling Alihu about the argument on the bus.
He laughed and laughed when I told him how it all ended.
Alihu laughed again as he said, "I can just picture the sur-
prise on their faces when she shouted out her complaint."

As he laughed, I repeated the highlights of what had happened -- the argument, the woman shouting, the people breaking out in laughter, the embarrassed silence which followed,
and the comparatively quiet ride on into Accra. We each
chuckled through the second rehearsal as much as we had the
first. After his last laugh, he and I got down to a serious
discussion of our own over some of the questions the men on
the bus had raised.

We began by talking about fasting.[19] I admitted to Alihu
that I didn't fast, but when he asked me why, I didn't quite
know what to say. He even surprised me by telling of how
often Jesus fasted. He referred to the forty day fast in
the wilderness and also the time Jesus rebuked His disciples
for not healing the deaf and dumb man (Mark 9:29). As he
talked on, I recalled how Jesus responded to a similar question on fasting. He had been asked why His disciples did
not fast and He replied, "Can the wedding guests mourn as
long as the bridegroom is with them? The days will come,
when the bridegroom is taken away from them, and then they
will fast" (Matt. 9:15f).

26

I looked upon myself as a disciple of Jesus, and yet, I had never seriously thought about fasting. I began to wonder if some of us Christians had misinterpreted what Jesus had said on fasting. It seemed to me we had wrongly concluded that Jesus was against fasting. The more I thought about it now, the more I realized He wasn't against fasting at all. He was more concerned that our fasting be channelled along lines that are pleasing to God. In the Sermon on the Mount, for example, He said,

> When you fast, do not look dismal, like the
> hypocrites, for they disfigure their faces
> that their fasting may be seen by men. Truly,
> I say to you, they have their reward. But
> when you fast, anoint your head and wash your
> face, that your fasting may not be seen by
> men but by your Father who is in secret; and
> your Father who sees in secret will reward
> you" (Matt. 6:16ff).

It became clear to me, all of a sudden, that Jesus wasn't speaking against fasting as much as he was condemning the ostentation and show which often went along with fasting. The display which accompanied the Muslim fast of Ramadan was no exception. I was tempted to throw this up to Alihu, but somehow I didn't feel it was quite right to do so just then.

What bothered me more was why I hadn't thought more about fasting myself -- why I should, or why I shouldn't fast. I told Alihu I would have to think about this whole question a little bit more, and maybe we could talk about it again some time. That was when I changed the subject and confessed my ignorance to Alihu about what Muslims know about Jesus. It really surprised me to hear him talk of Jesus' fast in the wilderness and His healing of the deaf and dumb man. I wondered just how much more Alihu knew about Jesus. That was why I said, "I didn't know you people knew so much about Jesus."

Alihu's account of Jesus was a fascinating one. He told me of how Jesus stood in a long line of prophets beginning with Adam and ending with Muhammad. There were some twenty-seven prophets, and among all these, Jesus was more than an ordinary prophet. He had a special place in the line of prophets -- a place of distinction which He shared with only three other prophets -- Moses, David, and Muhammad. Each of these four brought a special message to man -- Moses, the *Taurat*, or Law; David, the *Zabur*, or Psalms; Jesus, the *Injil*,

or Gospel; Muhammad, the Quran. Alihu went on to tell me
that Jesus, or Isa, as Muslims call Him, has a special place
even among these four. He alone was born of a virgin, the
Virgin Mary. He alone healed the sick and raised the dead.
And -- He alone is returning at the end of time.

By this time, my heart had warmed within me, and I was
even beginning to doubt my memory -- that I had just a few
hours previously heard a bitter argument between a Christian
and a Muslim. I began to wonder what all there was to argue
about, if in fact, we had so much to agree about. After all,
all that really mattered was that Jesus was our Saviour, and
if Muslims believed that Jesus brought the Gospel, then perhaps the matters that divided us weren't all that important.
I had no idea at all that Alihu, my next door neighbour,
knew so much about Jesus.

Then came the bombshell. I asked if it was true that
Muslims did not believe that Jesus died on the cross. Everything had been going so beautifully that I was hoping down
deep that Alihu would confirm our Christian faith, rather
than deny it. The Muslim on the bus had said that Jesus
hadn't died, but since some of the other things he said
were rather questionable, I wondered if he represented a
correct Islamic point of view on this question. It turned
out that he did, because Alihu acknowledged that Muslims
could not accept the crucifixion as fact. The reason for
this was that Jesus was a prophet. He was the Messiah and
the Word of God. Prophets were holy, and God could never
allow a holy prophet to be hung upon a cross. "Whoever
hangs upon a cross is a curse," Alihu said, "and God could
never allow one of His holy prophets to be desecrated and
shamed before men as a curse."

Thus, at the last moment, while the earth was in darkness,
God rescued Jesus. Somebody else was crucified in His place.
Jesus was taken to heaven, and from heaven He will return.
When Jesus returns, Alihu added, He will preach for a time
and everybody will become Muslim. Then He will die and be
buried alongside Muhammad. Soon after this, the end will
come.

I was outraged at this story, and at the same time, I was
amused. How could anyone believe what Alihu said when the
Bible was so clear on the subject of Jesus' death? Yet, it
was clear that Alihu was sincere. He wasn't making fun at
me, or anyone else. It was also clear that with one fell
swoop, he had demolished the very foundation of the Christian faith and hope. He had done this by denying it.

I asked Alihu how it was ever possible to reach such a
conclusion. He asked if I hadn't read the Quran. I said,
"No."

"Well, you ought to read Sura 4 (157) sometime, the
chapter entitled *Nisa'a*. It tells you that the Jews tried
to kill Jesus, but somebody was substituted for him."

I asked who this might have been.

"Nobody knows for sure. Some think it was Judas; others
think it was a man from North Africa who was called Simon."

By this time, I will have to admit, I was flabbergasted.
I wanted to tell Alihu what Jesus meant to me, and where he
was wrong. I wanted to tell him that he was so wrong, and
so utterly mistaken. But I wasn't sure if that kind of approach would help anything. The only thing I was positive
of was that Jesus had died for me, and that Jesus had died
for Alihu as well -- whether he recognized this fact or not.
I had learned from Jesus that we all have a precious value
upon our souls and that Alihu was precious also in the sight
of God.

I thanked Alihu for sharing those thoughts with me, but I
said I had to disagree with him. To me, the most wonderful
news in the world was that Jesus had died for my sins. The
very thing which Muslims found so hard to accept -- that a
prophet of God could become a curse -- was the very fact
which brought such joy and happiness to me. He took my sins
and guilt upon Himself, and became a curse that I no longer
need to fear God's judgment.

All along, as I was giving this testimony, I hoped the
Holy Spirit might get through to Alihu, that he might fall
upon his knees in repentance, and take Jesus into his heart
as his Saviour. But, this didn't happen. He just listened
quietly while I spoke. When I finished, he excused himself
by saying that it was almost time for prayer. He picked up
the teakettle and the sheepskin he'd put down by the side of
the road, and strolled on down toward the Hausa mosque. I
looked up at the sun. It would soon be setting.[20]

While I continued on home, I was bothered by a question I
would have to ask Alihu sometime. What do Muslims understand
by the Gospel? They believe that Jesus brought the Gospel,
but surely, if they deny the crucifixion of Jesus, the Gospel
can't mean the same to them that it does to us. What, then,
does the Gospel mean to a Muslim?

PROBLEMS WITH A COMMON VOCABULARY[21]

Yakubu's last question zeros in on a major obstacle to
effective communication. When Christians and Muslims talk
with each other, they use the same terminology, but it carries different meanings. Yakubu was thrilled to hear Alihu
acknowledge the fact that Jesus brought the Gospel. His
rejoicing was short-lived, however, for no sooner had Alihu
made this announcement when, from Yakubu's point of view,
He commenced to deny the very thing he had affirmed.

To Yakubu the Gospel meant the Good News of God's redeeming love in Christ Jesus. Apparently, it meant something
quite different to Alihu, who testified to his belief that
a substitute had died in the place of Jesus. The question
that bothered Yakubu was this: If you take the death of
Jesus and all that it signified -- his conquering of death
and the resurrection -- out of the Gospel, how can you then
still call what is left the Gospel?

When you observe the distance that separates Christians
from Muslims in their usage of this one term, the Gospel,
you wonder if this is the only designation that causes a
problem, or if the same kind of problem applies to the
whole vocabulary of terms which Christians and Muslims use
in common. Ordinarily, people assume that words carry a
more-or-less consistent meaning, but our experience with the
word Gospel forewarns us of the kind of pitfalls inherent in
such an assumption.

What are some of the words that Christians and Muslims
use in common? The list could be almost endless, but for
our purposes, we shall note only the following:

Forgiveness	Hell	Prayer
God	Holy Spirit	Revelation
Gospel	Jesus	Sin
Grace	Judgment	Submission
Heaven	Law	Will

Our experience with "Gospel" should alert us to the fact
that we could have a problem with any one of these components
which fit together to make up the mosaic we call Islam, and
the similar but distinct mosaic we call Christianity. We
could broaden our field of comparison to include ethics and
ultimate concerns. In these areas, too, we might expect to
find deceptively similar and yet frustratingly different
definitions, emphases and conclusions.

Those who say "it's all the same" are in for quite a surprise when they start getting down to comparative details. Similar, yes, But "all the same," no! There are areas of similarity and sameness, but there are also crucial differences. These we want to explore -- which leads us into two intriguing questions: 1) What is the greatest similarity between Christianity and Islam, and 2) What is the greatest difference?

THE GREATEST SIMILARITY

This is not a simple question to answer. It would be much easier if it were posed in another way, perhaps like this: What are the similarities between Christianity and Islam? To ask what is the *greatest* similarity is to try to single out that one distinguishing feature shared by Islam and Christianity which makes them somewhat unique in the world of religious traditions and expressions.

We've already noted several similar components in Islam and Christianity. We've talked about belief in Satan and his power to deceive, and we've observed that both Christians and Muslims anticipate an end to the world and a final judgment. Is any one of these the greatest similarity between Christianity and Islam? Or, could it be quite another altogether -- a similarity which at the outset looks dissimilar -- the fact that Christians and Muslims *worship one God*, the Creator and Sustainer of this and all universes?

THE GREATEST DIFFERENCE

Before we pursue that question further, let us ask the opposite question: What is the greatest difference between Islam and Christianity? As with similarities, there are various levels of differences, from the trite and mundane to the highly significant. The following table illustrates the kinds of differences which people notice:

Christians	*Muslims*
Eat pork	Don't eat pork
Drink alcohol	Don't drink alcohol
Don't fast	Fast
Worship on Sunday	Worship on Friday
Rest on Sunday	No special rest on Friday
Marry one wife	Marry up to four wives
Wear tribal/Western clothes	Wear long robes/smocks
Pray any time	Pray five times a day

Christians	Muslims
Believe the Bible	Believe the Quran
Worship Jesus	Worship Muhammad
Jesus is the Son of God	Deny Jesus is the Son
Worship the Trinity	Deny there are three gods
Worship God	Worship Allah
Urinate standing	Urinate kneeling
Wear shoes during worship	Remove shoes for worship
Do not perform ablutions	Perform ablutions

Unfortunately, as with so much oversimplification and careless comparison, several of these differences are more apparent than real, or they are generalizations which are only half-truths, or even false. It's true, for example, that many Christians do not fast, but it's also true that many Christians do fast. It's true that many Muslims wear long robes and Northern smocks, but it's also true that many Muslims wear Western clothes, and it's true that many Christians wear Northern smocks.

For another thing, several of the suggested differences are misleading, or even untrue. For example, Muslims do not worship Muhammad as Christians worship Jesus.[22] In fact, many Muslims are unhappy with the name "Muhammadan" for this very reason. They say, "It is correct to call you Christians because you worship Christ, but it is incorrect to call us Muhammadans because we do not worship Muhammad. Call us simply Muslims."

ONE GOD?

It is the same with the supposed difference that Christians worship God, while Muslims worship *Allah*. Allah is simply the Arabic name for God. It should be noted that Arab Christians also worship Allah, and He is for them, as for us, the Father of our Lord Jesus Christ. We should also observe at this point that more and more Muslims use the name of God which is current in the language they are speaking. Thus, a Muslim who is speaking Twi refers to God as *Onyankopong*, or *Nyame*, while a Muslim who is speaking Yoruba refers to God as *Oluwa*. A Muslim who is speaking English refers to God as God, and a Muslim who is speaking Arabic, or Hausa, refers to God as Allah.

The suggestion that Christians worshipping the Trinity stands in contrast to the Muslim denial of three Gods is totally untrue. The Christian, as does the Muslim, rebels

against the idea that there are three Gods. This wrong
kind of equation arises out of a Muslim misunderstanding of
the doctrine of the Trinity, although it's quite possible
that a lot of Christians contribute to this misunderstanding by their own inadequate presentation to others of what
the Scriptures really teach and of what they themselves
really believe.

In spite of the apparent confusion in understanding on
this point, we submit that the greatest similarity between
Islam and Christianity is that Muslims and Christians worship one God. In bowing down before the one God, the Creator, both Christianity and Islam follow in the train of
their spiritual ancestor, Judaism. If we want to use the
word monotheist, it is quite correct to speak of Christians,
Muslims and Jews as being monotheists. In fact, we are prepared to go even one step further, a step which at the outset disturbs many Christians and some Muslims. Not only is
the greatest similarity between Christianity and Islam the
worship of one God, but it is the worship of the same God.
Yes, Christians and Muslims worship the same God![23]

Now, what disturbs many Christians is that Muslims deny
that Jesus is the Son of God and that He, along with the
Holy Spirit and the Father, are one God. The Quran is
quite explicit on this point in several places. An example
is Sura 112, which is memorized by all Muslims and is frequently recited:

> In the Name of God, the Merciful, the Compas-
>   sionate,
> Say: "He is God, One,
> God, the Everlasting Refuge,
> who has not begotten, and has not been begot-
>   ten,
> and equal to Him is not any one."

The Christian asks, then, "if God is not the Father of
our Lord Jesus Christ, and if He is not the Trinity revealed
in the Holy Scripture, then is He God? Even if you call
this Creator whom you have in mind God, He is still not God.
God is God the Father, God the Son, and God the Holy Spirit.
Any being other than this -- whether designated God or
Allah, or whatever -- is not God." This is the very reason
some Christians and Muslims insist on calling the God of the
Christians God, and the God of the Muslims Allah. It is a
way of trying to indicate that they are worshipping different Gods. To them, the God of Islam and the God of Christianity are not the same.

For those who hold to that conclusion and are unwilling
to acknowledge that Christians and Muslims worship the same
God, there is great appeal in the kind of confrontation between Elijah and the prophets of Baal. You will recall how
Elijah challenged the people of Israel, "How long will you
go limping with two different opinions? If the Lord is God,
follow Him; but if Baal, then follow him" (I Kings 18:21).
To some Christians, the Allah of the Muslims is like the
Baal of the Old Testament time, a false deity whose ears
are silent to the pleadings of men.

ONE JESUS?

The same kind of argument is brought to bear upon the
name and person of Jesus. When a Christian talks with a
Muslim, should he insist upon using Jesus, or *Yesu*, rather
than the name with which Muslims know Him, the name *Isa*?[24]
Some Christians feel that to use the name Isa is compromising the truth, for the Muslim Isa is not the same person as
the Christian Jesus. Not only does this question come up in
conversation, but it also arises in Bible translation. What
would be your recommendation, for example, to a translator
working among the Walas in the Northwest of Ghana? The
Walas are heavily Islamized and so the name of Jesus -- as
Isa -- is commonly known in their midst. Should a Bible
translation in their language reflect the Muslim influence,
or should it rather utilize the name Yesu which is widely
used in other Christian communities throughout the country?

Those who argue against using the name Isa insist that
Jesus and Isa are two different persons. Isa is *only* a
prophet in Islam; Jesus is *the* eternal Son of God. Isa is
only a great teacher and a pattern for holy living in Islam;
Jesus is really *the* Teacher and *the* source of eternal salvation (Heb. 5:9). Isa is *only* a man in Islam; Jesus is *the*
God-man, Redeemer of mankind,

> *the* Name which is above every name, that at the
> Name of Jesus every knee should bow, in heaven
> and on earth and under the earth, and every
> tongue confess that Jesus Christ is Lord, to
> the glory of God the Father (Phil. 2:9ff).

Since the Isa of Islam is only a distorted caricature of the
true Jesus, it would be better to introduce Muslims to a
wholly new person, Jesus, or Yesu, rather than to encourage
them in their own inadequate understanding of the "Alpha and
the Omega ... the Lord God, who is and who was and who is to
come, the Almighty" (Rev. 1:8).

We are faced with essentially the same problem when it
comes to the use of the term Gospel, or the name of Jesus,
or the name God (*Injil, Isa, Allah*). Should we use the same
words when talking with Muslims, even though the words have
different meanings to them than they have to us? Unfortunately, as some would hope, the situation is not corrected
by insisting on using a different vocabulary. God is still
God, whether we call Him God, or *Allah*, or *Onyankopong*.
Jesus is still the same Jesus, whether we call Him Jesus, or
Isa, or *Yesu*. The Gospel is still the same Gospel whether
we call it Gospel, or *Injil*, or *Asempa*.

Similarly, what the Muslim reads into the name *Isa*, he
will as well read into the name Jesus when it is introduced
to him. What meaning he attaches to *Injil* will as well be
read into Gospel. His understanding of the Supreme Being
will not differ whether he calls Him God, or *Allah*. All
this is true because Jesus and the Gospel fit as different
components into the religious systems we know as Christianity on the one hand, and as Islam on the other.

It should be quite clear from our discussion thus far
that a common Christian invitation, "Believe in Jesus," can
be received by a Muslim as something trite and shorn of any
special meaning. If he is a knowledgeable Muslim, he, of
course, "believes in Jesus."[25] He may even accept John 14:6
as a valid insight into the person and work of Jesus, "I am
the Way, the Truth, and the Life." The phrase which follows
-- "no man comes to the Father but by Me" -- creates a problem for many Muslims because of their discomfort with the
Father-Son terminology. Some, however, are ready to look
beyond that terminology to find a deeper truth in that passage, the truth that Jesus is a guide, a pattern, and an
example *par excellence* for all the "children of God" to follow.

It surprises many Christians to find that Muslims "believe in Jesus" but it shouldn't surprise us once we know
that, to Muslims, Jesus is the great prophet who brought to
man the Gospel. Not only that, He lived the Gospel He
brought in such a way that His life is an example to be
copied in holiness, piety, humility, kindness and gentleness.

The great mystery concerning that fund of knowledge which
the Muslim has about Jesus is that in the process of accumu-
lating that knowledge, rehearsing it around the evening fire-
side, setting it forward as illustrative of a beautiful life
which is to be duplicated, the *Muslim has never met the real*

*Jesus. He has never come face to face with the whole per-
son of Christ!* Herein is centred the problem and the challenge in Christian-Muslim relations.[26] Is it possible for
a Christian to give a faithful testimony concerning his
risen Lord and Master to his Muslim neighbour who already,
in all sincerity, feels that he has met the Christ of whom
we are speaking, and in fact, has the advantage over us in
that he has the last and final revealed word from God on
the subject of Christ?

Introducing your neighbour to Jesus, or *Yesu*, while turning your back upon *Isa* doesn't solve the problem, or meet
the challenge at all. It rather, more than likely, creates
new problems. It's far more reasonable and honest to meet
your Muslim neighbour where he's at. His picture of Jesus
may be warped and distorted. Let's not forget that ours,
too, is often warped and distorted. His understanding of
what the Gospel is and means and how it is to be used and
applied may be unclear, but so again and again is ours. His
vision and apprehension of God and His Being are stratified
in tradition and limited by human definition, but so also
is ours. Yet, in spite of all the pitfalls, it is by way
of the inadequate tool of language, hampered by the heavy
weight of tradition, prejudice and institutionalized con-
cepts that our witness must be made. It might seem easier
to begin with a new vocabulary altogether, by which technique we would try to alleviate the problems caused by the
same words, but different meanings. Such developing of new
vocabulary, however, would destroy an important communication advantage which a faithful witness should seek not to
lose -- immediate points of contact. Therein is an open
door to a continuity in life and experience which can be
built upon, rather than severed and destroyed.

CONCLUSION

To return to the questions which led us into this discussion: What is the greatest similarity between Christianity
and Islam? What is the greatest difference between Christianity and Islam?

The greatest similarity is that Christians and Muslims
worship one God. We have gone one step further: They not
only worship one God; they worship the same God. In the
author's own experience, the strongest evidence for this
conclusion comes from the Christians who were previously
Muslims. The author has yet to meet a single such individual who has the feeling that he came to meet a new God when

he became a Christian. The experience in every instance has
been the same -- that God, who was far off, has suddenly come
close to him in Christ. It is interesting to see with what
accuracy and exactitude the writer to the Hebrews (1:1f) describes the experience of a great many "Muslim Christians."
"In many and various ways God spoke of old to our fathers
by the prophets; but in these last days He has spoken to us
by a Son." The God of Islam is the God whom Christians, too,
serve, worship and adore.

If so, what then is the greatest difference between Islam
and Christianity? The greatest difference is not listed in
the table that appears above. We listed there the obvious,
the differences that quickly meet the eye. The greatest
difference is not so immediately obvious. This in no way
minimizes its importance. In fact, the subtlety of this
difference should somehow prepare us to take it all the more
seriously.

Strangely, this difference is one which is rarely touched
upon in conversation between Christians and Muslims, or in
the writings about Christian-Muslim dialogue. A great number of fine efforts have been made, and continue to be made,
to try to define the similarities and the differences between Christianity and Islam with a view toward bringing
more peace, harmony and understanding to each community. Unfortunately, many of these efforts achieve only minimal success because they neutralize their potential by dealing in a
big way with problems that are only peripheral, and never
really get down to the very heart of what distinguishes Islam
from Christianity.

It's quite possible that more Christians have not put
their fingers squarely upon this distinguishing factor because of the confusion that exists even in Christian circles over this very matter. We are speaking of the place
of the Law of God in the life of man. As with the doctrine
of the Trinity, so also with the use of the Law, we find
great confusion both in doctrine and practice among Christians of different denominations, and even within denominations.

The intriguing thing we come to discover is that even as
we sit in judgment upon Islam, we are sitting in judgment
upon ourselves, for the problems of Islam as relate to the
Law are not unlike the problems of Christianity as relate to
the Law. Basically, it boils down to the problem of Law versus Grace, or Law versus the Gospel. We submit that the

greatest difference between Islam and Christianity is that in Islam emphasis is on the Law, whereas in Christianity it is on the Gospel. Another way of saying this is that in Islam man's salvation rests upon his own shoulders and his obedience to the Law, while in Christianity it rests purely and solely upon the Grace of God. Islam is a religion of Law; Christianity is a religion of Grace. Islam tells man what he must do to earn salvation; Christianity tells man what God has done to give him salvation. The emphasis in Islam is on what man must do; in Christianity, on what God has done. Islam is a call to obedience; Christianity, a proclamation of God's initiative.

Again we encounter the problem which has been troubling us all along -- the problem of words and meanings. Sometimes they sound so much the same, but are so different. Sometimes they sound so different, yet are so very much the same. Hopefully, words and meanings will become clearer and clearer as we move on in the next chapter in an effort to get to the heart and meat of the matter. In the process, we shall thrill to that which is no accident, no mere coincidence -- the fact that Jesus is named, both in the New Testament and in the Quran, "Word of God."[27] The God who spoke of old by the prophets speaks to us today by a Son, His living Word to man.

4

Getting to the
Heart of Things

The "holy" people were almost finished taking their communion.

I had gone along with Matthew on one of those rare occasions when he went to church. It happened to be one of
the four-times-a-year communion Sundays. Matthew went to
communion, but on the way to church he joked about how he
had to pay up his last six months dues before he was permit-
ted to go. He apologized that I might not be allowed to
participate since, even though I was a Christian, I was a
member of a different church. Matthew said that, as far as
he was concerned, he had nothing against my going, but he
knew it was an official policy of the church that you had to
be a confirmed member there. As with so many churches, if
you haven't been confirmed by them, you are not allowed to
go to communion. My church had the same policy, but this
morning, in particular, I felt the hurt of that policy. As
I sat before God's holy throne in Matthew's church, it became more and more difficult for me to rationalize the necessity for treating fellow Christians the way we often
treat them -- as somehow outside the embrace of God's love.

We had heard a beautiful sermon entitled "Under Law or
Under Grace?" The text was Ephesians 2:8-10:

> For by grace you have been saved through faith;
> and this is not your own doing, it is the gift
> of God -- not because of works, lest any man
> should boast. For we are His workmanship, cre-

ated in Christ Jesus for good works, which God
prepared beforehand, that we should walk in
them.

The pastor spoke of how helpless we are in trying to weigh
out the balance of divine justice in our favour when left to
our own resources. Even our good works, he quoted from
Isaiah 64:6, are "like filthy rags." In fact, even the
faith with which we apprehend God's promises to spare and
deliver us, is not a work for which we ourselves can take
any credit. It, too, is a "gift" from God to us. He concluded:

> Praise God for His wonderful promises! Praise
> Him for His wonderful faithfulness in looking
> upon us with His favour in spite of our being
> "dead through trespasses and sins" (Eph. 2:1)!
> Praise Him for making us "fellow citizens with
> the saints and members of the household of God"
> (Eph. 2:19)!

> Now, in that unity which is also His special
> gift to His people, the Church (Eph. 4:1-6),
> let us come forward and together share that
> body which was broken for us, and comes to us
> in this bread. Let us drink from this cup of
> the new covenant sealed by His blood, the re-
> membrance of which is with us in this wine.
> Here, before this altar, as you eat His body
> and drink His blood, may you find your own
> inadequate resources refreshed and renewed
> through Him who is the very Source of our be-
> ing.

With that invitation and my personal need for strength
and reassurance, I wanted so much to go to the Lord's Supper. I wanted to express and rejoice in the unity which is
God's gift. I wanted to kneel with Matthew my neighbour and
confess our inadequacies at being the kind of Christian
neighbours and witnesses to the love of Christ which God had
ordained us to be. I wanted to be forgiven together with
him. I wanted to be sent back into our neighbourhood with
its tensions and its polarizations "in joy and in peace."
BUT, it could not be. I was not a member of this church.
All of a sudden, it seemed so ironic to me that the Holy
Communion which ought to unite us, so often serves rather to
divide us.[28]

As others went forward -- friends, neighbours, business
associates, even a family of relatives, I had strange feelings inside of me. I felt so alone. It was as if I was
part of this "family," and yet the "family" was excluding
me from an important and essential "family" activity. Funny,
even Matthew would have been excluded from his own "family"
if he hadn't paid his church dues up to date.

Before long, however, I saw that I wasn't the only one
excluded. There was also Tawiah over across the aisle. When
his wife and three children got up for communion, he just
remained seated. Somehow he looked so forlorn, and so alone.
I wondered if this is how it would be on Judgment Day. Of
course, I should have known he wouldn't be allowed to go
either -- he was a polygamist. He'd inherited his first
wife from a senior brother who'd been killed in a lorry accident some ten or twelve years previously. I looked around
to see if she was here, but then I remembered she was a member in the Catholic church. I wondered what kind of thoughts
were going through Tawiah's mind. Had he been touched by
the sermon as much as I was? Was he -- filled with his helplessness and guilt -- longing for a touch of assuring forgiveness from the Lord as much as I was? The tragedy of the
situation was that some of the men who were piously going
forward for communion were far more unfaithful to their one
wife than Tawiah was to his two. Yet Tawiah was excluded
because he had't met all the necessary "human" requirements.

To add to my perplexity, something that was as disturbing as it was humorous happened in the benches just ahead
of us. As the ushers moved down the side aisles, they came
to three girls who had come home from college for the week-
end. Two of them were in mini-skirts and the third was wearing slacks.[29] Apparently, the stewards hadn't been aware
that the girls were planning on going to communion, or it
surely seems that someone would have hinted to them beforehand that they would not be allowed to commune unless they
went home and changed clothes. You should have seen the
animated discussion when their way forward to the communion
rail was blocked. Some young men a few benches away got up
to argue with the ushers and just when it looked as if it
might disrupt the whole church service, the girls finally
acquiesced and quietly sat down. I thought to myself, I'll
bet those stewards won't be around when this service ends.
If they can, they'll be miles away from those girls -- they
won't want to face them again.

By the time the service came to a close, I was feeling
very uncomfortable. So much of our actual church practice
seemed so inconsistent with the glorious Gospel message we
had just heard. The Gospel is so simple and undemanding,
so reassuring and inviting and all-embracing that it seemed
to me nothing less than tragic that we had seen fit to
"protect" and "preserve" the integrity of the Gospel by
hemming it in with all manner of rules and regulations. We
had made so many efforts to keep our congregations "pure"
in doctrine and practice that we almost forgot that Jesus
came into the world to save sinners. We had even institutionalized our "purity" in the kind of procedures and regulations that surrounded our practice of Baptism and the
Lord's Supper.

If the Lord's Supper is really a means of grace by which
God blesses His people, why did Tawiah and the three girls
and I have to be denied that blessing when it was offered?
If we have to be in a kind of state of "purity" to receive
those blessings, is it right that our man-made standards and
criteria define that "purity" and set up regulations to insure it? The Table is the Lord's. It's odd, isn't it,
that we decide who is "worthy" to receive His blessing?

I raised some of these questions to Matthew as we relaxed
for a few moments in his house following the services.
Matthew said, "You know, in some ways we're no different
than the Muslims. They're always talking about how you have
to live to balance out your account before God.[30] 'Do this,
avoid that, then God will be merciful.'[31] The Bible, on the
other hand, shows God being merciful to us without any pre-
requisites at all -- even our faith is a free gift -- and we
turn right around and impose requirements on ourselves and
others for what God gives freely."

"I know," I said, "that's exactly what bothers me. God
is so wonderful to us, and we turn right around and take the
wonder out of His love."

A HISTORY OF BITTERNESS

Yakubu and Matthew were getting down to a very basic question: What is the place of the Law in the life of a Christian? We're talking here about Law with a capital "L," the
Law of God written in the hearts of men (Rom. 2:14f) and
revealed through the Scriptures. It is different from the
laws of men, although it stands as an inspiration behind
many of these laws. The written form in which we know this

Law most concretely and concisely is the Ten Commandments, but the five books of Moses, and even the rest of the Old Testament, are a part of that Law. Besides setting forth specific laws, they stand as an expanded commentary on the Law of God and its application to man-to-man, God-to-man, and man-to-God relationships. The scope of its concern and substance penetrates into every activity and area of life.

There is little disagreement between Christian and Christian, or Christian and Muslim over the general substance of the Law. What happens beyond that basic agreement, however, is a story of antagonism, agony, bitterness and actual battle with innocent victims suffering unjust persecutions at the hands of irate interpreters and defenders of the Law of God. The mentality that has prescribed force, persecution, and even death, has understood itself, to put the best construction on it, to be submissive and subservient to God's will as incorporated in His Law.

Many was the occasion, for example, when bloodcurdling cried of *Allahu Akbaru, Allahu Akbaru* rang out across fields of battle, shattering the confidence of those who were the enemy. The cries were, as the words said, a praise to God, "God is the greatest, God is the greatest." Islam swept all before it in the early centuries of its existence, and as it did, the concept of *jihad* (holy war) loomed more and more important.[32] For a long time, even Muslim theorists debated whether or not *jihad* was among the prescribed "pillars of the faith" -- one of the requirements to be fulfilled if one were to complete his "submission" before God. For, Islam means "submission" and a Muslim is "one who submits."[33]

How much that bitter chapter in Christian history known as the Crusades was a reaction and a response to the foregoing, or how much it was initiated by the plain working of Satan upon the hearts of Christian men, we shall not debate here.[34] The simple fact is that a bitterness grew up between Christians and Muslims, which as we have seen, persists even to the present time in many quarters. It has nurtured hatred and strife. It has created mistrust and suspicion. It has built walls of misunderstanding. So much so, that often the finest Christian witness is maligned as simply another sly attempt on the part of Christians to convert Muslims to Christianity.

We have noted that Islam, as is Christianity, is a "witnessing" religion. There is a compulsion to testify. There is a driving urge to take what has been received and to pro-

claim it to the world. We have also hinted that it is perhaps this dimension that has helped to keep Christians and
Muslims inflamed and in a state of battle against each other
on so many fronts for so many centuries. Whether the battles
have been physical or verbal, whether they've been bitterly
or blithely fought, they still have been battles. The language to describe them depicts conflict and tension, a joc-
keying for position, and a thirst to prove superiority. In
the background and in the convictions of each opponent has
hovered a vision of loyalty, submission and obedience to the
Law of God.

Some of this battle history is reflected in our hymnology
and our writings. We sing "Onward Christian Soldiers,"
"Stand Up, Stand Up for Jesus, Ye Soldiers of the Cross,"
and "Soldiers of the Cross, Arise." We speak of the battle
between Christianity and Islam for the hearts of men. We
talk of religious "encounter." All of this sounds so unlike
the Christ who said to Peter, "Put your sword back into its
place; for all who take the sword will perish by the sword"
(Matt. 26:52).

ATTEMPTS TO BRIDGE THE GAP

There have been various attempts on the part of Christians
to bridge the gap between Islam and Christianity. One writer
has attempted to show how the Christ of Islam and the Christ
of Christianity are compatible -- in spite of the fact that
Islam denies the death of Christ upon the cross (Parrinder
1965:120f,172f). Another has endeavoured to lead Christians
into a new witnessing relationship with Muslims by way of
hearing in the muezzin's calls to prayer an appeal for understanding, service, retrieval, interpretation and patience
(Cragg 1956). The shortcoming in this approach is that it
is so easy to read our own interpretations into what the
muezzin is saying. When all is said and done, we still find
ourselves standing outside the pale of Islam. A third scholar has proposed that we remove the word "religion" from our
vocabularies, replacing it with "tradition and faith." We
would then focus attention less upon religious systems and
more upon the individuals in whom "tradition and faith" are
united (Smith 1964:47f,141,175f). What this argument overlooks, however, is that merely changing vocabulary doesn't
significantly alter anything. "Tradition and faith" are
just as vulnerable to misunderstanding as is "religion." We
could go on to speak of the contributions of many others,
each of whom has helped open the door of understanding between Christians and Muslims a little bit wider. The mys-

tery remains, however, that while in so many ways we have
come to stand so close to Islam, we are yet standing so far
away.

DIFFERENT STARTING POINTS, DIFFERENT CONCLUSIONS

The simple truth is that different starting points lead
to different conclusions. These are not always easy to
isolate and identify, especially when it comes to religious
systems. What appears to be equivalent from one system to
another may not be equivalent at all. For example, the role
of Jesus in Christianity and that of Muhammad in Islam appear to be almost identical, as is the case also with the
Bible and the Quran. What appears to be simple and straightforward, however, turns out to be much more complicated.
Thus, it is quite possible to argue that St. Paul, not Jesus,
is more like Muhammad, and that Jesus is more like the Quran
since "in the Islamic system the central focus of revelation
is the Koran, God's gift to man and the heart of the religion" (Smith 1960:52). In Christianity, on the other hand,
the central focus is Christ.[35] Carrying these comparisons
a step further, the New Testament and the *Hadīth* ("Apostolic
Tradition," according to Rahman 1968:43) seem to parallel
each other more than do the New Testament and the Quran.

The kind of difficulty presented here shows itself all
along the line as Christians and Muslims seek to relate to
each other. Whether you talk about prayer, or the Gospel,
you are talking about terms that have the same form, but
different content. Because of the exasperation which grows
out of this difficulty, you find many Christians and Muslims
avoiding any kind of encounter with each other at all. There
are others who will talk with each other, but sidestep any
kind of conflict by simply acknowledging that everyone is
entitled to his own belief, and that God will surely be
pleased with the sincere efforts of every man. When this
happens, you find neither the Christian nor the Muslim being
really true to his basic convictions as a Christian or a Muslim, i.e., if he really believes that Christ is the only Way
of salvation, or that to acknowledge Christ as that Way is to
commit *shirk*, the most grievous of all sins in Islam -- the
"associating" of someone or something with God.

A FRESH LOOK AT SOME OLD CONCEPTS

Given these difficulties, the following effort lays no
claim to having discovered a new secret as to how a Christian
is to relate to a Muslim, or how he might more effectively

witness to a Muslim. It represents, rather, simply one more
Christian trying to enter the conversation that others far
more learned in Islam have long ago started. To this discussion which has been going on at more serious depths recently, we shall add something which is sometimes mentioned,
but very seldom seriously explored. We are referring again
to the contrast between the Law and the Gospel. The concept
of Law is central to Islam and holds the key to a fuller understanding of the Muslim; the concept of Grace is basic for
an understanding of the Christian faith. The first concept,
that of Law, has been uniquely developed by Islam and is
known throughout the Muslim world as *Shari'a*. The concept
of Grace, while not unknown among Muslims, has become a living and experienced reality among Christians in the person
of Jesus Christ. As unique as the development of the first
concept, the *Shari'a*, is to Islam, so is that of the second
to Christianity. As we shall see, however, the problems
raised by the concept of *Shari'a* are not unique to Islam.
They are an essential part of the human problem, the result
of which puts Christians and Muslims alike under the damning
judgment of God. And although the second concept is unique
to Christianity, the plan of God which is summed up therein
embraces also the world of Islam. It is the meaning and far-
reaching ramifications for faith and life of these two con-
cepts that we shall seek to explore in the remainder of this
book.

The *Shari'a*

   According to Fazlur Rahman, former Director of the Islamic
Research Institute, Karachi, Pakistan,

> The most important and comprehensive concept
> for describing Islam *as a function* is the con-
> cept of the Shari'a or Shar'. This word origi-
> nally means "the path or the road leading to
> water," i.e., a way to the very source of life.
> The verb shara'a means literally to chalk out
> or mark out a clear road to water. In its re-
> ligious usage, from the earliest period, it has
> meant "the highway of good life," i.e., reli-
> gious values, expressed functionally and in
> concrete terms to direct man's life.

He goes on to add,

> From the very beginning, a definite practical
> intent was part of the concept of the Shari'a:

> It is the Way, ordained by God, wherein man is
> to conduct his life in order to realize the
> Divine Will ... It comprehends both faith and
> practice: assent to or belief in one God is
> part of the Shari'a just as are the religious
> duties of prayer and fasting, etc. Further,
> all legal and social transactions as well as
> all personal behavior, are subsumed under the
> Shari'a as the comprehensive principle of the
> *total way of life* (1968:117f).

The history of how the *Shari'a* came to occupy this position of centrality in Muslim life and thought is extremely
interesting. This development is all the more intriguing
in view of how little the word *Shari'a* is used in the Quran.
Rahman's account of this development makes fascinating reading (1968:75-95,117-138). The whole process parallels in
many ways the development of the Talmud in Jewish life and
thought, with one significant difference.[36] The *Shari'a*
is not codified.

During the lifetime of Muhammad, there was no need to
debate any interpretation of the Quran, or any application
of the Quran to life. Muhammad himself was the final authority, and his example was the embodiment of perfect
islam (submission). When Muhammad died, the position he
had held as an arbiter of right and wrong came to be occu-
pied by his Companions. The authority for them and their
actions was still the Prophet. They acted as they did because they had seen the Prophet act in this way, or they
knew that if he were still alive he would act in such and
such a way.

When these Companions began to die one by one, the Community (*Umma*) sought to retain a connexion with the Prophet
and the Companions by means of the Hadith -- this body of
tradition which grew to an unbelievable number of some
20,000 items by the end of the Second Century A.H.[37] Each
of these traditions follows a similar pattern, as illustrated by the following which explain the importance of
Friday and the seriousness of neglecting it:

> Suwaid b. Nasr has informed us, on the author-
> ity of Abdallah, from Yunus, from az-Zuhri,
> who said that Abd ar-Rahman al-A'raj related
> how he had heard Abu Huraira say that the
> Apostle of Allah -- upon whom be Allah's
> blessing and peace -- once said: "The sun

rises on no better day than Friday, for on it
Adam -- on whom be peace -- was created, on it
he was put in the Garden, and on it he was ex-
pelled therefrom."

Humaid b. Mas'ada has informed us, on the authority of Bishr, from Dawud b. Abi Hind, from
Abu'z-Zubair, from Jabir, that the Apostle of
Allah -- upon whom be Allah's blessing and
peace -- said: "It is incumbent on every man
who is a Muslim to take a bath one day in
seven, and that day is Friday."

Ya'qub b. Ibrahim has informed us, on the authority of Yahya b. Sa'id, from Muhammad b.
'Amr, from 'Ubaida b. Sufyan al-Hadrami, from
Abu'l-Ja'd ad'Damri, who was on friendly relations with the Prophet -- upon whom be Allah's
blessing and peace -- that Allah will put a
brand on the heart of anyone who passes three
Fridays in neglect (Jeffery 1958: 182ff).

As these Hadith developed -- both the Hadith of the Prophet
and the Hadith of the Companions -- Islam maintained a ten-
uous link with the Prophet's supreme example of what it was
to live the "surrendered life."

The Quran and the Hadith, however, did not answer every
question as to how to live the life of "Islam." As time
and circumstances changed, new situations called for new interpretations and application of Islamic Law. Hence, there
grew up a "Third Root" of the Law, the *Ijma*, i.e., the "con-
census" or "agreement" of the Community. Thus, if an unanswerable question arose, being unanswerable in the sense that
neither the Quran nor any of the Hadith spoke directly to a
new and particular situation, the Community met, debated the
issues, and discovered the answer on the basis of what the
Quran and the Hadith said. It was soon realized that something more was needed to supplement the Quran and the Hadith,
something to stand alongside *Ijma* as an interpreter of the
details of the Divine Will for man. That something came to
be known as *Qiyas* (analogical reasoning). The process of
Qiyas was closely associated with another idea, that of
Ijtihad (original thinking).

The procedure was this: When any problem arose --
whether of divorce or punishment or whatever -- the first
appeal was made to the Quran. If no answer was found, the

Hadith were scanned and searched in the hope that somewhere in the life and practice of the Prophet or his Companions this very problem had previously been encountered and an answer given. If this search was in vain, however, the *Ulama* (religious teachers) met to reach some kind of conclusion on the basis of earlier precedents. If this process could not solve the matter either, a final effort to adjudicate the situation was made on the basis of "original thinking" and"analogical reasoning," an attempt to arrive at a new and appropriate decision on the basis of conclusions derived from an analogy of how the Prophet or the Companions would have acted in a similar situation.

The sum of all these answers which define perfect surrender to God is the *Shari'a*. The fact that it is not written orderly in a single set of volumes does not make it any less real or binding. It is there to determine and order life all the same. It is just that discovering the answer isn't always that easy, but the answer is there, somewhere in the Muslim past.

As mentioned above, the development of the *Shari'a* closely parallels that of the *Talmud*, not in time, but in manner. As the Hebrews approached the Law of Moses, they too were faced with a multitude of difficult questions. The Law said, for example,

> Remember to observe the Sabbath as a holy day.
> Six days a week are for your daily duties and
> your regular work, but the seventh day is a
> day of Sabbath rest before the Lord your God.
> On that day you are to do no work of any kind,
> nor shall your son, daughter, or slaves --
> whether men or women -- or your cattle or your
> house guests (Ex. 20:8-10).

The commandment was simple enough until you started to ponder the question "What is work?" The more seriously you took the matter of your obedience, the more zealous you would be in your pursuit of an answer to that question. What could you do on the Sabbath without breaking the Law? What could you not do? You had to do some walking about -- was this work? And what about eating? The history of how the Jews answered some of these questions appear in Jesus' denunciation of some of the Talmudic formulas in His preaching and teaching. Others can be studied in the copies of the Talmud still extant and used today.

We do not, however, have to go far out of our own Christian tradition to understand the kind of problem we are talking about here. Christians, too, have had their difficulties defining the application of God's Word to real life situations. Within our various traditions (Lutheran, Baptist, Assemblies of God, etc.) various definitions of what it is to live the Christian life have crept in. They have, in some instances, become just as binding upon the Christian as have Talmudic formulas upon the Jew, and promulgations of the *Shari'a* upon the Muslim.

Those churches, in particular, which have a guiding set of confessions (for example, the Roman Catholic with its Decrees of the Council of Trent, various papal pronouncements, and a long history of tradition, and the Lutheran Church with its Book of Concord of 1580) continue to apply answers to modern-day situations patterned after the approach to answering similar problems in the past. Even church and missions that have rejected creeds and confessions (Church of Christ, Assemblies of God, Sudan Interior Mission) have developed their own formulations of what is lawful and what is not, just like the others. Oddly, many of the strictures which have emerged in Christian circles have become as confining to the Christian as have the Talmud to the Jew and the *Shari'a* to the Muslim. This is regrettable because while there are the similarities noted above, there is still something basically different in the way a person who is in Christ ought to approach the Law from the way a Muslim or a Jew and, in fact, many Christians do.

In that which follows, we shall attempt to isolate that difference and, hopefully, this analysis will prove as helpful to the Muslim as it is to the Christian as we seek together to discover God's will for us and His approach to dealing with us. As the discussion proceeds, we shall come to realize what an overwhelming mystery the grace of God is, and how tremendously meaningful the concept of His grace is, both as it relates to God's dealings with man and as it prompts new relationships between the Christian and his fellowman (2 Cor. 5:18-21).

Much New Testament discussion revolves around the question of the place of the Law in God's plan for man. In this connexion it is crucial that we seek to understand, as well as possible, the whole argument of Romans and Galatians -- not only that we might fulfil our own "surrender" and obedience more perfectly, but that we might become the kind

of people God in His mercy has called us to be -- also to
the millions who are part of the world of Islam.

The Law

The overriding concern of the scribes and Pharisees
rested in a determined devotion to the Law of God. For
all the sincerity and regulated religiosity which went into this devotion, however, there was only a strong and
seemingly unsympathetic condemnation from Jesus. In the
blistering attack of Matt. 23, He called them "hypocrites,
blind guides, serpents, brood of vipers." He accused them
of appearing outwardly as righteous men, but being inwardly
full of hypocrisy and iniquity. Their regularity in tith-
ing did not excuse them from "the weightier matters of the
law -- justice, mercy and faith. These you ought to have
done," Jesus said, "without neglecting the others" (Matt.
23:23).

The Book of Romans begins with a frightening description
of what happens when people insist on following their own
natural inclinations in rebellion against the truth of God.
The portrayal is a disturbingly graphic account of how sin
leads to sin, and perversity leads to greater perversity.
The picture is such that a great many "religious" people
who have identified with God's Law in one way or another
fail to see themselves as part of the "base mind and im-
proper conduct" (Rom. 1:28) to which God gives up the
wicked. This makes the revelation which follows all the
more startling: "All have sinned and fall short of the
glory of God" (Rom. 3:23). The distance that separates
the glory of God and the works of men is so great because
"all men, both Jews and Greeks, are under the power of sin"
(Rom. 3:9).

While it is a shattering experience to discover that
one's accomplishments and efforts have fallen short of God's
expectations, it is tremendously exciting to know that God
has brought to bear upon this human predicament His own
plan of salvation. The terrible indictment which goes with
the Law of God is rehearsed in Galatians 3:10 (LB): "Cursed
is everyone who at any time breaks a single one of these
laws that are written in God's Book of the Law." The despair which would naturally accompany such a condemnation,
however, is dispelled with the announcement that "Christ
has brought us out from under the doom of that impossible
system by taking the curse for our wrongdoing upon Himself.
For it is written in the Scripture, 'Anyone who is hanged

on a tree is cursed'" (Gal. 3:13 LB). That stirring declaration lies behind the liberating proclamation of Romans
8:1, "There is therefore now no condemnation for those who
are in Christ Jesus." In view of what has happened in Christ
-- His fulfilling of the Law in our behalf, His satisfying
the penalties demanded in the Law by His becoming the curse
-- all of this stands in the background of Paul's dynamic
pronouncement: *"Christ is the end of the Law"* (Rom. 10:4).

Many of us tend to take that pronouncement with all of
its straightforward simplicity, and add a "but" to it.
"Christ is the end of the Law, but ..." Then we go on to
attach to that "but" all kinds of strange requirements which
have an uncomfortable resemblance to the "do not taste, do
not touch" stipulations condemned in Colossians 2. "For
freedom Christ has set us free," says Paul (Gal. 5:1). Unfortunately, that dimension of freedom, which ought to char-
acterize all of our living, tends to become buried under an
avalanche of legalism. When this happens, that very quality
of life which should distinguish the Christian life from
every other becomes hidden.

We tend to become erratic in our use of this freedom and
judgmental of those who are using their freedom in a way
different from ours. It is difficult for us to recognize
the validity of other patterns of worship and ways of administration. We tend to institutionalize our spiritual
experiences as normative and demand that others have the
same kind of experience. In our attempts to "protect and
guard" the Truth, we create untruths, hedging in our freedom with all kinds of rules and regulations.

These rules and regulations have to do with matters as
diverse as church dues and pre-baptism requirements. They
set up criteria by which the Christian life is defined in
terms of "dos" and "don'ts" which upon closer analysis are
nothing more than "the precepts of men" (Matt. 15:9). The
doctrines which warn against giving offence to the weaker
brother become catchalls for all manner of sanctimonious
piety which stands in sharp contrast to the admonition of
Romans 14:17: "The Kingdom of God does not mean food and
drink, but righteousness and peace and joy in the Holy
Spirit."

The tragedy of the situation does not rest as much in the
rules and regulations themselves as in the use that is made
of them. They gradually come to press as a damper upon the
free and joyous expression of the forgiven life. More unfor-

tunate still, they come to stand as a barrier between the
Gospel and the individual, even a wall between God's mercy
and the full enjoyment of that free grace by those who are
its designated recipients, the "broken and the contrite"
(Ps. 51:17), the "labouring and the heavy laden" (Matt.
11:28), the "hungering and thirsting after righteousness"
(Matt. 5:6). It is this grace which is bestowed upon man
without requirement, that Law having been fulfilled in
Jesus (Matt. 5:17). He now is "the end of the Law, that
everyone who has faith may be justified" (Rom. 10:4).

As in so many religious systems (including Christianity),
so in Islam, the Law still holds center stage. Among the
most common Muslim names are those which have an *abd* as
part of them. *Abd* means slave.[38] *Abdullah* is the "slave
of God." *Abdurrahman* is the "slave of the Merciful," *Abdul
Karim,* the "slave of the Generous one," and so on. To "do
your Islam" is to bind yourself to God as a slave is bound
to his master. Your total submission to God's will incorporated in the *Shari'a* is the response that the Master demands. The haunting question arises, however, as it did to
Luther: How and when do I know that my submission is complete, that my debt of gratitude to God has been paid?

The Gospel

God spoke to Luther's uncertainty even as He had previously spoken to Paul and countless others from the time of
Abraham onwards. His answer rested in the announcement of
His grace, the Gospel. It is no different with us today
The count of our trespasses has not been computed. The
satisfactions we have tried to render have not been measured.
Even with them, our being weighed in the balances would be
found wanting. God, in His freedom to act, has taken the
initiative. The joy of forgiveness is His to give, ours to
receive, for "God was in Christ reconciling the world to
Himself, not counting their trespasses against them" (2 Cor.
5:19). The dilemma of our uncertainty because of our failure to keep perfectly God's Law has been resolved. God in
his grace has been both Initiator and Actor in the human
predicament.

Paul uses the very word which is so precious to Islam in
his reasoned and warmly emotional testimonial concerning his
own people and their relationship to God. He bears witness
that "they have a zeal for God, but it is not enlightened,"
and then, putting his finger upon the very heart of man's
basic problem, he says, "being ignorant of the righteousness

that comes from God, and seeking to establish their own,
they did not *submit* to God's righteousness" (Rom. 10:2f).
What, we ought to ask, is God's righteousness? It is that
wonderful gift of which Paul speaks when he says, "It depends not upon man's will or exertion, but upon God's mercy"
(Rom. 9:16). God's righteousness is God acting on man's
behalf, taking him as he is, forgiving him his failures,
offering him a new humanity, for "no human being will be
justified in His sight by works of the Law" (Rom. 3:20).
God's righteousness means that the question of knowing
whether and when we have satisfied God's requirements has
been answered. There are no requirements beyond submission
to God's righteousness, that is, faith in Christ's sacrifice.
Christ has fulfilled all! Praise the Lord!

In the new situation that exists because of God's initiative, the Law which condemns and damns does not now begin
serving a new purpose. It still condemns and damns. It
still points up our inadequacy and inability to work out
our own salvation. It still serves as a mirror to continually and realistically reflect our true position before
God, a position of shortcoming and imperfection.

The fact that we have been freed from that which held us
in slavery means that we are now part of a new humanity.
"If any one is in Christ, he is a new creation; the old has
passed away, behold, the new has come" (2 Cor. 5:17). Because "that which is born of the Spirit is Spirit" (John
3:6), there is a power available to man that was not there
before. He is no longer left to his own human resources,
and it is on the strength of this new kind of possibility
that Paul holds out the inviting way of life described as
follows:

> I appeal to you, therefore, by the mercies of
> God, to present your bodies as a living sacri-
> fice, holy and acceptable to God, which is your
> spiritual worship. Do not be conformed to this
> world but be transformed by the renewal of your
> mind, that you may prove what is the will of
> God, what is good and acceptable and perfect
> (Rom. 12:1f).

It is not by our own strength, but "by the mercies of God"
that we are able to live out our lives to the fullest in a
new dimension of righteousness, God's righteousness, not
under compulsion, but under the freedom of God's grace.

To those who have experienced this new release on life,
God gives a responsibility of "ambassadorship," a theme we
shall explore at greater depths later on. The joy of living
in the forgiveness of God is a blessing to be shared with
others, not as a pilgrim who is still groping for the Way,
nor as a conqueror who has won the battle of life, but as
an ambassador who is every moment standing in as dire need
of the message he is preaching as is the man to whom he is
reaching. That message is not to be, as it is so often
formulated, a call to obedience to the Ten Commandments
(and the many others we unconsciously tack on). Such an
approach "makes trial of God by putting a yoke upon the
neck of the disciples which neither our fathers nor we have
been able to bear" (Acts 15:10). The faithful ambassador,
rather, being himself as much a recipient of God's proffered
love, proclaims, "We believe we shall be saved through the
grace of the Lord Jesus, just as you will" (Acts 15:11).

As hatred breeds hatred, and bitterness spawns bitterness,
so love nourishes love. The practical fruit of God's righteousness, as outlined in Romans, is a debt of love which in
the process of being paid, finds ever new commitments yet
to be met (Rom. 13:8). This love which flows from a never
empty well of gratitude to God for His mercy is that which
sends the ambassador forward, sustains him in his witness,
lends power to his appeal to men to be reconciled to God.

That appeal, which is as new to us each morning as it is
to those to whom we extend it, loses its freshness or its
vitality whenever we lag back into a pitiful and hopeless reliance upon ourselves and our own feeble efforts to fulfil
the Law. We are, then, right back where we started and in
need of the whole process being again renewed in our lives.
Because of our constant experience of failure and renewal,
we never stand above those to whom we witness. We stand with
them -- as urgently in need of God's continuing grace as they
are. To that need the Gospel speaks anew each day.

The beauty of this situation is that as the wonder of
Christ's resurrection blossoms forth in our lives each day,
it reassures us of our place in the new humanity which God,
through His grace, has called into being. Its call is to
"serve, not under the old written code, but in the new life
of the Spirit" (Rom. 7:6). Its joy is to "spread the fra-
grance of the knowledge of Him everywhere" (2 Cor. 2:14).
Its hope is "an inheritance which is imperishable, undefiled,
and unfading, kept in heaven for you, who by God's power are
guarded through faith for a salvation ready to be revealed
in the last time" (I Pet. 1:4f).

UNDER LAW OR UNDER GRACE?

One of the most deceptive traps Satan, the father of lies (John 8:44), puts before men is a false security in a hoped-for obedience to God's will as revealed in His Law. That Law, first planted in the consciences of men and later spelled out more fully in spoken and written revelation, serves quite another purpose, however -- "that every mouth may be stopped, and the whole world may be held accountable to God" (Rom. 3:19).[39]

As Paul's "spirit was provoked within him" when he saw how the people of Athens were trying to settle their accounts with God by way of idol worship (Acts 12:16), so Paul was astonished and angered as he saw how people were trying to pervert the Gospel of God into an instrument of bondage (Gal. 2:4). This was a new kind of idolatry, and in many ways a more dangerous kind, for while they "exchanged the truth about God for a lie and worshipped and served the creature rather than the Creator" (Rom. 1:25), they also severed themselves from Christ, their very hope of right-eousness. "You who would be justified by the Law," Paul says, "you are severed from Christ; you have fallen away from grace" (Gal. 5:4). "Note then," says Paul,

> the kindness and the severity of God: severity
> toward those who have fallen, but God's kind-
> ness to you, provided you continue in his kind-
> ness; otherwise you too will be cut off. And
> even the others, if they do not persist in
> their unbelief, will be grafted in, for God
> has the power to graft them in again (Rom. 11:22f).

We have been grafted in, "called out of darkness into His marvelous light" that we might declare His wonderful deeds (I Pet. 2:9). This is what the Gospel is all about, and this is what ambassadorship is all about. Drinking deeply of His goodness, His love, and His forgiveness, it is becoming "all things to all men" (I Cor. 9:22). It is being prepared "to make a defense to any one who calls you to account for the hope that is in you" (I Pet. 3:15). It is giving "no offense to Jews or to Greeks or to the Church of God" (I Cor. 10:32). It is being "entrusted with a com-mission" (I Cor. 9:17). It is representing Him "who desires all men to be saved and to come to the knowledge of the truth" (I Tim. 2:4).

As Paul says, "We have this treasure in earthen vessels, to show that the transcendent power belongs to God and not to us" (2 Cor. 4:7). As Jesus was vulnerable to man's animosity and hatred, so are the ambassadors He sends forth in His name today. But it is partly in this very vulnerability that the strength of their testimony lies, for they themselves stand as living examples of people upon whom God's grace in Christ has operated, transforming them into a new humanity.

Under Law or under Grace? "In many and various ways God spoke of old to our father by the prophets; but in these last days He has spoken to us by a Son" (Heb. 1:1f). "From His fullness have we all received, grace upon grace. For the Law was given through Moses; grace and truth came through Jesus Christ" (John 1:16f). In that grace we live; to that Christ we witness!

5

You Are
My Witnesses

Jonathan was all excited. He'd just scored a double
victory, he said -- one over a Catholic; the other, over a
Muslim.[40] He'd given them each something to think about,
and if they were damned to hell, it couldn't be said that he
hadn't tried. "They're the hardest people to convert, you
know," and he rambled on about his "successful witness."

Jonathan had heard that one of Pius' friends was a
mechanic, or a fitter as we called him, so he popped over to
Pius' house to find out more about the man. Pius had just
come home from work and was having a drink. He invited
Jonathan to join him. Jonathan went in and sat down but,
of course, refused a drink.

"No sooner had I sat down," Jonathan said, "and I began
to feel a compulsion to witness to Pius. I asked him if he
didn"t know that drunkards would never inherit the Kingdom
of God. They were going straight to hell, and not only
that, but because they led others astray by their example,
they were going to bear an even heavier punishment. I came
right out and told him," Jonathan said, "you can't call yourself a Christian and hold a bottle of beer in your hand. The
two just don't go together."

Jonathan said he knew the Spirit of God was working while
he "witnessed" because Pius just sat there quietly. He interpreted the silence as a sign that Pius knew he was guilty
of breaking God's Law. That's when Jonathan told him he
should repent, and if he would give up the habit, he could
be assured that God would be forgiving. If not, he'd just

have to bear the consequences of his actions. The consequences were everlasting hellfire. "I had to be frank
with him," Jonathan said, "You know, the Catholics are almost worse to convert than the Muslims." That statement
opened the door for Jonathan to speak of his second "victory."

The two Ahmadis had stopped by each house in the neighbourhood to pass out some literature on Islam. They were
also selling copies of the Quran. "I told them where to
get off," Jonathan boasted. "They came to witness to me,
but I witnessed right back to them. By the time they left,
they knew they'd heard the Word of God. They heard it loud
and clear.

"When you're dealing with people who are hardened to the
Gospel," Jonathan explained, "that's the time you can't go
soft on your witness. You're in a power encounter, and unless you recognize it for what it is, you're not going to
make any headway. That's why I came right out and told
them I didn't want any literature from their fake prophet
littering up my house and confusing my family about the
truth. I told them the Bible warned us that false prophets
would come, and that Satan himself would put words into
their mouths."

Jonathan went on, "I quoted the Bible to them -- you know,
where it says, 'By their fruits you will know them.' Then,
I said, look at how your prophet taught you to pray -- out
on the street corners for everybody to see. 'When you pray,'
the Bible says, 'you must not be like the hypocrites, for
they love to stand and pray in the synagogues and at the
street corners, that they may be seen by men' (Matt. 6:5).
I didn't leave out the next part either," Jonathan continued,
"'In praying do not heap up empty phrases as the Gentiles
do; for they think they will be heard for their many words'
(Matt. 6:7).

"You're no different than the Catholics," Jonathan told
the Ahmadis. "They recite all their prayers in Latin and
you recite all yours in Arabic, and none of you really knows
what you're saying. You recite the same thing over and over
again, and you think you will be heard for your much speaking, but it's all really nothing but 'empty phrases, many
words.'

"I knew God was with me so I went right on to condemn
their beggars and their show of charity. It's all there in
the Sermon on the Mount, you know, 'When you give alms,

sound no trumpet before you, as the hypocrites do in the
synagogues and in the streets, that they may be praised by
men' (Matt. 6:2).

"I finally summed up my witness with the words, 'Beware
of practising your piety before men in order to be seen by
them; for then you will have no reward from your Father who
is in heaven' (Matt. 6:1). I could see they were beaten,"
Jonathan said. "They couldn't even bring one argument to
defend themselves, or their false prophet. Praise God! It
was a great victory for Christ in both cases."

I'll have to admit -- I felt really disheartened after
Jonathan's visit. I couldn't share in his enthusiasm, and
I was puzzled over how he gloated over his supposed victory.
To me it seemed like a strange kind of victory, if you could
call it a victory at all.

Jonathan's "witness" seemed to be such a totally negative
kind of witness. In fact, it seemed to me that if I had
been in the shoes of any of the people to whom Jonathan had
"witnessed," I would have been turned off altogether from
the Gospel, rather than turned on by it.

What seemed to be the most tragic part of the two conversations was that the Gospel never once came through in
anything that Jonathan said. It was all Law, presented
judgmentally from a position of assumed superiority.
Jonathan was speaking down to the people in a "witness"
tinctured with pride. The very "practice of piety" he was
condemning in others dripped and glowered from every word
he spoke. Jesus must have meant something other than this
when He said, "You shall be my witnesses" (Acts 1:8).

I wasn't convinced either that all Muslim prayer was a
matter of hypocrisy or that holding a glass of beer in your
hand was incompatible with being a Christian. I could see
how someone might say that Muhammadu's prayer was hypocrisy,
but people could as well say the same about Matthew's. As
for Alihu, I found it hard to apply that judgment of Jesus
upon him. He was just too fine a man of integrity. If it
was hypocrisy, Alihu certainly wasn't aware of it. He was
too honest and sincere a man for anybody to label any aspect
of his life hypocritical.

While I was still mulling over what Jonathan had told me,
and thinking about what ought to go into a faithful witness
to the Gospel, who should walk in but Pius. After the nor-

mal greetings, he sat down and asked, "What kind of a nut
is this we've got for a neighbour? This guy Jonathan comes
over this afternoon, I offer him a drink, and what does he
do? He goes into a tirade against drinking. I just let him
rant and rave, but all along I was thinking, I've got my
faults, but I still don't think a drink once in a while is
worse than the prejudice, the pride, and the narrow-minded
piety Jonathan has. You know, he doesn't have a stroke of
love for Muslims, and he doesn't have any use for Northerners, and yet he goes on and on about the evils of smoking
and drinking and mini-skirts. I almost told him where to
get off, but he still is my neighbour. We still have to
live across from each other, so I thought the best thing to
do was just to let him have his say."

Before I could respond, Pius went on, "Speaking of Muslims, they're not so dumb, are they?" He'd met Abdullahi
on the way over to my house, and he asked Abdullahi when he
was going to go along with him to church sometime. Abdullahi
said he'd think about it, but he didn't know why we Christians played drums in church and shouted all the time. Pius
knew right away that Abdullahi was talking about Ama and
Kwesi's spiritual church, and so he said, "Well, don't let
that bother you, Abdullahi, that's just how some of these
so-called Christians do. They claim they've got the Spirit
of God, but once you investigate, you find they've mixed in
all kinds of paganism with their Christianity. What's left
isn't Christianity anymore. The thing for you to do is to
come over to our church sometime, or go along with Yakubu.
You'll find out what church is really all about. Don't,
whatever you do, get mixed up with one of those spiritual
churches. One other thing, don't judge the Christian church
by what you see there."

Pius thought for a minute, and then he said, "You know,
we've got to start standing up with a united front against
these spiritual churches.[41] They've already confused a lot
of Christians, and now they're starting to confuse the Muslims as well. In fact," Pius concluded, "I even told
Abdullahi that he was probably better off where he was as a
Muslim than to get all involved with one of those crazy
spiritual churches. People are only going there to get
money and, at the same time, every one of their prophets is
just filling his own pockets. It's a case of the blind
leading the blind."

Pius said he wanted to walk over to see his friend, the
fitter, and forewarn him about Jonathan. He asked me to

walk along, so I agreed. As we walked past the market place,
Pius nudged me and asked, "Aren't those the two who have
been selling Qurans and passing out Muslim literature in the
neighbourhood?" Sure enough, there were the two Ahmadis.
One of them was preaching while the other was sitting at a
little table with a white table cloth and a Bible and a
Quran. From time to time the preacher made reference to
one or the other. His friend was having a problem keeping
the kerosene lamp properly lighted.

We stood in semi-darkness at the back of a group of
twenty to thirty people. The younger of the two was talking
about how Islam is misrepresented and under attack, especially by Christians. He said, "The Quran says there are
people who take our religion 'in mockery and as a sport'
(Q. 5:60). They hear our call to prayer and they ridicule
our willingness to demonstrate our faith and our submission
to God as a testimony for all to see. They attack us for
our kindness and our charity. As the Quran says, 'Some of
them find fault with thee touching the free-will offerings;
if they are given a share of them they are well-pleased,
but if they are given none, they are angry' (Q. 9:58). Some
of them, even as the Quran says here, 'hurt the Prophet,'
peace be upon him, but 'know they not that for those who
oppose God and His Apostle, is the fire of hell? -- wherein
they shall dwell' (Q. 9:61,63)?

"It doesn't do any good to argue with such critics because, as the Quran says, 'They are a people who have no
understanding' (Q. 5:61). 'What, do they desire another
religion than God's' (Q. 3:83)? The Quran gives us an
answer to give them:

> We believe in God, and that which has been sent
> down on us, and sent down on Abraham and Ishmael,
> Isaac and Jacob, and the Tribes, and in that
> which was given to Moses and Jesus, and the
> Prophets, of their Lord; we make no division
> between any of them, and to Him we surrender.
> Whoso desires another religion than Islam, it
> shall not be accepted of him; in the next
> world he shall be among the losers ... But
> those who repent thereafter, and make amends
> -- God is All-forgiving, All-compassionate"
> (Q. 3:84-89).

The speaker continued, "Some of these detractors say
they believe in Jesus. They believe Jesus brought the Gos-

pel. The Quran confirms right here in Sura 5:49 that Jesus
brought the Gospel confirming the Torah of Moses. This is
why we Muslims accept the Bible along with the Quran. Moses
brought the Law, Jesus brought the Gospel confirming the
Law and the Quran was brought by Muhammad, confirming both
the Law and the Gospel." As the preacher said this, he held
up both the Quran and the Bible for everybody to see.

By this time, ten to fifteen more people had crowded
around. They were all men, mostly young men in their
twenties and thirties. It also looked like more members
of the Ahmadiyya had arrived. From the whispers to the
right of us, there seemed to be a group of Christians preparing to challenge the speaker when he finished.

While the speaker held the Bible and the Quran high,
another Ahmadi stood up, "If any of you in the crowd tonight are Christians, the Holy Quran has a special message
for you. Did you know that the Holy Quran has a special
title for you -- a title of honour and respect? It calls
you 'People of the Book' because you, along with the Jews,
were singled out of all the people upon the earth to receive a special revelation from God.[42] The Jews were given
the Law and the Psalms by Moses and David. We Muslims were
given the Quran by Muhammad. You were given the Gospel by
Jesus. The Quran asks, 'People of the Book, do you blame
us for any other cause than that we believe in God, and what
has been sent down to us, and what was sent down before'
(Q. 5:62)?

"You Christians criticize us on so many counts, but as
for you, everything is not right in your own household. What
the Quran says is true:

> When they come to you, they say, 'We believe;'
> but they have entered in unbelief, and so
> they have departed in it; God knows very well
>   what they were hiding.
> Thou seest many of them vying in sin
> and enmity, and how they consume the unlawful;
>   evil is the thing they have been doing.
> Why do the masters and the rabbis not forbid
>   them to utter sin, and consume the un-
>   lawful?
> Evil is the thing they have been working (Q. 5:64f).

"Have you," the same fellow continued, "seen the kind of
division Christians have brought into the world? Their

churches are at enmity with each other. Protestant doesn't
get along with Catholic. Presbyterian doesn't get along
with Pentecostal. Spiritual church is fighting spiritual
church. The Christian church hasn't solved the racial
problem either. It even supports white against black, as is
demonstrated in South Africa. We've seen what it has done
on the side of government to rape and rob our people and our
lands of our very own resources. The former Colonial Government even dragged our own people into war when the Christians
were warring with each other in Europe. Sura 5 has a special word for Christians:

> As often as they light a fire for war, God
> will extinguish it. They hasten about the
> earth, to do corruption there; and God loves
> not the workers of corruption. But had the
> people of the Book believed and been god-
> fearing, we would have acquitted them of
> their evil deeds, and admitted them to Gar-
> dens of Bliss. Had they performed the Torah
> and the Gospel, and what was sent down to
> them, and what was beneath their feet. Some
> of them are a just nation; but many of them
> -- evil are the things they do (Q. 5:67ff).

"The situation is by no means hopeless," the Ahmadi brought
his speech to a close. "The reason we are standing before
you tonight is to appeal to you to follow the Messenger of
God, Muhammad, Peace be upon him, as we are following him.
He was given a message to deliver:

> O Messenger, deliver that which has been sent
> down to thee from thy Lord; for if thou doest
> not, thou wilt not have delivered His Message.
> God will protect thee from men. God guides
> not the people of the unbelievers (Q. 5:70).

"God protected Muhammad, Peace by upon him, as He protected
the other prophets before him. The message he delivered to
us, we deliver to you:

> People of the Book, you do not stand on any-
> thing, until you perform the Torah and Gospel,
> and what was sent down to you from your Lord
> (Q. 5:71).

"The Gospel is more than words to be believed. It is a
message to be lived. That's why we do our prayers five

times in the day. That's why we confess there is no God
but God and Muhammad is His prophet. That's why we fast
during the month of Ramadan, and go on pilgrimage to Mecca.
That's why we give our money to the poor. Surrender your
life. Do your submission -- now before the Judgment comes!
For those who submit, the Quran offers you this blessing:

> Surely they that believe, and those of Jewry,
> and the Sabaeans, and those Christians, who-
> soever believes in God and the Last Day, and
> works righteousness -- no fear shall be on
> them, neither shall they sorrow" (Q. 5:72).

As I lay on my pillow that night thanking God for His
protection and care during the day, dozens of confused
thoughts were swimming through my head. We had a clear
command in the Scriptures. Jesus told us we were His witnesses, but we Christians had such different conceptions of
what a "Christian witness" is. To Jonathan it was a particular life-style as opposed to his own. Some of the truths
he pointed to were valid and important, but even then I
questioned their appropriateness in the situations in which
he had used them. I questioned also the unqualified condemnation of Muslim prayers and charity, as if we Christians
are never guilty of the same failures. Of course, we never
see ourselves as others see us, but what made Jonathan's
testimony all the more hollow-sounding was that, just like
Pius said, he was "prejudiced, proud, and narrow-minded."
He made a big thing out of certain externals, while others
he overlooked altogether, as for example, the simple matter
of speaking with a measure of respect to both Pius and the
Muslims. When I had once hinted to Jonathan the wisdom of
an approach of reverence, he said, "Yes, but remember the
mandate we've been given, 'Thus saith the Lord.' Anything
less than that is a compromise of the Truth."

While I struggled with some of these thoughts in bed,
the word of Jesus came to me:

> Woe to you, scribes and Pharisees, hypocrites!
> for you are like whitewashed tombs, which out-
> wardly appear beautiful, but within they are
> full of dead men's bones and all uncleanness.
> So you also outwardly appear righteous to men,
> but within you are full of hypocrisy and iniquity
> (Matt. 23:27f).

I finally turned on a light to look for those words in the
Bible since I had forgotten their context. I found them
preceded and followed by other passages which were equally
relevant to the subject of witness.

I put down my Bible, but my thoughts still wandered. It
struck me as unfortunate that Jonathan hadn't gone to the
market with me rather than Pius. He would have gotten an
answer, at least, to one of his conclusions -- that the
Muslims couldn't answer him because they knew he was in the
right. Their whole talk in the market place was a response
to what Jonathan had told them, only Jonathan didn't have
a chance to hear them. It was all there, though -- a reaction to Jonathan's remarks about other Christians (Christians can't get along with each other), a response to his
attack upon the Muslim pillars of the faith (Confession,
Prayer, Almsgiving, Fasting, Pilgrimage), and his condemnation of Muhammad. They also gave a reason for why they
hadn't answered Jonathan's attack. In their estimation, he
wasn't deserving of an answer because there are some people
who "have no understanding."

Then, there was Pius -- so warm and friendly and neigh-
bourly, and yet so antagonistic to the spiritual churches.
Ironically, he exhibited the same kind of judgmental attitude he was criticizing in Jonathan. The only difference
was that instead of being upset about drink and Muslim
prayer, he questioned the very right of spiritual churches
to exist.

I had to admit there were a lot of things about spiritual
churches that had me mystified. Many, if not most, of their
prophets were unqualified -- spiritually and otherwise. In
fact, some of them were spiritually bankrupt and openly corrupt. Then, too, many of the people who patronized their
churches were looking for the wrong things. They were looking for money and power and pregnancy, and I don't know what
all. They had to be missing something in our churches, however, or they wouldn't be flocking out of our doors to satisfy their needs elsewhere. Maybe our fault was that we put
too much emphasis on heavenly things while their fault is
that they put too much emphasis on earthly things.

I asked myself, can we generalize and judge all spiritual
churches as being bad? I certainly couldn't pass any judgment on Kwesi and Ama's church -- nor could Pius, for that
matter. Neither of us had ever visited their church. We
knew about it only by rumour and by what few things Kwesi,

Ama and others had told us. But, even if a closer examina-
tion revealed all was not good, or right, with their church,
I wondered if all was good and right with our own churches.
Certainly, our church had made mistakes in the past, and
too,the Catholic Church's history is filled to overflowing
with wrongdoing. When that thought hit me, I even had to
laugh. Here is Pius -- attached to that very Church which
initiated the Inquisition, killed and terrorized reformer
after reformer, sentenced Luther to death, proclaimed the
Pope infallible. It amused me that this very Pius, my good
neighbour, could disassociate himself from all that and sit
in judgment on *all* the spiritual churches in Ghana. And get
this, *when* he hadn't even visited one of them.

   The Muslims were "witnessing." Jonathan and Pius were
"witnessing." In all of the "witness" I'd heard, I felt
something was missing, but I couldn't quite put my finger on
what made me unhappy.

   All of a sudden, the thought popped into my mind -- what
about my own witness? What kind of witness did I myself
give to others -- to Muslims, to Christians, to pagans, to
everybody?

   As I dropped off to sleep, there was a prayer on my lips:
"Lord, show us the way. Help me to be the kind of person
You want me to be. Help us all to be the kind of witnesses
that will bring glory to your Holy Name. Amen."

THE PEOPLE WHO ARE GOD'S WITNESSES

"You are My witnesses" (Is. 43:10,12; Luke 24:48; John
15:27; Acts 1:8). There is much confusion among Christians
as to what Christian witness is all about.

For one thing, the biblical description of the people
who are God's witnesses is so different from ours. In our
sinful pride and blindness we are inclined to promote a different kind of an account altogether. We want to emphasize
our goodness, our brotherliness, our generosity, our kindness, our truthfulness, and our morality. We want to point
to our buildings, our organs, our choristers, our choir
robes, our hospitals, our schools, and our church offices.
Failures? Yes! But usually they're someone else's. When
confronted with our own mistakes, we are inclined to declare
that "to err is human." Even then, we so often retain the
impression that our accomplishments far outshine our failures.

The scriptural picture is quite another altogether. In
a most candid way it exposes what is really in our hearts --
how tainted with selfishness our motivations, how corrupted
with greed our achievements, and how tinged with pride our
feeblest efforts. Like a giant knife, the Word cuts through
the cloaks of deceit and petty goodnesses with which we sur-
round ourselves:

> The Word of God is living and active, sharper
> than any two-edged sword, piercing to the
> division of soul and spirit, of joints and
> marrow, and discerning the thoughts and in-
> tentions of the heart. Before Him no crea-
> ture is hidden, but all are open and laid
> bare to the eyes of Him with whom we have
> to do (Heb. 4:12f).

God's Word reveals to us our true nature. It shows us who
we really are.

That picture is not always a beautiful one. It is a picture of people whose lives are not only filled with failure
and disregard for the Law of God, but who openly rebel against
God. They forget Him and live in thanklessness. They exalt
themselves as being no longer dependent upon Him. Even when
trouble comes, they turn their backs upon Him and look elsewhere for help. Elevating themselves in pride, they boast as
if they themselves had provided the resources they selfishly
use. He who is the Source of life itself and every human re-
source becomes to them just another name, a name often taken
in vain.

The mystery of God's love and plan for man is that He calls
upon people like this to be His witnesses.

WHAT KIND OF WITNESSES ARE WE?

We have just seen some typical examples of *how* many Christians witness. Some of us are witnesses just like those we
read about. *We* are the Jonathans and the Piuses and the
Yakubus in our own neighbourhoods. What kind of Christian
witness were they giving? What kind do we give?

To the Ahmadis, Christ came off as a stern taskmaster who
criticized severely even when people tried to do their very
best to please God. They had to have been puzzled by such
an attack, however, because to them the *Shari'a* was so explicit in detailing every procedure of the very practices

Jonathan condemned. The riddle for the Muslims would rest
in their conviction that Jesus and the *Shari'a* said the
same things. Given this basic assumption, it would be difficult for them even to conceive of Jesus attacking the
Shari'a. Their conclusion would have to be that Jonathan,
or somebody, had tampered with the Scriptures and perverted
their true message.

The Quran, too, condemns hypocrisy, but what Jonathan
was doing was accusing the Muslims of hypocrisy -- *as if*
Christians are never guilty of the same. It may be true
that Christians do not stand on street corners to pray, but
it is certainly not true that they don't demonstrate a lot
of show in their giving. Just visit a typical harvest festival! You'll see far more of the very practice Jesus was
condemning inside a Christian church than you ever see outside a mosque.

To both Abdullahi and the Ahmadis, each of the Christians
in the neighbourhood came off as part of a church which was
at war with itself. The Catholics were under attack by the
Protestants, the spiritual churches by the Catholics. The
divisive issues, as presented, were not unique to Christians
-- as Muslims well know, for they have plenty of the same
kind of troubles. What is unfortunate, however, is that the
beautiful fact and phenomenon of the unity of the Church is
lost altogether when Christians paint this kind of picture
of the Church.[43] What meets the eye helps to confirm erroneous suppositions that the Church as an organization is
no different from any other. It appears torn by factionalism
and petty jealousies. It gives an impression of being divided into segments, each proudly confident of its own superiority and righteousness. It also gives the appearance that
each segment is blissfully unaware of the possibility that
it might sometimes be in the wrong, and not always exclusively in the right. When this happens, some of the beauty
of the Gospel is thrust aside and lost to view.

What was missing in the testimony of Jonathan and Pius
was the honesty which Christ called for and the humility
which He lived. When God's people give a faithful witness
to others, these qualities are at the heart of every testimony -- whether the witness is a verbal confession or an act
of love.

HONESTY

One of the reasons we feel so at ease in the company of intimate friends is the lack of need to put on a show. We don't have to wear a mask. We don't have to put on a front. We can be ourselves.

Even then, however, we are often not ourselves. We say things we don't mean, and what is often the truth we don't say. We're not talking only of the pose we put up before others. We often put up a pose before ourselves. We have an enormous capability for convincing ourselves that we are something we are not. In fact, we are so clever at the art of manipulation, misrepresentation, and deception that we never know whom to trust or what to believe. Even our own personality, motivated by feelings, imaginings, ambitions, hopes, prejudices, disappointments and desires, succumbs to constant delusions as to who we are, and what our role, status, purpose and end in life is and ought to be. You might even say we are several personalities wrapped up into one. There is one or more we offer to the world, there is another we offer to ourselves, and finally, there is our real personality behind it all.

The Scriptures frequently recognize and call attention to this common human problem and failing. Jeremiah says,

> The heart is deceitful above all things, and
> desperately corrupt; who can understand it?
> "I the Lord search the mind and try the heart,
> to give to every man according to his ways,
> according to the fruit of his doings" (Jer.
> 17:9f).

An important thrust of the Scriptures is to plead with man to be honest with himself. When he is honest with himself, he can be honest with God and with his neighbour.

From the foregoing we come to see why sincerity is such a poor criterion by which to judge the rightness or the wrongness of people's actions, religious convictions, or whatever. People can be ever so sincere, and yet totally in the wrong. Because the heart is "desperately corrupt" and because it is "deceitful above all things," people can even be in the wrong and convince themselves that they are in the right.

HUMILITY

"Do not become proud, but stand in awe" is the oft-
unheeded advice of the Apostle Paul to the Christian (Rom.
11:20).

Christians in Africa are very proud. In some ways, they
have much for which to be proud. They have played significant roles in building commendable school systems. They
have established hospitals and clinics in many lands. They
have contributed scores of leaders who have taken healthy
initiatives and given earnestly of themselves to local and
national and even international development.

By contrast they ask, "What have Muslims done? What have
they contributed? Instead of being a progressive element in
society, they have been a regressive element. Their children do not go to our schools, except in token numbers. The
masses of their people are illiterate, lazy, backward, and
unproductive."

Unfortunately, as with all generalizations, this kind of
assessment disregards many of the useful contributions Muslims have made to African society.[44] Among these are an
early appreciation for the art of writing and education,
the production and preservation of important historical documents, and the early opening up of the resources of many
lands for international trade purposes.

Setting aside these contributions, let us suppose for a
minute that it would be possible to defend the thesis that
Christian contributions to national life far exceed Muslim
contributions. The word of Paul would still apply, "Do not
become proud, but stand in awe." Scripture again and again
warns us of the pitfalls of pride. If any glory is deserved,
it is not for us to take. It is rather for us to give. It
is to be given to the Lord. "Let him who boasts, boast of
the Lord" (I Cor. 1:31).

WITNESSES TO GOD'S MIGHTY ACTS

Isaiah prefaced a most awe-inspiring description of God's
supremacy over man and His creation with the words, "Behold,
the Lord God comes with might, and His arm rules for Him."
It was that message and its significance that Zion, as a
"herald of good tidings," was to proclaim (Is. 40:9ff). Zion
had experienced God's mighty acts in her midst.

God reminds the nations that, before Him, they are "like a drop from a bucket," and their inhabitants "like grasshoppers" (Is. 40:15,22). Then, singling out the people of Israel for special mention, He says to them,

> I, I am the Lord,
> > and besides me there is no saviour.
> I declared and saved and proclaimed,
> > when there was no strange god among you;
> > and *you are My witnesses.*
> I am God, also henceforth I am He;
> > there is none who can deliver from My hand;
> > I work and who can hinder it (Is. 43:11ff)?

The reason why the people of Israel were singled out in this special way is because they had heard His declarations and had witnessed His saving actions. The great event of which they were witnesses was the return to Israel of the people who had been carried away captive into Babylon. The hopelessness of their plight because of their own inadequte resources magnified all the more the wonder of their deliverance by the mighty act of God.

As the people heard this proclamation, they had to have been reminded of the other unexpected and dramatic deliverance they had experienced as a people, the exodus out of Egypt. There, too, they had been slaves in a foreign land, helpless, hopeless, incapable of finding the strength to free themselves from the bondage of slavery. It was God's initiative, God's act, that brought liberation.

The New Testament speaks of another kind of liberation. It, too, came at God's initiative. It, too, was accomplished by God's mighty act. It, too, is authenticated by witnesses, as were God's mighty acts of the Old Testament. It, too, came to a people who were helpless, hopeless, and incapable of charting their own course to freedom. We are speaking of God's mighty deliverance of man from sin and the consequences of his sin! His "slavery" to sin (Rom. 6:20) was coupled with his being "dead" through trespasses and sins (Eph. 2:1), a "deadness" which consisted not only in the verdict, "The soul that sins shall die" (Ezek. 18:4), but in man's whole inability to muster the spiritual resources to alter his pathway to inevitable destruction.

The Good News is that God intervened. His intervention into the human dilemma of inescapable death and condemnation came by way of Christ's death as man's substitute.

Jesus, the Messiah, was not substituted for -- HE WAS THE
SUBSTITUTE! He became a curse that we need not be accursed
(Gal. 3:13). He died an earthly death that we need not die
an eternal death. He "thirsted" (John 19:28) that we need
not thirst in Hell (Luke 16:24). He resurrected as a sign
that our peace has been made and that forgiveness of our
sins is a reality. His resurrection confirms God's promises to raise us, too, from the dead.

This is the New Testament liberation, the cosmic significance of which extends across all the ages of man. Adam,
Noah, Abraham, Moses and David did not know its details,
but they trusted in God's mercy and compassion. "These all
died in faith, not having received what was promised, but
having seen it and greeted it from afar" (Heb. 11:13). To
these great men of faith could be added the great women of
faith -- Sarah, Ruth, Rahab the harlot, Anna the prophetess,
and a host of others.

These witnesses to God's mercy in Christ by virtue of
their faith in His promises are joined in the New Testament
by that chosen group of people who walked by Jesus' side.
They were the people who received the Truth of God from His
very lips. They were the people who looked awkwardly and
helplessly on while the events of His Passion erupted swiftly
and furiously before their very eyes. They were the people
who anguished through the moments which stretched into days
as they wrestled with the improbable possibility, "Is He
really alive?"

Their witness in the New Testament is the same as that
we meet in the Old Testament -- a testimony to the unfolding
of God's mighty acts in history. The details of the witness
are different, but the core of the message is still the same:
God saves and delivers through His mighty power. Peter, for
example, gave testimony to this when he spoke to the Roman
centurion Cornelius (Acts 10:34-43).

The single outstanding mighty act of the New Testament is
the resurrection of Jesus Christ from the dead.[45] It is no
accident that this event formed the basis for the witness of
the disciples of Jesus (Acts 1:22; 2:32; 3:15; 4:33; 5:32;
10:39; 41f; 13:31). They had followed Him, and He was a
great man. They had concluded He was someone special --
perhaps even the long-awaited Messiah.

This conclusion was not easily reached. In spite of all
the miracles Jesus had done, He was so very, very human.

When He walked all day, He became tired. When He went without food, He became hungry. When His friend Lazarus died,
He cried, and the most shattering blow of all -- when they
nailed Him to a cross, *He* died. That totally unexpected
end to a Life that was so beautiful, so good, so promising
and so on the brink of great expectations, completely shattered their confidence and even their faith.

   Broken, disheartened, fearful, ashamed, they hid behind
locked doors afraid of what might happen next. Gone were
their dreams of being part of the kingdom they had anticipated Christ would establish. They had coveted and even
argued over the positions they thought would come. Gone
was the confidence which had once asserted, "Lord, do You
want us to bid fire come down from heaven and consume them"
(Luke 9:54). Gone was the faith which had promised, "Lord,
I am ready to go with You to prison and to death" (Luke
22:33). Left was guilt, failure, perplexity.

   The evidences of Jesus' death were so final and so con-
clusive that when reports started to come in that Jesus was
alive, "these words seemed to them an idle tale, and they
did not believe them" (Luke 24:11). Even the two disciples
who met Jesus on the way to Emmaus were so convinced that
He was dead that they did not recognize Him in their midst
(Luke 24:16). Earlier, some of the women had gone to anoint
the body of Jesus. Finding the tomb empty, "they went out
and fled from the tomb; for trembling and astonishment had
come upon them; and they said nothing to any one, for they
were afraid" (Mark 16:8). Finally, when they were convinced
that Jesus was really risen from the dead, Luke reports,
"they still disbelieved for joy" (Luke 24:41).

   These were not fools who pinned their hopes upon frustrated
ambitions or uncertain threads of imagination. They were men
and women whose imaginations were crushed by the total hopelessness of the situation. Even the statements which Jesus
had made to sustain them through this time were empty and
meaningless for they had all seen Jesus dead, totally dead.
They had seen Him die, condemned by "church" and state --
slowly, painfully, irrevocably.

   To them at that time the mighty acts of Jesus were nothing more than memories past. The hope that He might use the
unusual power He possessed to right the situation and bring
order out of chaos -- as He had done on so many occasions --
proved fruitless. He died, and their hopes died with Him.

This is the background of Peter's doxology, "Blessed be
the God and Father of our Lord Jesus Christ! By His great
mercy we have been born anew to a *living hope* through the
resurrection of Jesus Christ from the dead" (I Pet. 1:3f).
The mighty act of God which brought a total reorientation
to the lives of the disciples was the event of the resurrection. This mighty act became the starting point of their
New Testament witness. It was, in fact, the central point.

LIVING DEMONSTRATIONS OF GOD'S ACTIONS

According to the Bible -- and our own experience bears
this out -- people without a fear of God are fearful beings,
undeserving of the title "human." Capable of all kinds of
evil, they are more like "irrational animals, creatures of
instinct, born to be caught and killed" (2 Pet. 2:12; Jude
10). "They exchange the truth about God for a lie and worship and serve the creature rather than the Creator" (Rom.
1:25). "Although they know God they do not honour Him as
God or give thanks to Him, but they become futile in their
thinking and their senseless minds are darkened" (Rom. 1:21).
"For this reason God gives them up to dishonourable passions"
(Rom. 1:26).

What Paul says, as he continues his description of "godless" man, reads like an account of modern-day society in
one of our daily newspapers:

> Since they do not see fit to acknowledge God,
> God gives them up to a base mind and to impro
> per conduct. They are all filled with all man-
> ner of wickedness, evil, covetousness, malice.
> Full of envy, murder, strife, deceit, malignity,
> they are gossips, slanderers, haters of God,
> insolent, haughty, boastful, inventors of evil,
> disobedient to parents, foolish, faithless,
> heartless, ruthless. Though they know God's
> decree that those who do such things deserve
> to die, they not only do them, but approve
> those who practise them (Rom. 1:28-32).

The evidences of the unhappy picture Paul describes are
everywhere about us. The startling thing is that this is
how we, too, would be *if* God had not intervened in our
lives with His mercy, making us who were "no people" *a people,*
"God's people."

This is what Christian witness is all about. It is about
the misery of sin and its consequences. It is about helplessness and hopelessness and despair. It is about what
happens when God's mercy touches despondent lives with His
love. It is about people who were "no people" becoming
"God's people." It is telling what Jesus did by His death,
burial, and resurrection to make men fit for God's presence
and God's life.

The Good News is that God rescues people from the misery
of sin. He meets them where they are -- fallen and not
able to rise. He lifts them up from where they were --
crushed and unable to generate hope. He recreates their
personalities and reorients their lives. He takes them and
constitutes them into a new kind of nation, a unique nation
unbounded by geographic markers. For the people of this
new nation, it is a new day with all kinds of new possibilities. As Paul describes it:

> If any one is in Christ, he is a new creation;
> the old has passed away, behold, the new has
> come. All this is from God, who through Christ
> reconciled us to Himself (2 Cor. 5:17f).

Or, as Peter said:

> You are a chosen race, a royal priesthood,
> a holy nation, God's own people, that you
> may declare the wonderful deeds of Him who
> called you out of darkness into His marve-
> lous light. Once you were no people, but
> now you are God's people; once you had not
> received mercy but now you have received
> mercy (I Pet. 2:9f).

It is the latter quantity which is the uniting factor in
this unusual nation, this new entity whose presence is alive
in the world as a "yeast" (Matt. 13:33), a "salt" and a
"light" (Matt. 5:13f). This new nation is the Church,

> built upon the foundation of the apostles and
> the prophets, Christ Jesus Himself being the
> cornerstone, in whom the whole structure is
> joined together and grows into a holy temple
> in the Lord (Eph. 2:20f).

As we differentiated earlier between Law with a capital
"L" and law with a small "l," so now we differentiate be-

tween Church with a capital "C" and church with a small "c."
Church with a capital "C" is "the Holy Christian Church,
the communion of saints" -- the existence and the reality
of which we confess regularly in the Apostles' Creed. Church
with a small "c" is that visible, all-too-human institutionalized structure we meet in our neighbourhoods, the human element making it as vulnerable and susceptible to
every human foible and failure as is any other human institution.

The mystery for us is that we are as much a part of the
one as of the other, the exception being that while all
church members may not be a part of the "Body of Christ,
the Church," all who are part of the Church are also part
of the visible church on earth. The "Church" is made up of
all believers in Christ, and *only* believers. The "church"
or the "churches" are made up of both believers and hypocrites. This distinction is not a new one. It is the kind
of distinction Jesus made when He spoke of "the weeds among
the wheat" (Matt. 13:25) and the bad fish among the good
(Matt. 13:48).

We should note at this time that nowhere in the Scriptures are God's people called upon to witness to themselves, or to put this in a modern idiom, "to preach Christianity."[46] Christianity, like every human being and every
human institution, is riddled with failure. It has been
proud and it has been possessive. It has killed and it has
maimed. It has lied and it has cheated. It has honoured
and dishonoured God. It has brought glory to His Name as
well as shame.

Muslims are often quick to point out to Christians the
failures of Christianity -- the wars which "Christian" rulers and people have initiated, the prejudices and injus-
tices which "Christian" people have nourished and promoted,
the wealth which "Christians" no less than others have
greedily coveted and selfishly controlled. Unfortunately,
whenever we are challenged about any of these failures, we
often take it as a personal affront. We immediately arise
to defend our cause whatever the cost -- even at the cost
of the truth. In the process we give in to our natural inclinations as men. We meet retort with retort, abuse with
abuse, insinuation with denial, truth with untruth, and insult with insult. We so easily set aside the humility and
the honesty which our Lord wills for us and which were so
much a part of His life. "When He was reviled, He did not
revile in return; when He suffered, He did not threaten"
(I Pet. 2:23).

Another reaction to such charges is to try to avoid the blame by laying it at the feet of the people who are Christian only in name. This attempt, however, is as unfair as it is dishonest. Born-again Christians are just as susceptible to sin and failure as are those who are Christian only in name. Rather than try to escape the guilt which is ours by pinning it upon others, the honest thing is to acknowledge our faults for what they are -- evidences of how far we still fall short of the glory of God. They only illustrate how much we are still utterly dependent day after day upon God's grace to keep us from evil and the Evil One.

The simple truth is that the visible church on its pilgrimage through time is as much a demonstration of God's action among men as is the life of any individual Christian. Our call is not the impossible task of defending Christianity as a faith, or a religion, or an organization which has no failures. Our call is daily to repent of our failures and daily to begin life anew in the Spirit.

History is filled with examples of how the visible church, oblivious to its failures or in spite of them, has again and again succumbed to the temptations of exalting its own position. Divided into its many parts, it has been as intensely "nationalistic" as has any other human organization. This nationalism has exerted itself in different fashions. Some parts of the visible church have looked upon themselves as the true Church outside of which there is no salvation. Others have not gone so far as to state that no one can be saved outside their own ranks, but they have still insisted that theirs is "the true visible church on earth." Beginning in the Old Testament, God warned His people of the dangers of that kind of presumption. Consider the following excerpts from the record.

THE WARNINGS AGAINST SELF-RIGHTEOUSNESS AND PRIDE

After their forty years of wandering in the wilderness of Sinai, God was ready to give His people another chance to move into the promised land. They had ruined their first opportunity by their "faithlessness" and their"murmuring" against God (Num. 14:26-35). With lightning-like rapidity, His curse fell upon them and they were turned back into the desert to die off one by one while their children under twenty grew into manhood in the rigorous and austere school of desert deprivation. When they were finally ready -- after forty years of training -- to tackle the assignment of conquering "seven nations greater and mightier" than them-

selves (Deut. 7:1), God forewarned them of the nationalistic pride which would be their daily companion, a constant
threat to their faith and loyalty to Him. God specifically
warned them of three areas of danger: Pride in their own
righteousness (Deut. 9:4-7), pride in their own power and
might (Deut. 8:17f) and pride in their numbers (Deut. 7:6ff).
Israel's "boast" could be nowhere but in the Lord! This is
the story of God's people throughout the ages. Stubborn
and rebellious, bereft of strength of their own, few in
number -- they have been themselves a living demonstration
of God's action among men.

The picture Isaiah paints confirms the same conclusion.
He speaks of God's people as being nothing but a "worm"
(41:14). He describes them as being "blind" and "deaf."
They see many things, but do not observe them; their ears
are open, but they do not hear (42:18ff). Yet, these are
the same people God designates as being created for His
glory (43:7). They are His servants and His witnesses
(43:10). They are themselves living demonstrations of His
mercy at work in the world.

Although as God's witnesses we are "a chosen race, a
royal priesthood, a holy nation, God's own people" (I Pet.
2:9), every basis for nationalistic pride or feeling of
superiority is destroyed by the knowledge of how totally
dependent we are upon His goodness. Paul, who was himself
so intensely aware of how little credit he could take for
what God had made of him (I Cor. 15:9, Eph. 3:8, I Tim.
1:15f), could hardly have spelled this out for us more
clearly:

> Consider your call, brethren; not many of you
> were wise according to worldly standards, not
> many were powerful, not many were of noble
> birth; but God chose what is foolish ... weak
> ... low and despised in the world ... so that
> no human being might boast in the presence of
> God. He is the Source of your life in Christ
> Jesus, whom God made our wisdom, our righteous-
> ness and sanctification and redemption; there-
> fore, as it is written, "Let him who boasts,
> boast of the Lord" (I Cor. 1:26-31).

These are some of the reasons why God's witnesses speak
to the world from a position which more often appears to be
one of weakness than of strength. As Paul says,

> We have this treasure (the light of the knowl-
> edge of the glory of God in the face of
> Christ) in earthen vessels, to show that the
> transcendent power belongs to God and not to
> us (2 Cor. 4:7).

It is now that we begin to understand more fully what Jesus
meant when He said,

> Unless a grain of wheat falls into the earth
> and dies, it remains alone; but if it dies,
> it bears much fruit (John 12:24).

Have you ever dug into the groud to observe this mystery in
its beginnings -- a sprout of new life emerging from a rot-
ting, dying, decaying seed?

While there are many spectacular things in the world, few
are as awe-inspiring as the miracle of new life. As we are
well aware, we live in an age in which science has given us
some outstanding and almost unbelievable achievements. Yet,
with all our modern scientific knowledge, technique, and
prestige, we stand as humble and fascinated before the mysterious wonder of birth as did our ancestors long ago. Men
all over the world marvel at this miracle.

What God does with the witnesses He has chosen is just as
marvellous. He finds them full of fears, afraid of forces
working to hurt and destroy them. He sees them restless,
running here and there in search of peace. He meets them
going and coming from sacrificing themselves and their
worldly goods on thousands of useless altars with no more
certainty of peace after the sacrifice than before. These
were God's creation, but they are God's creation gone astray.

The miracle of new birth is how God takes these people as
they are, remaking and remolding their broken and disar-
ranged lives. He breathes into them His Spirit and from
this new birth issues forth the "fruit of the Spirit -- love,
joy, peace, patience, kindness, goodness, faithfulness, gentleness, self-control" (Gal. 5:22). Their lives are no
longer hidden and sheltered in fear, but they are open letters "to be known and read by all men ... written not with
ink but with the Spirit of the living God, not on tablets of
stone, but on tablets of human hearts" (2 Cor. 3:3). Gone are
pride and self-righteousness which are "buried with Him by
baptism into death." In their place is the realization "that
as Christ was raised from the dead by the glory of the Father,
we too might walk in newness of life" (Rom. 6:4). *Such are
the witnesses of God.*

6

Truth and Freedom

IS MUHAMMAD A TRUE, OR A FALSE PROPHET?

I really didn't want to answer the question at all.

We were sitting on the front verandah of my house --
I, the two Ahmadis, and Alihu. The two Ahmadis had finally
made it to my house with their Qurans.

Just before they arrived I had been telling Alihu of
their preaching in the market the night before. Alihu
wasn't too favourably impressed. He said the Ahmadis had
confused a lot of things, and since 1923 when they first
came to Ghana there had been nothing but trouble in the
Muslim community. Alihu said he didn't know what they
were after. Somewhere along the line they were misled by
a false prophet in India who was named Ahmad. That's why
they were called Ahmadiyya.

I told Alihu I thought they were doing some pretty good
things. They had a secondary school in Kumasi and they were
building several clinics and hospitals in different parts
of the country. Alihu was about to tell me what he thought
about those projects when we heard a shout of Agoo, Agoo at
the gate. It was the two Ahmadis.

After the usual greetings, they handed me a Quran and
suggested that I look through it. They were sure that I
would want to buy a copy. I noticed it was printed in
Lahore, Pakistan. It had English on one side; Arabic on the
other.

I had wanted a copy of the Quran, but for some reason I
didn't want to look like I was too anxious to buy one. Besides, I felt a little uncomfortable with Alihu being there.
I knew he didn't have much respect for the Ahmadis in the
first place, and secondly, he didn't think the Quran should
be translated -- that's why he didn't like this idea of
English and Arabic together. I didn't know if that was his
main opposition to what they were doing, or if he rather
was unhappy over how they were selling the Quran up and
down the neighbourhood just like it was any ordinary book.
Alihu felt very strongly that you had to treat the Quran
with great respect. After all, it was a copy of the Sacred
Text in heaven. You just didn't tamper with it like you
might with any other book.[47]

Alihu had once remarked to me how surprised he was to
see how we handled our Bibles. We just picked them up and
put them down without any ablutions. By way of contrast,
I observed one night how careful he was in handling his
Quran. He had just finished his prayers (so, of course,
he had done his ablutions) when a young man came to ask a
question. The Quran was brought and with considerable ceremony and extreme care, Alihu unwrapped it from the cloth in
which he kept it, found the appropriate *ayat*, wrote it down
for the man, and then with equal care, wrapped the Quran up
as it had been at the first.

I remembered how one time when we were at Muhammadu's,
Muhammadu had brought out the Quran to show something to
Alihu. Alihu refused to touch it saying he hadn't performed
his ablutions. This made me all the more surprised when
Alihu took one of the Ahmadiyya Qurans just like that and
began to page through it. I suspected he didn't think
their Qurans were the real thing. The English took something away from their sacredness, I was sure, but perhaps
besides that, he might think they didn't have the true
Quran. He had told me on another occasion that he didn't
see how they could have the same Quran and teach and practise so differently from the rest of the Muslims all over
the world. I didn't know what all Alihu had in mind, but
he mentioned something about their way of praying being different, their funerals being different, and that they always
celebrated Muslim holidays on different days. Besides, the
Ahmadis would never pray with them at the Central Mosque.
In spite of the disagreements between the Muslim Mission and
the Muslim Community, they at least prayed together, Alihu
remarked.

While Alihu was mumbling off what seemed to me page after page of the Arabic text, the younger Ahmadi showed me a book on Muslim prayer and another on Muslim history. Then it was that he asked me what I thought of Muhammad -- was he a true or a false prophet? That question really put me on the spot.

I had more or less taken for granted that Muhammad was a false prophet, but if the fellow was going to ask me why I thought he was a false prophet, I would have to admit I didn't know. I hadn't really read the Quran, or for that matter, studied very much about Islam at all. Even as re-gards the crucifixion -- I didn't know if what Alihu had told me that other time was what Alihu thought, or what Muhammad said, or that it was written in the Quran, or what. The fact that Jonathan had called Muhammad a false prophet wasn't very convincing to me either -- given all the disagreements Jonathan and I had with each other on other subjects.

What little I had read in the Quran seemed quite all right to me, and so I finally responded to the question in the best way I knew how. I said I didn't really know. I knew that some Christians felt Muhammad was a false prophet, and I was sure they had some good reasons to reach that kind of a conclusion. The fact was that Jesus had told us to beware of false prophets (Matt. 7:15), and consequently everybody should be on their guard. At the same time, I said, I knew that Christians made mistakes as did everyone else, and perhaps some of my fellow Christians had erred in their judgment of Muhammad. I hesitated to sit in judgment upon them or their judgment until I might have an opportunity to make my own. I added that I would be interested in get-ting a copy of the Quran for that very reason.

The two men seemed very pleased at this decision, the one even suggesting that since I was a special friend, they would reduce the cost of a copy just a little bit as a special favour for me. This, of course, made me all the happier over my purchase. I thanked them for their consi-deration and soon they were on their way. The parting word was that they'd be back one day to discuss some of the things in the Quran with me. After awhile, Alihu, too, begged to leave and soon I was alone with my new Quran.

I turned to *Nisa'a* which had stayed in my mind ever since Alihu had told me how Muslims understood the crucifixion of Jesus -- that Jesus had not died, but that someone had been

substituted in His place.[48] I read for some time before I
came to the very verse he had referred to. It was in a
section where the Jews were criticized for many things,
among them for

> their saying, "We did kill the Messiah, Jesus,
> son of Mary, the Messenger of Allah;" whereas
> they slew him not, nor crucified him, but he
> was made to appear to them like one crucified;
> and those who differ therein are certainly in
> a state of doubt about it: they have no defi-
> nite knowledge thereof, but only follow a con-
> jecture; and they did not convert this conjec-
> ture into a certainty (Q. 4:157).

It was Sura 4:158 in my new Quran, and it sure seemed to
me a difficult verse to understand. Muslims must have found
it difficult, too, because there was a long footnote which
called attention to how Jesus had made a miraculous escape
from the accursed cross, and how in searching for the lost
ten tribes of Israel he had gone to Kashmir where he finally
died and is buried to this day.

I knew that Alihu would shake his head over that footnote,
and while thinking about that, I wondered if the Arabic text
was the same in this Quran as in Alihu's. I wondered, too,
how much an orthodox Muslim interpretation of this text might
vary from that of an Ahmadi Muslim.

Before I put the Quran away, I looked at Sura 1, the
Fatiha, which I knew was a part of every Muslim prayer ritual:

> In the name of Allah, the Gracious, the Merciful.
> All praise belongs to Allah, Lord of all the
>   worlds,
>   The Gracious, the Merciful
>   Master of the Day of Judgment.
> Thee alone do we worship and Thee alone do we
>   implore for help.
> Guide us in the right path,
> The path of those on whom Thou has bestowed
>   Thy blessings,
>   those who have not incurred Thy dis-
>   pleasure,
>   and those who have not gone astray.

Actually, that's quite a beautiful prayer, I thought. Couldn't
we Christians use it as well as Muslims?

*The Fatiha whetted my appetite to read more. What would
I answer the Ahmadis the next time they asked me if Muhammad
was a true, or a false prophet? I wondered.*

"WHAT IS TRUTH?"

If you were acting the part of Pilate in the trial of
Jesus, what kind of expression would you put into his question, "What is truth" (John 18:38)? Was Pilate really seeking an answer? Or was he inwardly laughing in derision at
what seemed to him a noble, but naive goal in life -- "to
bear witness to the truth?"

Pilate had climbed high in the ranks of a government
which ruled over many diverse peoples. As such, he was part
of a system which gave the appearance of having learned how
to cope with relative truth at many different levels, including the religious.

The "truths" the Roman Empire embraced were many and
varied. As the Empire expanded, the Romans absorbed the
gods of whomever they conquered into their own galaxy of
divine beings. Thus, by the time of Jesus, religious pluralism was a significant feature of the Roman Empire.

As a man who had successfully moved up to the heights of
sizable responsibility and great reward in Roman politics,
it's quite possible that Pilate had developed a cynical attitude toward truth. Truth was something relative, not
absolute. It was something you could twist and manipulate
to suit your own purposes. What you lived before the world
was a lie -- the truth of what transpired behind the scenes
irrelevant to what met the eye. Rome's was a politics of
power where might made right, and Pilate had risen to the
rank of "colonial governor" in that system.

By the time Jesus was brought before Pilate, He had already been sentenced to death by the seventy-man Sanhedrin,
the Supreme Council of the Jews (Mark 14:64). Pilate could
see from their handling of Jesus that for all their sanctimonious religiosity, truth for them was only a decision of
momentary expediency. The imbalance in their priorities of
right and wrong did not perhaps strike Pilate as particularly
peculiar as much as it probably struck him as typical of how
people are -- religious or otherwise. You will recall how
the Jews clamoured for the death of an innocent Jesus while
at the same time refusing to enter Pilate's quarters (John
18:28). Pilate was a Gentile and their entering his judicial

court would defile them for the Passover festival. A strange
kind of "truth" this -- the life of a person held in less
regard than a rule of ritual purity, a set of values that
appraised a rule of ritual higher than the life of a man.
Here is the artificial religion God was condemning through
Amos (5:21-24) and the hollow religious practice God was
denouncing through Isaiah (1:11-15).

Let's remember that the men who were demanding the death
of Jesus for religious reasons were part of that large con-
tingent of people who had been designated God's witnesses in
Isaiah 43. It's quite possible they were sincere in what
they were doing, their sincerity propelling them into a
furious hatred of the blasphemies Jesus had supposedly ut-
tered. They were jealous for God and they knew full well
how fearful God's jealousy could be. Time and again His
jealous wrath had fallen upon them as a people.

To Pilate, however, they must have appeared less as God's
witnesses than as narrow-minded religious bigots. His efforts to release Jesus were countered with mob action demands, "Crucify Him, crucify Him" (John 19:6). We shall
never know how many of those who joined in that shout would
have individually looked Jesus in the eye and demanded the
same. It's always easier to cast judgment upon someone from
within the shroud of anonymity which surrounds a crowd. The
seeming security of the crowd induces people to act and react
in ways they would not attempt as individuals.

In unity there is strength, as the saying goes, but the
strength of this unity is as much used for Satan's purposes
as it is for God's. The mob which shouted for the death of
Jesus was in Satan's grasp. They were blind to every warning to stay the evil and unjust final act of judgment from
which there could be no turning back.

As part of the Roman government, Pilate, too, knew the
uses to which strength could be put. In his government,
strength as often determined the "right" as the "right" determined the use of strength. What was right was determined
by whoever was in control.

It must have been difficult for Pilate to adjust to the
ambiguities of that moment in the early morning hours of the
day Jesus was sentenced to death. He was in control -- and
yet, he was not in control. He should have been in control,
and that was for him, perhaps, the most difficult feature of
that hour. With all his military, he had lost control. He
had lost control to a mob.

Pilate's assessment of the predicament in which both he and Jesus found themselves in the wee hours of that morning was perhaps most accurately summed up in his "What is truth" comment to Jesus. He may have been asking a searching question, but it seems more likely that he was making a final judgment upon the hopelessness of using truth as a criterion for justice. The "truth" of the situation rested with the mob, and it was their voice of "justice" which prevailed -- not the much-heralded Roman justice of that period in history. Had Jesus been a Roman citizen, it might have been different, but as a colonized subject he had no such rights. Even then, whether Pilate would have used his military to defend a man in the face of a mob is an open question.

When Pilate mumbled "What is truth," he spoke more from a position of weakness than of strength. Had he recognized a greater truth than the "truth" of the moment, the outcome of Jesus' trial might have taken another course altogether. As it was, he could only indicate his displeasure by washing his hands of the crime. The "truth" that Jesus was a blasphemer and that whoever blasphemed was to die for his fault prevailed.

TRUTH TODAY

If we move from Pilate's courtroom into one of our own, we again confront the constant search for this continually elusive quantity called truth. Daily, judges and magistrates sort through masses of evidence in efforts to discover the truth in different situations. If it were not for the fact that people are able to lie with such straight faces, adroitly hiding and misrepresenting the truth, the work of a judge would not be so difficult. Since people are so adept at bending the truth to suit their own purposes, however, legislative and judicial processes -- from formulating laws to enforcing and interpreting them -- are extremely complicated. The truth is often buried under avalanches of conflicting opinions and differing points of view. Unravelling the slim and fragile threads of truth from such entangled mountains of half-truths is not only difficult, but frequently humanly impossible.

One of the ways in which society has tried to cope with the problem of truth versus untruth is by incorporating the truths its people have grasped into a system of customs, laws, and traditions. There is a way of doing things that is right, and there is a way that is wrong. The vast array of legalities which emerges, comprising a formidable assort-

ment in each and every society, serves the purpose of pre-
serving order in the midst of what would otherwise be chaos.
These legalities represent an attempt on man's part to safeguard the truths he has discovered, or which have been revealed to him through one divine channel or another.

In traditional African society these truths have been
handed down in song, dance, ritual, proverb and Ananse
stories. Chiefs, elders, fetish priests and storytellers
played roles as interpreters of the truth. In modern urbanizing society we find a mixture of the old with the new
of parliaments, legal codes, courts, lawyers, judges,
churches and mosques, priests, prophets, *qadis* and *malams*.

These various agents and agencies contribute to the well-
being of society by curbing outbursts of lawlessness. Such
outbursts would otherwise be the order of the day were these
restricting factors not in force. The stronger the hold of
these various persons and institutions upon society, the
more stability there is, and stability in turn generates
confidence that what is right and true is in control. When
people lose that confidence, disorder erupts. This may take
the form of simply neglecting the customs which then gradually fall into disuse, or it may result in open rebellion
against the authorities who are in positions of leadership
and the mores, or standards of morality, behaviour and
ethics they represent.

TRUTH AND CONSCIENCE

Underneath the surface of the turmoil which goes into
man's struggle to apprehend, know, enforce, protect and retain the truth is that mysterious force called conscience.
The drama of the trial and execution of Jesus provides some
intriguing illustrations of troubled consciences at work
along with various efforts to relieve the pressures of conscience. Pilate tried to ease his conscience by washing his
hands of the truth. The Jews who shouted for the death of
Jesus tried to ease their consciences by giving careful attention to the seemingly minor detail of not defiling themselves by entering Pilate's compound. Peter tried to ease
his conscience by bitter weeping (Luke 22:62). Judas alone
gave up hope of any relief. In despair he hanged himself.

Conscience is an interesting combination of learned behaviour and inherent inclinations. The Bible tells us that
God

> will punish the heathen when they sin, even
> though they never had God's written laws, for
> down in their hearts they know right from
> wrong, God's laws are written within them;
> their own conscience accuses them, or some-
> times excuses them (Rom. 2:12ff, LB).

Thus man has a basic sense of right and wrong which is as
much a part of his being as are his physical organs and pro-
perties. The problem is, however, that just as he yields up
his "members to impurity and to greater and greater iniquity"
(Rom. 6:19), so also he allows his conscience to be used as
a servant of Satan. Since "his heart is deceitful above all
things" (Jer. 17:9), he ends up enshrining in his customs,
laws and traditions not only truth, but also error and untruth.

Because man's deceitful heart is capable of misleading
his conscience, neither conscience nor any of the legislative forms it helps to create -- whether custom, or law, or
tradition -- is a reliable embodiment, interpretation, or
application of ultimate truth. Conscience has within itself
an awareness of ultimate truth, but unless that awareness is
sharpened and deepened, it remains at best only an inadequate
guide for what is fulfilling in life and what is pleasing to
God.

Pilate, Peter, Judas and the mob provide good examples of
consciences at work. Among these, Peter and Judas were far
more affected by the tumultuous events which unfolded so
rapidly in the life of Jesus than were either Pilate or the
Jews who sent Him to His execution. The Jews relied for
security of conscience upon the law of Moses, as they interpreted it -- as well as upon the anonymity of the crowd;
Pilate, upon the expediency of the "truth" of the moment as
dictated by the mob. Peter and Judas, on the other hand,
knew Jesus intimately. They had walked with Him through the
school of life and had had their consciences honed and tuned
by the Word of God which flowed from His lips. They knew
the falsehood of the charges. They knew the integrity of
His life. They saw a lie unfolding before their very eyes,
each of them playing a part in it, their consciences tor-
menting them for their roles in this drama of injustice.

The problem disturbing the consciences of Peter and Judas
wasn't a question of how imperfectly they had fulfilled the
Law of God. It wasn't a matter of how infrequently they had
said their prayers or how unzealously they had given alms.

It wasn't how little they had confessed their faith, how
irregularly they had fasted, or how few pilgrimages they had
made. It was purely and simply a question of what they were
doing with Jesus. For them, the full truth of the situation
rested in their relationship with Him -- broken and shattered
not by Jesus, but by them. By their own choice, they had
broken the links in the covenant of God's grace which had
enfolded them.

There was adequate cause for bleeding and torn consciences,
for this was He of whom John later testified.

> In the beginning was the Word, and the Word
> was with God, and the Word was God. He was
> in the beginning with God; all things were
> made that was made. In him was life, and
> the life was the light of men. The light
> shines in the darkness, and the darkness
> has not overcome it.
>
> The Word became flesh and dwelt among us,
> full of grace and truth ... From his fulness
> have we all received, grace upon grace. For
> the law was given through Moses; grace and
> truth came through Jesus Christ (John 1:1-5,
> 14,16f).

This is the same Jesus who said before Pilate:

> I have come into the world to bear witness to
> the truth. Every one who is of the truth
> hears My voice (John 18:37).

It was then that Pilate said, "What is truth?" and not "hearing" the voice of Jesus, he went on to sentence Jesus to
death. Peter and Judas heard that voice, their consciences
each stricken with grief.

TRUTH AND RELIGIOUS PRACTICE

There was another who heard that voice -- a Samaritan
woman, a loose woman at that, for she had been married to
five men and the man with whom she was then living was not
her husband. She posed a typical question to Jesus, a question which arises when people of different cultural backgrounds discuss their religious differences: Which is the
correct way? "Our fathers worshiped on this mountain," she
said, "and you say that in Jerusalem is the place where men
ought to worship."

Jesus responded to the woman by pointing her sights beyond the physical acts and motions of worship:

> The hour is coming when neither on this mountain nor in Jerusalem will you worship the Father ... the hour is coming, and now is when the true worshippers will worship the Father in spirit and truth, for such the Father seeks to worship Him. God is spirit, and those who worship Him must worship in spirit and truth (John 4:20-24).

The woman was so impressed that she invited others in the town to come and meet this Jesus, who had told her the truth about herself and had challenged her to worship God "in spirit and truth."

The kind of question which troubled the Samaritan woman is not unlike the questions Christians and Muslims ask of each other today. Attention is easily focused on external matters -- the direction and the frequency of prayer, the performance of ablutions, the wearing of certain garments, the choice of certain names, the avoidance of certain foods, the recitation of certain formulas. Which is the correct way? Is one a way of truth and the other of error? Or is there truth in each? What is the truth?

GOD AND TRUTH

We today tend to think of truth as the opposite of falsehood. "He's telling lies" is almost like a game with children, but even then, there are times when it becomes a very serious game. Tempers flare. Accusations and countercharges surface. What started as a game becomes a fight. When this kind of quarrel bursts upon the adult scene, it has a potential for the most serious consequences, and when it happens on the world scene, it creates the possibility of war.

There is a proverb which says "Talk is cheap." It is easy to make assertions, insinuations and promises. It is quite another thing to prove what one has asserted, to document what one has insinuated and to fulfil what one has promised. This is the difference between the "truth" of God and man's "truth."

For a proper understanding of this important distinction we need to explore the usage of a key biblical concept. It comes to us through a variety of words, but they all derive

from the same basic Hebrew and Greek roots. The most common
of these words has been adopted into almost every language
on the face of the earth. This is the word "Amen." Two
others -- *emeth* and *emunah* -- are closely related to it, but
we rarely catch the connexion. For one thing, we don't know
the Hebrew language, and therefore are not capable of noting
the similar derivation. For another, we're misled by the
King James Version which, following the Septuagint, trans-
lates *emeth* and *emunah* as "truth" when the more accurate
equivalent in most cases would be "faithfulness."

In our multilingual society we daily wrestle with the
problem of communication across linguistic boundaries. As
we all know, sometimes even the simplest expression is muti-
lated and distorted in the process of translation. It is
difficult, almost impossible, to get an exact equivalent for
every word.

"Truth" is an exact equivalent for *emeth* only if we are
going to read all the meaning into the word truth that the
Hebrews read into the word *emeth*. While this is not absolutely impossible to do, it is complicated in view of the
usage to which truth is daily put in the vocabularies of
people around us. For the majority of them, truth is something which stands as the opposite of falsehood. Truth is
the opposite of a lie.

Christians and Muslims are as much a part of the cultural
milieu about them as is anyone else. Hence, when Christians
and Muslims, too, talk about truth, it is usually in the
framework of "true" versus "false." Was Muhammad a true
prophet or a false prophet? Did Jesus die upon the cross,
or did He not? Did the Jews change the message of the Old
Testament, and Christians alter the message of the New? Was
Muhammad the Comforter promised in John 15:26? Is Jesus the
Son of God? Was man born with original sin? Is the original
copy of the Quran in heaven?

The nature of the questions implies that if you can answer
the questions correctly, everything is alright between you
and God. As students succeed or fail in examinations on the
basis of more true answers than false, so when the Final
Judgment comes, successful candidates will be those who are
able to recite the right answers. To many, this is what it
is to "know the truth."

As a result of this perspective, many of our inquirer and
catechetical classes become nothing more than rote recitation

of certain formulas which have been drawn up and propounded as capsule summaries of the "truth." Since Africans are especially adept at memorization, many courses of instruction have become just that -- memorization sessions. The unhappy result is that many Christian people amass a great amount of information, but never go beyond that. They never take the second step of transferring their knowledge from "head" to "heart."

Martin Luther and his heroic predecessors and successors rescued the Gospel from the tyrannical hold of a widespread ignorance which threatened to destroy its sweet simplicity and beauty. After surviving the struggle which saw him placed under the ban and execution order of both Church and State, Luther sought to make a start at eradicating this ignorance by producing two catechisms. They were to be used by pastors in teaching their flocks and by fathers in teaching their households. It wasn't long before catechisms as aids to teaching spread among the Reformed and Roman Catholic churches as well.

While this practice brought many blessings into the lives of Christian people, it also brought certain dangers. One result was that many churches fell into the pitfall of labelling as "truth" and teaching as essential for salvation whatever particular doctrines appeared in their catechisms. Christians went on to preach that those who accepted these doctrines would be saved; those who did not were spurned as having a different spirit. This kind of practice is still with us today. Jealous of our own "truth," we protect it by limiting our fellowship and only reluctantly admit that other Christians may have a body of truth as acceptable to God as is our own.

The most disturbing aspect of this situation is that the "truth" we garner so carefully, defend so zealously, and protect so jealously is often far removed from the truth of which the Bible speaks. The Bible speaks of a Life which was lived -- not a set of intellectual equations. It tells of a Person who acts and moves on His own initiative of mercy to embrace and forgive men -- not One who is limited by our inadequate definitions of Who He is and how He moves. This is the God of history Who established a covenant with Israel and kept that covenant even when Israel failed. This is He who speaks and brings to pass what He has spoken. *He is faithful.* This is why He is the "God of truth" (Deut. 32:4; Ps. 31:5, KJV).

To the Greeks truth was intellectual. It was assertions which could be proved. It was formulations which could be tested in debate and affirmed. It was historical facts which could be verified. It was impersonal and objective. This is the understanding of truth which Christians and Muslims alike have borrowed from the Greek world of thought. Our general comprehension of truth as objective intellectual formulations bears out this contention. What is lost, unfortunately, is the rich meaning that Moses, David, and other Hebrew writers attached to the word truth.

While truth for the Hebrews had the Greek connotation of objective fact versus falsehood, there was something more. Truth had to do with character and personality -- it was not divorced from life. It was something to be experienced and something to be lived. It was a quality of life, the earmarks of which were dependability, reliability, trustworthiness, consistency, and faithfulness.

Truth in Hebrew thought is best exemplified in the relationships between God and man. The second half of the Book of Isaiah glories in the praises of Him Who "does not faint or grow weary" (40:28). He "defers His anger" (48:9) and does not "forsake the blind" (42:16). He does not "forget" His people (49:15) because He is "the Lord, Who is faithful" (49:7). What is so unusual in this quality of God's being is that "if we are faithless, He remains faithful -- for He cannot deny Himself" (2 Tim. 2:13).

God is "true" in that He is faithful. The signs of His faithfulness are seen in His fulfilling His Word to man. This is the central theme of Isaiah 40-66 where God issues a challenge to all the peoples of the earth. They are to bring their witnesses to testify to what their gods have accomplished, the primary test resting in their faithfulness. Have they been able to speak and to bring their words to pass?

Again and again, God uses the Prophet Isaiah to bombard His "witnesses" with the same question:

> Who told you this long ago?
>   Who declared it of old?
> Was it not I, the Lord   (45:21)?

Yes, God affirms,

> The former things I declared of old, they
> went forth from my mouth and I made them

> known; then suddenly I did them and they came
> to pass... I declared them to you from of
> old; before they came to pass I announced
> them to you (48:3,5).

God goes on to challenge Israel's attention anew:

> From this time forth I make you hear new
> things, hidden things which you have not
> known. They are created now, not long ago;
> before today you have never heard of them,
> lest you should say, "Behold, I knew them"
> (48:6f).

The obvious question comes next, "You have heard; now see
all this, and will you not declare it" (48:6)?

God's punishment would fall upon His people, but his mercy
would not fail them. Disaster would come to them for their
rebellion, but in His faithfulness He would not cut them off
forever. The assurances of this abiding, unfailing love are
frequent, beautiful, and clear. While looking toward the
future, God speaks to Israel as if her deliverance is taking
place in the present (Is. 54:7-10). This is how sure His
threats and promises are. This is how true the Word that He
speaks is. When "I Am Who I Am" speaks (Ex. 3:14), He causes
to happen what He announces. No wonder men are to "tremble
at His Word" (Is. 66:2,5).

JESUS AND TRUTH

It is no accident that Christians see the New Testament
Word, the Messiah, so vividly prophesied and portrayed in
that same second half of the Book of Isaiah. It was from
this prophecy that Jesus quoted when He announced His ministry to His "home congregation" in Nazareth (Luke 4:18f). It
is in this prophecy that we see, not a muted but a minutely-
detailed description of the Suffering, Death and Resurrection
of Christ. Not only are the facts there in accurate detail,
but the purposes for their happening are there -- and all of
this spoken some seven hundred years before Christ was born
in Bethlehem.

Aspects of the Word of prophecy concerning Christ were
actually authenticated long before His coming when God delivered the Jewish remnant from exile in far-off Persia.
They had been carried into slavery by Babylon, but even before their going, God had spoken of deliverance:

> Comfort, comfort my people, says your God.
> Speak tenderly to Jerusalem ...
>   that her iniquity is pardoned.
>
> A voice cries:
> "In the wilderness prepare the way of the Lord,
>   make straight in the desert a highway for
>   our God.
> Every valley shall be lifted up,
>   and every mountain and hill be made low ...
> And the glory of the Lord shall be revealed,
>   and all flesh shall see it together,
>   for the mouth of the Lord has spoken"
> (Is. 40:1-5).

This Word of God was fulfilled when Persia succeeded Babylon as the world power of that time and King Cyrus ordered his own military to assure safe passage for the Jews across the wilderness back to their old homeland. When God speaks, He brings His Word to pass.

As with so many prophecies, this prophecy had a New Testament fulfilment as well. Its fulfilment unfolded in a new and dynamic way when John the Baptist appeared "preaching a baptism of repentance for the forgiveness of sins" (Luke 3:3). But instead of proclaiming a highway of deliverance across the desert, he proclaimed a highway of deliverance through the crusts of sin and guilt which weigh heavily upon the hearts of men. He announced the salvation which was to come by Him who was the Lamb of God.

God's faithfulness had been proved in the First Exodus out of Egypt. In an equally remarkable way, it was renewed with the Second Exodus, the delivery out of captivity in Babylon. The most remarkable of all, however, was the Third Exodus -- man's deliverance out of the captivity of sin! In that process Satan's stranglehold upon man's allegiance was crushed. His sign of victory -- disease, and death -- was once and for all broken and destroyed. Looking forward to that day Isaiah had said, "He will swallow up death forever, and the Lord God will wipe away tears from all faces, and the reproach of His people He will take away from all the earth, for the Lord has spoken" (25:8). This is the background to the victory shout in the great Resurrection chapter of the Bible:

> Death is swallowed up in victory ...
> O death, where is thy sting?

> The sting of death is sin, and the power of
> sin is the law. But thanks be to God, who
> gives us the victory through our Lord Jesus
> Christ (I Cor. 15:54ff).

The "truth" to which Jesus came to bear witness is the
faithfulness and consistency of God. God is "true" to His
spoken Word. In a very special sense, Jesus is that Word
of God, for

> No one has ever seen God; the only Son, who
> is in the bosom of the Father, He has made
> Him known (John 1:18).

We can look at a person and make various judgments about
him from his appearance. We can tell whether he is tall or
short. We can tell whether he is black, or white, or yellow.
We can tell whether he is young or old, and a lot of other
things, but until he speaks, we are unable to tell whether
he is educated or uneducated, African, American or European,
whether he is a good man or a fool. As soon as he opens his
mouth, we begin to know who he is, and the more he talks,
the more he gives away about himself.

Words, however, are only a partial indication of a person's character and personality. Since "talk is cheap," it
is possible for a person to completely deceive another concerning his personality and his character. He can make himself out to be something that he is not. In the final analysis, it is his actions which lend credibility to his language.

Jesus not only communicated God's Word verbally -- He
lived that Word! He demonstrated its meaning so perfectly
that, as we have seen, He was given the unusual title "the
Word." His faithfulness to God's will carried Him to victory over death and in the process added yet even deeper
dimensions to that title. "The Word became flesh and dwelt
among us, full of grace and truth" (John 1:14). God's mercy
and God's truth took on new depths of meaning as Jesus died,
for God was faithful to the point of even allowing Christ to
go through death for us. It is "through Him," then, that we
"have confidence in God, Who raised Him from the dead and
gave Him glory" (I Pet. 1:21).

We "have confidence" in God because He is faithful. His
faithfulness and consistency are so unlike the capriciousness
and unreliability of the other spirits men and women worship.
Some of these are ancestral spirits; others, spirits of the

soil, or the air, or the rivers, or the trees. Men go to
great lengths to buy protection for themselves and their
households. Unfortunately, the reliability of that protection is no more certain than when and where lightning will
strike next. By way of contrast, God's faithfulness is
compared to the regularity of the dawn and the spring showers:

> Let us press on to know the Lord;
>   His going forth is sure as the dawn;
> He will come to us as the showers,
>   as the spring rains that water the earth
> (Hos. 6:3).

The supreme demonstration of God's faithfulness to men is
Jesus. He is "Emmanuel ... God with us" (Matt. 1:23). He
is "the Amen, the faithful and true witness" (Rev. 3:14).
"He who has seen Me has seen the Father," Jesus said (John
14:9), and again, "He who sees Me sees Him Who sent Me"
(John 12:45).

It seems so natural in the light of Jesus' special and
unique role in history that He would preface so many of his
statements with the Greek *Amen, amen, lego humin* -- familiar
to us as the "verily, verily, I say unto you" of the King
James translation. Truly, He is the One of Whom Paul exults:

> All the promises of God find their Yes in
> Him. That is why we utter the Amen through
> Him, to the glory of God (2 Cor. 1:20).

"I am the Way," Jesus said, "the Truth, and the Life"
(John 14:6). Although He probably spoke those words in
Aramaic, they are recorded for us in the Greek language,
which in its usage of truth (*aletheia*) puts an emphasis upon the factual and the intellectual. He was, however, talking to people whose background was Hebrew. Because He was
a Hebrew speaking to Hebrews, their understanding of whatever word he used had to have been coloured by their understanding of the equivalent Hebrew words *emeth* and *emunah*.
The primary emphasis in those words, as we have seen, was
upon the faithfulness, the dependability, and the consistency of God.

To "worship God in spirit and in truth," then, is more
than just to believe that Jesus lived and died. "Even the
demons believe," the Bible tells us, "and shudder" (James
2:19). This kind of belief, however, is not enough. What
God calls for is a faith which grows out of trust in His

faithfulness for there is a close relationship between God's faithfulness and our faith. To worship God in spirit and in "faithfulness" is to commit yourself into God's care as seriously as Jesus was committed. It is to "cast all your anxieties on Him, for He cares about you" (I Pet. 5:7). It is to be "buried with Him by baptism into death, so that as Christ was raised from the dead by the glory of the Father, we too might walk in newness of life" (Rom. 6:4). It is "to be justified by faith in Christ, and not by works of the Law, because by works of the Law shall no one be justified" (Gal. 2:16). It is to "live as free men, yet without using ... freedom as a pretext for evil" (I Pet. 2:16). It is to "continue" in His "Word" for

> If you continue in My Word, you are truly My disciples ... you will know the truth, and the truth will make you free (John 8:31f).

THE PROBLEM OF FREEDOM

Christian freedom poses problems not only for Christians, but also for Muslims. Muslims are bewildered by the wide range of freedom that Christians enjoy, interpreting this freedom as licence for wrongdoing and unwillingness to submit to the clear commands of God. Christians, on the other hand, often misunderstand and misuse their liberty, either excusing certain acts which make a travesty of their liberty, or just the opposite, making a mockery of their liberty by demanding the fulfilment of requirements which God Himself does not impose upon man.

Some of the Scriptural directives Christians have used to legislate all kinds of rules upon themselves are the following:

   a. You, therefore, must be perfect, as your
      heavenly Father is perfect (Matt. 5:48).

   b. Decide never to put a stumbling block or
      hindrance in the way of a brother (Rom. 14:13).

   c. Take note of those who create dissensions
      and difficulties in opposition to the doc-
      trine which you have been taught; avoid
      them (Rom. 16:17).

   d. Take care lest this liberty of yours some-
      how become a stumbling block to the weak
      (I Cor. 8:9).

e. Whoever ... eats the bread or drinks the
cup of the Lord in an unworthy manner
will be guilty of profaning the body and
the blood of the Lord (I Cor. 11:27).

f. All things should be done decently and
in order (I Cor. 14:40).

g. Come out from them, and be separate from
them, says the Lord, and touch nothing
unclean; then I will welcome you (2 Cor.
6:14,17).

h. I warn every one who hears the words of
the prophecy of this book: if any one
adds to them, God will add to him the
plagues described in this book, and if
any one takes away from the word of the
book of this prophecy, God will take away
his share in the tree of life and in the
holy city (Rev. 22:18f).

On the basis of these passages and others Christians have
gone to varying lengths creating pictures of what godly
lives are like. These portraits which are held up as ideals
to be emulated often turn out to be strange composites of
our own cultures, biblical cultures, survivals from previous
cultures, and various biblical interpretations and applications. What emerges in each circle of Christians is an attempt to turn these pictures into reality by way of adopting
certain policies. The ideal pictures stand as shadows behind the policies.

Some of the laws which govern policy and practice in each
society of Christians are written down in the form of creeds,
confessions, constitutions and bylaws. Others are unwritten,
although this doesn't necessarily mean they are any less
binding. Written and unwritten -- these regulations stamp
a mark of distinction upon each group of Christians giving
them a unique character all their own.

The fascinating diversity which comes out of these different groups with their various backgrounds distresses many
Christians and disturbs many Muslims. In itself, this diversity is not evil. What is to be lamented is the imposition
of these diversified forms and patterns upon others as essential rules to be followed in the ordering of their Christian
lives. New Christians are entitled to freedom just as much

as are old Christians, and they are entitled to just as much
freedom -- full individual freedom and full group freedom.
They are free in Christ to develop their own "worship in
spirit and in truth," their own lifestyle, and their own
service to the glory of His Name. If this assumption is
acceptable, we should hesitate to interpret diversity as a
satanic fragmentation of the Church's unity. We should
rather see in this prominent feature of present-day church
life a healthy sign of the freedom which God gives so liber-
ally to His people.

As with the rest of God's gifts, this gift can be mishan-
dled and misused. Here is where the problem comes in for
Christians. They value so much what they have that they
don't want to lose it. They have often had to struggle hard
to get where they are in their doctrinal formulation and in-
stitutional development. The oddity is that once having
gotten there, it is so easy to try to stabilize and formalize
practices and procedures in such a way that further exercise
of the very freedom which enabled them to reach that point
is stifled and crushed.[49] There is such a great fear of
losing what has come to be cherished that the slightest
abuse or misuse of freedom is construed as valid argumenta-
tion for curtailing and controlling freedom all the more.
Again and again, this kind of rationale has closed the door
to further development, enjoyment and practice of the very
freedom which in Christ is a precious and potentially productive gift of God to man.

FREEDOM VERSUS LEGALISM

The danger in all this is that the simple truth of the
Gospel is so easily camouflaged and buried under legalistic
stipulations which have no bearing whatever upon man's eternal welfare. This is why Peter asked in the first known
convention of the church:

> Why do you make trial of God by putting a yoke
> upon the neck of the disciples which neither
> our fathers nor we have been able to bear (Acts
> 15:10)?

This is why Paul insisted,

> For freedom Christ has set us free; stand fast
> therefore, and do not submit again to a yoke
> of slavery (Gal. 5:1).

And this is why Paul pleaded:

> Why do you submit to regulations, "Do not
> handle, do not taste, do not touch" (re-
> ferring to things which all perish as they
> are used), according to human precepts and
> doctrines? These have indeed an appear-
> ance of wisdom in promoting rigour of de-
> votion and self-abasement and severity to
> the body, but they are of no value in
> checking the indulgence of the flesh
> (Col. 2:20-23).

Peter responded to his own question by asserting:

> We believe that we shall be saved through the
> grace of the Lord Jesus, just as they will
> (Acts 15:11).

Similarly, Paul in a beautifully clear statement expressed
simply and concisely exactly why man's rules, regulations,
and works are altogether useless in determining or improving his relationships with God. A right relationship with
God, he explained, "depends not upon man's will or exertion,
but upon God's mercy" (Rom. 9:16).

Earlier we observed that "Christ is the end of the Law"
(Rom. 10:4). Paul spoke those words in the context of
speaking about his own people, Israel. He bore them witness
that they had "a zeal for God," but it was "not enlightened."
In delineating their dilemma and isolating the truth of their
situation he used a word which is very dear to Muslims --
the word "submit." Paul said,

> Being ignorant of the righteousness that comes
> from God, and seeking to establish their own,
> they did not *submit* to God's righteousness
> (Rom. 10:3).

We must be careful, however, that we do not conclude that
this "ignorance," this "seeking to establish their own," and
this unwillingness to "submit to God's righteousness" is a
peculiarly Jewish or Muslim problem. It is our problem. It
is the problem of man. It is the problem of man's righteousness versus God's righteousness. It is the problem of whether to serve God under the Law or under grace.

As we have seen, Paul deals at considerable length with
this anguishing problem both in Romans and in Galatians. He

analyzes the purposes which the Law serves and spells out
the meaning of God's grace. In his debate he wrestles with
a concept closely related to that of submission -- the concept of slavery. Earlier we noted how this concept reflects
itself in the names that many Muslims bear. The word *abd*
(slave) combines with the names of God to serve as names
for people -- indicative of their relationship to God.

Christians do not ordinarily think of themselves as
"slaves" of God, preferring rather to emphasize "sonship,"
"heritage," and "promise" as indicators of their new relationship with God in Christ (Gal. 3,4; Rom. 8). Jesus himself had said,

> No longer do I call you servants (*doulos*,
> the equivalent of *abd*), for the servant
> does not know what his master is doing;
> but I have called you friends, for all
> that I have heard from My Father I have
> made known to you (John 15:15).

Still, this new status and the freedom which comes with it
do not keep Paul from speaking of Christians as "slaves of
righteousness" and "slaves of God" in the context of trying
to discover and explain the meaning for man of what has happened in Christ.

FREEDOM AND THE NEW CREATION[50]

Christ came "while we were yet helpless" (Rom. 5:6). We
were helpless because we were "enslaved to sin" (Rom. 6:6).
It is this release from the dominion and control of sin
which frees man for an entirely new, dynamic and creative
relationship with God, a relationship which is so new and
dynamic and creative because it is no longer based upon Law,
but upon grace. "Sin will have no dominion over you, since
you are not under Law but under grace" (Rom. 6:14). "Having
been set free from sin, you have become slaves of righteousness" (Rom. 6:18).

The bondage of sin and the restrictions of the Law hold
man captive in a grasp of condemnation and death. Left to
his own resources, he is no freer than an animal in a cage.
He moves and manipulates his position as best he can as if
he were master of his own destiny, but the four walls are
still there along with the top and the bottom. His only
escape is through death, and what is on the horizon then,
he has no way of knowing -- unless he is willing to listen
to Someone who has crossed over that horizon and returned.

Here is the mystery of what happens when a person comes
to know Christ as His Saviour. He walks with Him through
death into life. He crawls out of the box in which the Law
had held him captive and serves God in a new and unrestrained
kind of freedom.

> You have died to the Law through the body of
> Christ, so that you may belong to another, to
> Him Who has been raised from the dead in or-
> der that we may bear fruit for God. While we
> were living in the flesh, our sinful passions,
> aroused by the Law, were at work in our mem-
> bers to bear fruit for death. But now we are
> discharged from the Law, dead to that which
> held us captive, so that we serve not under
> the old written code but in the new life of
> the Spirit (Rom. 7:4ff).

Laws restrict and restrain. Have you ever heard of anyone
doubling his income tax because he wanted to show his appreciation for what the Government has done for him? Yet,
there are Christians who have doubled the tithe required of
men under the Law of Moses. Laws set limitations and people
are expected to operate within those limitations. Some do
it gladly; others, grudgingly, but even then, you rarely
hear of people exceeding the requirements -- whether gladly,
or grudgingly.

It is different with those who "serve not under the old
written code but in the new life of the Spirit." They are
"slaves of God," but there is no limitation to their service. They are "slaves of righteousness," but there is no
restriction upon their obedience. They are free people --
free to serve and free to obey as the Spirit moves them.

"Who are you to pass judgment on the servant of another?"
Paul asks. "It is before his own master that he stands or
falls" (Rom. 14:4). It is in this kind of context that we
have to also understand Jesus's "Judge not, that you be not
judged" (Matt. 7:1) and Paul's "Let no one pass judgment on
you in questions of food and drink or with regard to a festival or a new moon or a sabbath" (Col. 2:16). The freedom
we have in Christ extends into so many of the areas over
which we are inclined to pass judgment on each other. It is
hard for us to recognize that other parts of the body of
Christ, although having different functions and capabilities
and characteristics, are fully as much a part of the body as
are we.

It may be difficult for some of us, for example, to understand and appreciate the spontaneous shouting which goes on
during moments of prayer in some Pentecostal and spiritual
churches. We may refer to the Scriptures and say that this
kind of practice is contrary to "all things being done decently and in order" (I Cor. 14:40). We may be inclined to
answer our Muslim friends as did Pius, "As for those so-
called Christians, they don't quite know what they're doing.
Come to our church, or to Yakubu's." The tremendous freedom which God gives to His people in Christ opens the door
for a multitude of religious forms and patterns of worship,
each as valid and acceptable to God as the other.

Once we begin to grasp something of the startling beauty
of the divine-human mosaic which appears to us in visible
form as the sum total of the churches about us wherever
God's Word is preached and lived, we can't help but begin to
feel very humble. We're part of a great plan -- a plan that
God in His freedom initiated, a plan which has as its purpose freeing man that man might be free to serve Him. "He
died for all," Paul writes, "that those who live might live
no longer for themselves but for Him who for their sake died
and was raised" (2 Cor. 5:15). The guidelines for this life
of service to Him are in the Law, but the emphasis in the
Law is no longer upon the Law as a set of requirements. In
Christ, the Law has a different dimension. It is "the perfect Law, the Law of liberty" (James 1:25).

This "Law of liberty" finds its fulfilment in love (Rom.
13:10). "You were called to freedom," says Paul, "only do
not use your freedom as an opportunity for the flesh, but
through love be servants of one another" (Gal. 5:13). "Bear
one another's burdens, and so fulfil the Law of Christ" (Gal.
6:2). The emphasis in these passages is so different from
how people talk about the Law of Moses, or the requirements
for membership in their churches. Here the emphasis grows
out of a response to God's faithfulness -- a faithfulness
freely demonstrated in his dealings with man. It is a faithfulness centred in the cross of Christ, and it is that faithfulness which serves both as invitation and pattern for our
own dealings with our fellow men.[51]

It is here in the cross of Christ that truth and freedom
meet. The cross becomes for Christians the symbol both of
God's truthfulness (faithfulness) to man and man's freedom.
"For the joy that was set before Him," Jesus the "Truth" of
God, the "Amen," "endured the cross, despising the shame"
(Heb. 12:2). Freely, of His own accord, He walked that way

of servitude. Thus it is that so much culminates in the
colossal event of the cross. The truth of man is there --
his sin, his guilt, his shame; the truth of God is there --
His innocence, His pure love and mercy, His glory. The
truth of man is there -- his bondage, his helplessness and
hopelessness, his misery, his agony of death; the truth of
God is there -- His initiative for man and His free joy at
taking up the cross of sacrifice. The truth of man is
there -- his help, his hope, his peace; the truth of God is
there -- His world-embracing demonstration of faithfulness,
freely planned, freely offered, freely given. The truth of
man is there -- relief for guilty consciences, reconciliation with God, the seeds of new creation; the truth of God
is there -- all His promises fulfilled. The truth of man
is there -- unfaithfulness, broken covenants, despair; the
truth of God is there -- His perfect healing, His renewal
of His perfect relationship with man.

This is the cause of the Christian's new freedom and joy
unbounded. There is no limitation to the good things he can
undertake in the Lord, no boundary to the kindness he can
unleash in the world. He is no longer a victim of the Law's
consequences, nor is he restricted by its limitations or its
requirements. With Paul he can say,

> We are the true circumcision, who worship God
> in spirit, and glory in Christ Jesus, and put
> no confidence in the flesh (Phil. 3:3).

All things are only secondary compared to gaining Christ.

> Whatever gain I had, I counted as loss for the
> sake of Christ. Indeed I count everything as
> loss because of the surpassing worth of know-
> ing Christ Jesus my Lord. For His sake I have
> suffered the loss of all things, and count them
> as refuse, in order that I may gain Christ and
> be found in Him, not having a righteousness of
> my own, based on law, but that which is through
> faith in Christ, the righteousness from God
> that depends on faith; that I may know him and
> the power of his resurrection, and may share
> his sufferings, becoming like him in his death,
> that if possible I may attain the resurrection
> from the dead (Phil. 3:7-11).

The only thing that counts is being part of the new creation.

> Far be it from me to glory except in the
> cross of our Lord Jesus Christ, by which the
> world has been crucified to me, and I to the
> world. For neither circumcision counts for
> anything, nor uncircumcision, but a new cre-
> ation (Gal. 6:14f).

Christians again and again lose sight of the centrality
of the cross in their lives and in their witness. In the
light of all that happened there, it seems so sad that we
so often get all wrapped up and excited over many things
which in the larger context of life and eternity have no
real significance. This is what Paul meant when he talked
about counting all things "refuse" and being "crucified" to
the world. In the new freedom he had in Christ these things
were no longer of any consequence.

In the freedom which is ours in Christ the emphasis is on
service and the motivation is love. It is a love which flows
ceaselessly and selflessly even in small matters like the
giving of a cup of cold water (Matt. 10:42). When this love
takes hold of you, you "do nothing from selfishness or con-
ceit, but in humility count others better than yourself. You
look not only to your own interests, but also to the interests of others" (Phil. 2:3f). This is the love of which
Paul so eloquently speaks in the great "Love" chapter of
the Bible:

> Love is patient and kind; love is not jealous
> or boastful; it is not arrogant or rude. Love
> does not insist on its own way; it is not ir-
> ritable or resentful; it does not rejoice at
> wrong, but rejoices in the right. Love bears
> all things, believes all things, hopes all
> things, endures all things (I Cor. 13:4-7).

When this love rules our lives, we are free to accept each
other as we are.[52] We are free to be the kind of faithful
witnesses God has really called us to be.

7

Conversion

"IS THE GOAL OF CHRISTIAN LOVE CONVERSION?"

*"Don't kid me about your Christian love being so special,"
said Muhammadu. "Why, your love is no different from the
love of anyone else in the world."*

*Ama rose up quickly to a defence of the love which she
herself poured out so generously into our neighbourhood.
"What do you mean, Muhammadu? Show me where you Muslims
have built even one hospital or clinic. Show me where
you've started even one school to train the young of this
country. Show me, if you can, if there is any such thing
as a Muslim love to compare with the kind of love Christians
have for people. Look what Christians have done -- and all
out of love."*

*"That's exactly what I mean," Muhammadu replied. "The
Christian's love is no different from the world's. The
world loves in order to gain something. I love my neighbours in order to get their business. The politician loves
people in order to get their votes. Christians love people
in order to get them to come to their churches. That's
what I mean, Christians love others only in order to convert
them."*

*"That's not true, Muhammadu. We, of course, are interested
in more people becoming Christian, but that's not the main
reason we build hospitals and schools and feed the hungry and
clothe the poor. We believe that because of what Christ has
done for us we are no longer to live for ourselves, but for
others. Jesus gave us an example of how we are to do when*

He washed the feet of the disciples (John 13:1-15). 'We
love because He first loved us' (I John 4:19). That's what
Christian love is all about."

"It's beautiful how you talk about it, Ama, and kind of
idealistic, but let's get down to practicalities. When I
was working in the North, I became sick. I had to go to a
hospital and the closest one was a Christian hospital. Every
morning we had to sit through church. I was afraid if I
didn't, I wouldn't be looked after properly. Even the
people who came as outpatients had to listen to a sermon before they could get attention. Is that love to force a man
to hear a sermon before you treat his wound, or give him
medicine?"

"Muhammadu," said Ama. "Let's say you had two very
precious gifts to share with your neighbour -- two keys, a
silver and a gold. Let's say the gold was the more precious.
It was the key to eternal life while the other was a key to
life on earth. You wanted your neighbour to have both, but
you had to give him one before the other. Now, if the medicine for his soul was the golden key, and the medicine for
his stomach was the silver key, wouldn't you feel that the
golden key should be given first?"

"It still seems to me you're taking selfish advantage of
people who don't have any other choice. I don't see how
you can claim Christian love is any different from how any
Muslim, or for that matter, any pagan loves his neighbour.
We're all out to get whatever we can -- let's admit it.
There's nothing wrong in that."

"But there is something wrong in that!" Ama thought
awhile before she continued. "I'll admit our Christian love
isn't always perfect. Our Master's was. Jesus' love was
perfect and His example is there for us to follow even though
we don't always succeed. Maybe we've sometimes let our love
be controlled by a selfish desire to win people for Christ,
rather than let it be controlled by Christ Himself. Whenever this selfish love is there, I think it is wrong --
whether it's a Christian, a Muslim, or a pagan. This is one
of the things that's hurting our country. Everybody is out
to get whatever he can. But, that's not right. That's
wrong!"

"Well, right or wrong, that's how it is, and I don't
think you or I are going to change this neighbourhood, or
the world." With that final analysis, Muhammadu shrugged

his shoulders as if he'd resigned himself to making the best
out of life in a world which lived by the philosophy of
"dog eat dog." As he sauntered down the road, a lorry
passed by with the inscription, *Duniya*. *Duniya* means "World"
in Hausa and the import of that one-word proverb had been
pretty well summarized by Muhammadu. That's how the world
is. You take it, or leave it.

Ama looked at me and asked, "Yakubu, didn't you have anything to say to help me out with Muhammadu? How do you convince a Muslim that our love isn't selfish?"

"I'm not sure," I replied. "Muhammadu confronted us with
some difficult questions. I can see how they would come up
from a Muslim point of view. I think there are times when
our love is discoloured. We're so anxious to get members
and we've only so much time and so much energy that we con-
centrate our attention where we hope to get the best results.

"Last week, for example, our Elders considered steps to
get more members. It doesn't seem we've been growing like
we were a few years ago. Everybody brought his own suggestion, but the ones which were the most seriously debated
had to do with whether to start a nursery school, or a
clinic, or both. Someone observed that this is why the
Catholic church is growing so fast."

"I know," said Ama. "We've been having the same discussions in our church, and there's a lot of difference of
opinion. Even Kwesi and I don't agree on this subject at
all. The more we've argued about it, the more it seems to
me that we're talking about two separate things. Getting
members is one thing; starting a school or a clinic is
another."

"I'll agree with you there," I chimed in. "They're two
different subjects and that's where a lot of the confusion
comes about, but that brings up another problem. Can you
really separate the two?"

"I think you can," Ama answered, "and that's what I think
we need to do."

"That's well and good," I replied, "but like Muhammadu
said, let's get down to practicalities. Jesus said we are
to go and disciple all nations. Right? If I am interested
in fulfilling the Great Commission and if building schools

and hospitals helps in that process, why should I be ashamed of admitting this to my Muslim neighbour? Why should we be ashamed of admitting this to ourselves? Why not even openly proclaim it to the world?"

"Something isn't quite right in that kind of a philosophy of missions, Yakubu. I still can't quite put my finger on what troubles me about it. Maybe our problem is that we don't understand what happens in conversion, or more especially what our particular role in conversion is. What I see happening around us, though, is that the Father makes His sun rise on the evil and on the good, and sends rain on the just and on the unjust (Matt. 5:45). I see Jesus healing the ten lepers even though only one returned to thank Him (Luke 17:18). I wonder if our love can be anything less -- outgoing, undemanding, unhesitating, embracing all men."

"But, Ama, be honest with yourself. Why do you embrace other people with this love? Isn't it that they in turn would embrace the Lord and become His disciples?"

"No," Ama reiterated. "It's not that." Then she thought a minute and she wasn't any longer so sure of herself. She repeated the question to herself in another form, "Is the goal of Christian love conversion? No," she answered, "it's not."

While I was awaiting a fuller explanation for her conclusion, one of Matthew's children came running up and said Ama was needed at home. Long after she had gone, I still sat paging through my Bible. I knew her question would haunt me until I found an answer. Really, it was my question, and not simply hers. She had only framed it more accurately, "Is the goal of Christian love conversion?" I felt I needed to know and would not rest until I did.

CONFUSION ABOUT CONVERSION[53]

Why do you suppose Muhammadu was turned off by the idea of conversion to Christianity? Did he have valid reasons for being suspicious of the motives for Christian love? Was he right in his assessment of Christian love as being no different from the love of the world? If the aim behind a Christian's loving his neighbour is gaining him for Christ, is this selfish and wrong? These are some of the many questions Muslims and other non-Christians force Christians to face.

Christians themselves are bothered by yet other questions.
How can Christians convert more Muslims? Why are Muslims
so difficult to convert? Is there any reason to try to convert Muslims when they have their own religion already? Why
do Muslims allow their sons to marry Christian wives, but
refuse to let their daughters marry Christian husbands? Why
do Muslims disown and disinherit their children who become
Christians?

There is much confusion among both Christians and Muslims
regarding conversion to Christianity. Muslims feel threatened by the possibility and Christians feel frustrated by
what seem so few results from so many efforts. To remedy
the situation, Christians often move from one evangelistic
effort to another, while Muslims withdraw even further out
of reach into the protective security of their own enclaves.

For Muslims, conversion to Christianity has ominous over-
tones. It is associated with a denial of Muslim values,
and Muslims who convert to Christianity are sometimes regarded by fellow Muslims as traitors. Muslim parents take
various precautions to safeguard their children, even to
the extent of keeping them out of school. With the still
growing need for an educated working force, this refusal
and neglect are a costly price for individuals, families
and nations to pay in an effort to preserve their religious
principles. As long as this continues, it means that Muslims will be further handicapped in keeping up with the
rapid pace of national development and in contributing their
fair share.

WHAT HAPPENS IN CONVERSION

Much of the confusion about conversion comes because
Christians and Muslims alike have a mixed-up understanding
of what happens in conversion. It seems so unfortunate that
two large groups of people who have strong religious convictions and at the same time are ready to hearken to the word
of Jesus should fall into such discord over what Jesus described in these words, "I tell you, there is joy before the
angels of God over one sinner who repents" (Luke 15:10).
Shortly before that interpretive statement regarding the
parable of the lost coin, Jesus had told the parable of the
hundred sheep of which one was lost. When the sheep was
found, the owner invited his friends and neighbours to be
happy with him, saying, "Rejoice with me, for I have found
my sheep which was lost." Jesus followed that with an even
stronger interpretation, "Just so, I tell you, there will be

more joy in heaven over one sinner who repents than over ninety-nine righteous persons who need no repentance" (Luke 15:6f). Christians have often demanded more for conversion than God Himself demands. We have gone into this in some detail in previous chapters, but because there has been such widespread abuse of Christian freedom in this regard, we cannot just pass the subject by at this point without additional comment.

In the previous chapter, we concluded that the love which God has given us in Christ calls for us to accept our neighbour as he is. If this is so, and he wants to become a Christian, does he have to comply with all our rules and regulations in order to be accepted by God in Christ? Does he need to change his clothing, his food, his name and sometimes his neighbourhood in order to become a Christian? Does he need to learn to speak another language? Does he need to change the whole rhythm of his life? In other words, when it comes to conversion, of all our living habits, which things are important and which unimportant in the larger context of life and eternity?

We shall go into these matters at greater length in a later chapter, but we should remind ourselves once again that these things are the "yoke" of which Peter was speaking and the "bondage" to which Paul was referring. We have said it before, but we must emphasize it once again, *"Christ is the end of the Law"* (Rom. 10:4), and that is the end of the Law in all its parts. For those who are in Christ, the only rule is the freedom to love: "Owe no one anything, except to love one another" (Rom. 13:8). That perspective casts a damning judgment upon many of our requirements for church membership and "good Christianity."

CONVERSION IS NOT OUR ACT

One of the most unfortunate misconceptions surrounding the phenomenon of conversion is that we are the authors and initiators of this act. Christians who are in love with their Lord and long that all men might come to know Him and to "worship Him in spirit and in truth" carry a great burden on their hearts for everyone who does not know the Lord. They want the truth to be known and proclaimed. They want to do their share, and are open to doing even more than their share -- if only someone can teach them a sure way, a tested method, or a proven pattern by which to operate so as to convert people to the Lord.

Conversion is not, however, that kind of manipulation of
human minds, nor is evangelism a matter of tested methods
and proven patterns.[54] Evangelism is a manner of living
and proclaiming the Word, and conversion is a matter of responding to that Word in a way that relieves a person from
the anxiety and uncertainty of relying upon himself for a
right relationship with God. In this process, one's life
is reoriented from service to self to sacrifice for others.
But this is not man's act; this is God's act!

Thus it is a gross presumption on the part of Christians
to assume that they have within themselves the power to convert others, or that they can somehow gain the key to this
kind of mastery over the minds and hearts of men. The way
some Christians talk about conversion and church growth, it
is as if the key to success lies somewhere within the grasp
of man. We must, however, remind ourselves again that conversion is not our act. It is a sovereign act of God! It
is as God spoke to the small colony of people who had returned to the Promised Land from their exile in Persia,
"Not by might, nor by power, but by My Spirit" (Zech. 4:6).

God had set before this remnant of His people, Israel,
a gigantic task -- the rebuilding of Jerusalem and the rebuilding of the Temple. They were discouraged by the magnitude of the task and the few workers to undertake it. The
Lord's assurance came through these words to Zerubbabel,
the Governor, "Not by might, nor by power, but by My Spirit,
says the Lord of hosts."

It is not by the "might" of our arguments, nor by the
"power" of our logic that we are going to convince any Muslims to accept Jesus as more than a Prophet.[55] It is not
by the "might" of our evidence, nor by the "power" of our
persuasion that we are going to force them to bow before
Him as their Lord and Master. It is "not by might, nor by
power, but by My Spirit, says the Lord of hosts."

CONVERSION AND CHRISTIAN WITNESS

While it is presumptuous for Christians to conclude that
conversion is an act which they control, it is wrong to divorce conversion from Christian witness altogether. There
is a relationship, but it is a relationship which is greatly
similar to what we have already seen between God, man and
salvation. When a man enters into a right relationship with
God, a position which is termed "righteousness," it is not
because of his fulfilling certain requirements, or even lend-

ing God an assist. It is totally God's doing. It comes
completely at His initiative. It is His act from beginning
to end! Similarly, we are in no position to take the credit
for someone's conversion anymore than we can take credit
for our physical birth, or our own conversion.[56] The glory
-- ALL -- belongs to God. Even our faith is His gift to us
(Rom. 12:3; Eph. 2:8f).

The beginning step in this new relationship of righteousness is conversion. There is a connexion between Christian
witness and conversion, but when conversion comes, it is
God's act. He call us to be faithful in our witness, to be
honest to others about His action and interaction in our
own lives and experience, but it is He who takes that witness and uses it to His glory. Thus, conversion happens at
His initiative.

When you read about the church at Corinth, you are almost
surprised to find any church there at all. The church was
beset behind and before by problem after problem. Among the
difficulties were what must have been very exasperating
problems in leadership. Not only that, there were dissensions within the family of God, not unlike some of the dissensions which divide Christians today. Some said they belonged to Apollos; others said, "No, we belong to Christ."

In speaking to this problem Paul asked a question not
only crucial to that situation, but also crucial to ours as
we look at our role as witnesses to Christ and the connexion
between our witness and conversion. Paul asked, "What then
is Apollos? What is Paul?" His answer puts a distance between our witness and conversion which has to keep us very
humble:

> Servants through whom you believed, as the Lord
> assigned to each. I planted, Apollos watered,
> but God gave the growth. So neither he who
> plants nor he who waters is anything, but only
> God who gives the growth (I Cor. 3:5ff).

Christian witness is connected to planting and watering, but
it is God who takes the seed and makes it grow.

The picture Paul gives about conversion and church growth
helps us in another way as well. It helps us to understand
conversion as a cumulative process in which more than one
Christian witness may participate. There is also a time
element involved, a warning for patience on the part of God's

people. Perhaps one of the things which has put a distaste
for the thought of conversion in the minds of many is the
urgency with which many Christians press people for immediate decisions to accept, or reject Christ. Unfortunately,
this kind of pressure forgets, or overlooks, the fact that
Christian witness is like the planting of seeds in the
ground. Sometimes it takes a seed a long, long time to
germinate and grow.

PRAYER AND THE HARVEST

It is God who brings the growth and who also brings the
fruit to fruition. Just as there is a time for planting,
so there is a time for harvest, and as the disciples of
Jesus have a role to play in the planting, so also they
have work to do in the harvest. Jesus said, "The harvest
is plentiful, but the labourers are few; pray therefore the
Lord of the harvest to send out labourers into His harvest"
(Luke 10:2). Generally we use this passage as a mission
text to inspire people to offer themselves as harvesters in
the Lord's vineyard, but that was not Jesus' emphasis. He
was calling for prayer, urging God's people to put the work
of harvest before Him in prayer. It is His harvest. He is
the Lord of the harvest. It is He who has prepared the
fruit for harvest. It is He who will provide workers to
bring home the harvest. Moreover, Jesus speaks of the harvest as being already prepared. The priority, thus, is not
to pray for a harvest, but to pray for labourers who will
bring in the harvest. God will give the harvest when we
pray for labourers. A lack of opportunity doesn't keep the
harvest from coming in -- rather a lack of workers.

The first order of the day is prayer; the second is to
go forward into the harvest. The time between planting and
harvest may be long, but this is no excuse for the disciples of Jesus to delay going forward into the fields. "Do
you not say," Jesus said,

> "There are yet four months, then comes the har-
> vest"? I tell you, lift up your eyes, and see
> how the fields are already white for harvest ...
> For here the saying holds true, "One sows and
> another reaps." I sent you to reap that for
> which you did not labour; others have laboured,
> and you have entered into their labour (John
> 4:35,37f).

Harvesting is a gathering process, and it must not have been
until after Pentecost that the full significance of Jesus'
words came through to the disciples. With Pentecost, the
Holy Christian Church "built upon the foundation of the
apostles and prophets, Christ Jesus Himself being the cornerstone" (Eph. 2:20), broke forth into history with a new
kind of visibility. The harvesting process is the work of
gathering those who are ready for the harvest and incorporating them into the Church, the Body of Christ.

CONVERSION AND THE CHURCH

Paul tells the story of the Church, this gathering and
incorporating process, as follows -- it is the story of all
of us who are part of the Church:

> Jesus came and preached peace to you who were
> far off and peace to those who were near; for
> through Him we both have access in one Spirit
> to the Father. So then you are no longer
> strangers and sojourners, but you are fellow
> citizens with the saints and members of the
> household of God (Eph. 2:17ff).

The conversion process reaches a climax in a single moment of time, but it may be difficult or even impossible to
point with any kind of accuracy to that particular moment.
Nor is it necessary. What is important is that at a particular precise moment in history a particular individual sees
the hopelessness of living any longer outside the covenant
of God's grace. Immediately, when that happens, his hunger
and thirst for a right relationship with God open the door
for Christ to enter into his life with the invitation, "Follow Me."

Building up to that moment may take days, weeks, months,
and even years. It may involve a countless number of named
and nameless Christian witnesses. Or, it may happen in the
twinkling of an eye. It can also happen so early in life
that the person does not remember a time when he was not a
follower of Jesus.

When that moment of time comes, however long or short the
process, that person becomes immediately a part of the
Church. He is incorporated as a full member into the Body
of Christ -- baptism or no baptism, certificate or no certificate, laying on of hands or no laying on of hands, approval
of the Elders or no approval. His sins are forgiven and his

guilt is behind him. His release from the bondage of sin
and its consequences is total. His spirit soars through
the air like a bird with a freedom and peace he could discover in no other way. The conversion process is completed
at that moment in time.

As a full member of the Body of Christ, he is immediately
entitled to all the rights and privileges of such membership. The Sacraments of the Church are his to enjoy. The
fellowship of the Church is his in which to participate and
through which and in which to exercise his new rights and
privileges. One of those rights and privileges is the freedom we have already discussed at some length. The newly
converted "follower of Jesus" is entitled to embark upon
his new life of discipleship without any strings attached
whatsoever. "If the Son makes you free, you will be free
indeed" (John 8:36)!

CONVERSION AND THE CHURCHES

There are no strings attached, but it must be remembered
that the new convert is incorporated into the Body of Christ,
the Church. The Church is invisible, a spiritual temple in
the Lord, incorporating into one Body -- with Christ as the
chief cornerstone and the Head -- all believers and only believers in Him. The divine institution is invisible, but it
has its visible manifestations whenever and wherever the
Word of God is preached for it does not return to Him "empty"
(Is. 55:10f). It is calling men to faith (Rom. 10:17) and
discipleship (Matt. 4:19). It is laying bare and exposing
their innermost thoughts and purposes (Heb. 4:12f). It is
instructing them in the way of salvation through faith in
Christ Jesus and training them in righteousness (2 Tim.
3:15ff). It is gathering them into a fellowship with Jesus,
for where two or three are gathered in His Name, there is He
in the midst of them (Matt. 18:20).

Many people who say they are Christians are today disas-
sociating themselves from fellowship with other Christians.
They bring all kinds of excuses for their separation. They're
not happy because there are so many different churches, or
they're not happy with the pastor. They don't like the pattern of worship, or they can't find the time. In their defence they say they read the Bible and pray at home. They
listen to church services on the radio or TV. We hear
people saying these words all around us, especially in the
cities, but these are strange words to be coming from true
disciples of Jesus.

The disciple of Jesus never lives in a vacuum. He is part of a fellowship where the emphasis is on "we" and not "I." The work of that fellowship is to embrace the brother in love, encourage him in his faith, admonish him in his error -- all to the glory of God who has called that fellowship into being.. Here is a fellowship which walks together, a recipient of God's grace. It is a fellowship in which Christians strengthen each other through prayer, mutual worship and confession as they gather regularly around the Word of Christ in anticipation of His Second Coming (Col. 3:11-17; Heb. 10:22-25).

Now is the time to honestly ask ourselves: Is this the kind of fellowship into which we are inviting our Muslim friends and neighbours and anyone else who is not a part of the fellowship which Christ offers? How much do we and our churches reflect the "new nature created after the likeness of God in true righteousness and holiness" (Eph. 4:24)? Or how much do we reflect the "old nature" -- immorality, impurity, passion, evil desire, and covetousness, which is idolatry; anger, wrath, malice, slander and foul talk (Col. 3:5,8)? We have to be concerned about these questions because conversion not only brings people into the fellowship of the Church; it brings people into the fellowship of our churches.[57] For this reason, the Church and the churches are always in a kind of tension. The "all believers and only believers in Christ" who make up the Church are also members of the churches

This is not to say that you cannot be a member of the Church without being a member of one of the churches. You can! But, once you are a member of the Church, you are also part of the visible church, whether you identify with it, or not. Not to identify with it is a risky undertaking

> for we are not contending against flesh and
> blood, but against the principalities, against
> the powers, against the world rulers of this
> present darkness, against the spiritual hosts
> of wickedness in the heavenly places (Eph.
> 6:12).

"Let any one who thinks that he stands take heed lest he fall," the Apostle Paul reminds us (I Cor. 10:12). Trying to stand on your own as a follower of Jesus with the heavy stakes which are involved and the great forces which are in opposition is a gigantic and a lonely task. Christ stood alone in going to the cross, but He was forsaken in order

that we need not be forsaken. We need each other; hence,
the fellowship of the Church! We find this fellowship in
our churches. Jesus once told a group of faultfinders an
important truth about the sabbath" (Mark 2:27). We so
easily forget this truth when it comes to deciding what is
necessary for acquiring church membership, as well as retaining church membership. The problem we need to face is
that our rules and regulations for membership tend to take
positions of prominence which they do not deserve, thus
obscuring the real substance of what happens in conversion.
What happens there is that God calls a man out of darkness
into His marvelous light! A miracle takes place which in
some ways overshadows even the miracle of creation.

We've all had the experience of playing in mud, making
our own creations, shaping our own designs. Have you ever
tried to wet down again the mud from a broken vessel that
had been shaped by a potter and fired in his kiln? It's
an impossible task for us -- far easier to start from the
beginning with new clay than to try to take the old broken
down vessel and remake it. But, this is what God has done
with man! He takes the broken down clay of man's fallen
nature, with all the hardness of heart, the stubbornness,
the prejudice, the unwillingness to repent and walk in the
way of God, and God remakes that man. Conversion marks
the moment when that miracle happens. "Not by might, nor by
power, but by My Spirit," says the Lord (Zech. 4:6). "What
is impossible with men is possible with God" (Luke 18:27).

The regulations which govern entrance into the life of
our churches should reflect something of the excitement of
that change. A new birth has taken place. A baby in Christ
has been born. The story surrounding his rebirth becomes
part of God's witness to the world that He still acts and
moves among men, even as He did when He brought Christ from
the dead into the resurrection of a new life. Is it necessary for us to add yet other requirements to that person's
conversion than simply to acknowledge the miracle which God
has already accomplished? Is there more to do than simply
to embrace him and welcome him, in Christ, into our fellowship?

CONVERSION AND SOCIAL DISLOCATION

The problem of church membership regulations is closely
related to another -- the problem of social dislocation.

The life of every congregation is coloured by its origins,
its history, its social environment, and the people who are

a part of it. This worshipping community develops its own
tradition, sanctions certain life styles, and determines
what is necessary for membership. It approves certain worship forms, including the kind of music to be used, and
agrees upon certain emphases and interpretations of Scripture. This is all well and good, except when it comes to
the matter of that congregation's trying to take seriously
the Great Commission of Jesus. Even then there is no problem as long as efforts are made to invite into that fellowship people who come from similar homes and similar social
backgrounds. When efforts are made to reach out beyond
that cultural-linguistic group, however, some real difficulties are encountered. The evangelizing group has at
least two choices: 1) They can preach a Gospel that gives
to anyone who follows Jesus all the freedom that belongs to
the Gospel, or 2) they can attach to the Gospel, as essential to it, all that is associated with the church in their
own society. When the latter happens, a social dislocation
is connected to the Gospel that the Gospel itself does not
demand.

Jesus phrased the demands of the Gospel in many different
ways, but one of His most pointed declarations was, "If any
man would come after Me, let him deny himself and take up
his cross daily and follow Me"(Luke 9:23). Jesus spoke
often and again about suffering, the suffering which would
come to Him and the suffering which would come to His followers. He spoke about rejection, their rejection by those
to whom they would offer the Gospel. He spoke about hatred,
the hatred of the world.

When speaking of suffering, Jesus was not speaking of the
kind of suffering Christians often impose upon new converts
-- the "suffering" of grappling with new and strange worship
forms, the "hatred" of all the good things they had previously
valued and enjoyed in their society, the "rejection" of
their whole former way of life including clothing, food,
living quarters, manner of living, and companions. The
"come out and be separate from them" of 2 Corinthians 6:
14-17 was not calling for this kind of social dislocation.
Yet, this is a pattern of "conversion" which Christians
have again and again, often unknowingly and unintentionally,
but nevertheless cruelly, forced upon those who have come to
join them in new discipleship. No wonder Muslims have been
afraid of conversion!

The kind of problem we are talking about here is well
illustrated in Ghana. By and large, the churches in the

North and South of Ghana have a "Southern flavour." Because the bulk of the worshipping community is Southern, the languages of worship are largely Southern. The form of dress for worship is largely Southern -- because this is the normal dress of the Gas, Ewes, and Akans who helped in many instances to found the congregations in which they now worship. Even in the North, regulations, policies, church architecture, hymn tunes, liturgies, instruments of worship, and forms of administration have been borrowed, for the most part, from the South. Other things, like clerical collars and choir robes, have been borrowed from churches in Europe and America without any attention as to the "why" or "what" for the use of this or that alternative. In many cases, it wasn't even a matter of alternatives. There was one way of doing things, and this way was imposed without meaning or interpretation. When customs or traditions are carried forward by people who do not understand them and imposed upon still a third party, the end result is a feeling of yet even greater strangeness. No wonder a Northerner feels out of place when he steps into a Christian church! Only in some of the villages of the North and in a few scattered urban areas of the South do we have any exceptions to this kind of church planting.

Without a doubt, this matter of opening the door to evangelizing all the diverse peoples who make up the population of Ghana is the greatest single challenge facing the churches in Ghana today. The first problem, however, is to convince Christians that there *is* a problem. In spite of the fact that people live with cultural diversity day in and day out, and confront the complications which arise from cross-cultural contacts in the market place, on the buses, at their places of work and in the neighbourhood where they live, Christians are somehow reluctant to face up to the realities of this problem as it relates to church growth.

Thus, very few Christians are disturbed by the fact that thousands upon thousands of people who live in Accra, Kumasi, Sekondi-Takoradi, Cape Coast, Koforidua, and Tamale do not feel at home in worship services conducted in English, Akan, Ga, or Ewe. These are key languages, but far from adequate to meet the needs of all the diverse people in these places. A similar situation prevails in a host of other urban centres across the continent of Africa -- the cities and towns which have multitribal populaces. Unhappily, change will not come until the Christians who now fill the churches in these places become more concerned about taking seriously

their part in the Great Commission (Matt. 28:19f). If and
when that happens, there will have to be a rethinking of
the whole task of mission -- more in terms of the desires,
preferences, and traditions of those who have yet to hear
the Gospel, than in terms of those who already are in the
church. Is this perhaps part of what is meant by the servant role to which Jesus calls His followers?

Once the problem is realized and seriously faced, Christian creativity and imagination may come up with alternatives other than the three suggested here, but each of
these deserves to be seriously considered. The first is
the more ideal; the second, the more practical; the third,
an alternative that can flourish alongside, or independent,
of the other two. Each offers the new follower in Christ
the full measure of the freedom which is his in the Gospel
while minimizing the problem of social dislocation.

The first solution is to think of each congregation more
in terms of being a parish of many congregations, each unit
serving a distinct sociocultural-linguistic group within
the community. This means that there would be certain joint
functions, but many, many separate functions. Each group
would be free to develop its own programme of worship and
service under its own leaders, but would not need separate
costly facilities. Elders (deacons) from each separate
group would report to each other from time to time. Their
relationship with each other would be comparable to how
Peter describes himself as an elder among elders (I Pet.
5:1). Theirs would be a team ministry with each "minister"
having special responsibilities for his own sociocultural-
linguistic group. The advantage of this solution is that
it gives the local congregation an opportunity to reflect
to the world one of the beautiful characteristics of the
Communion of Saints -- "the unity of the Spirit in the
bond of peace" (Eph. 4:3). It does this while embracing in
its fellowship people from all the diverse elements which
comprise that community.

The second solution is to simply plant more churches --
a separate church for each separate sociocultural-linguistic
group within the community. This means that the established
churches will have to take seriously the challenge of re-
cruiting and equipping a solid corps of able workers who
will give themselves to the difficult task of becomming missionaries to the diverse groups within the larger community.
The solution calls for a commitment, an initiative, and a
zeal which is willing to "become all things to all men"
(I Cor. 9:22). It may mean learning another language or

adopting another life-style -- whatever is necessary to become a bridge of God into each separate community of people.[58]

Closely attached to both the above patterns of mission
and ministry is the third -- the idea of people movements,
whole groups of individuals from one sociocultural-linguistic
background coming forward at the same time to announce a
decision for Christ.[59] The harvesters whom the Lord assigns
should always be alert for such movements of the Spirit, for
as we have seen, "the fields are already white to harvest."
Whenever this miracle of grace happens and large numbers of
people are ready to come into the church by way of multi-
individual decision, the problem of social dislocation can
be greatly minimized if each group is steered into a congregation of its own particular socio-linguistic-ethnic unit,
or is given the freedom to form its own semi-autonomous
group within a larger established congregation. This calls
for an open readiness on the part of those who receive these
new disciples into the body of Christ to gladly grant them
the full freedom they have in Christ. Given the leadership
to implement these kinds of possibilities, "congregations"
of largely "Muslim-Hausa" people could become commonplace
in Ghana.

THE REAL OBSTACLE TO CONVERSION

The really sad part about requiring social dislocation
as a concomitant to conversion is that this is a totally
unnecessary obstruction to the free reception and expression
of the Gospel in the lives of new converts. There is, however, an obstacle to conversion which cannot be avoided,
the preaching of the cross. This was called by Paul "the
foolishness of God," and it is this "folly" which God's
witnesses sooner or later have to present in their testimony. As Paul said,

> The Word of the cross is folly for those who
> are perishing, but to us who are being saved
> it is the power of God ... For Jews demand
> signs and Greeks seek wisdom, but we preach
> Christ crucified, a stumbling block to Jews
> and folly to Gentiles, but to those who are
> called, both Jews and Greeks, Christ the
> power of God and the wisdom of God   (I Cor.
> 1:18-24).

In many ways, the preaching of the cross is a greater stumbling block for Muslims than for people of other religious
backgrounds.

Muslims know the Name of Jesus and they know a little about Him as a great Lawgiver. But, in all they have said and known, they have never met Him as the Living and Reigning Christ! They have never met the Suffering Servant who "came not to be served but to serve, and to give His life as a ransom for many" (Matt. 20:28). The wealth of His revelation in the Bible has yet to be appropriated by them. After we have made all possible adjustments to Muslim culture, it is still necessary for Muslims (and our own children, too) to believe on, accept, receive, and trust Jesus as Lord and Saviour. In nothing we have said do we intend to minimize this obstacle. It is real. How are we ever going to convince Muslims that this Jesus of whom we are speaking is the real Christ they have yet to meet?

The disciples asked Jesus a similar question. They were talking about the young rich man who had walked sorrowfully away from Jesus after receiving a command for perfection which is not among the original Ten Commandments at all. He had asked what needed to be done in order to insure eternal life for himself. When he declared he had faithfully kept all the commandments, Jesus told him that there was yet another, "Go, sell what you possess and give it to the poor, and you will have treasure in heaven; and come, follow Me" (Matt. 19:21). As the young man went sorrowfully away, for we are told that he had great possessions, Jesus commented,

> Truly, I say to you, it will be hard for a rich
> man to enter the kingdom of heaven ... It is
> easier for a camel to go through the eye of a
> needle than for a rich man to enter the kingdom
> of God (Matt. 19:23f).

We might breathe a sign of relief at that word of Jesus, thanking Him that we don't have such a problem because we have so little wealth. Perhaps we may even glory in the kind of denunciation Jesus speaks upon the rich. Not so, however, with the disciples. They saw in the commentary of Jesus a word which applied to each and every one of them, for they were well aware of the streak of covetousness, greed, and selfishness which runs deep in each one of us. Hence, they asked, "Who then can be saved?" It is the same question we puzzle over as we ponder the subject of Christian witness to Muslims and Muslim conversion. Jesus' answer to the disciples is just as appropriate for our problem as it was for theirs, "With men this is impossible, but with God all things are possible" (Matt. 19:26).

This is the second time in the Gospels an answer like
this is given to explain a situation which defied all human
experience and explanation. The first time was when the
Angel Gabriel spoke to Mary and cleared up the mystery as
to how she would have a child when she had not slept with a
man. The angel told her that "with God nothing will be impossible" (Luke 1:37). Similarly the question of conversion
and new birth in the Spirit is answered: "That which is
born of the flesh is flesh, and that which is born of the
Spirit is spirit" (John 3:6). It is God's initiative! It
is God's act!

Who of us, for instance, would have had the courage to
witness to a learned Pharisee called Saul who had gone on a
rampage of death and destruction against Christians? Yet,
God met him and changed his life, turning it around so completely that he glorified and spent the rest of his life in
the service of the Christ whom he had persecuted. "What is
impossible with men is possible with God" (Luke 18:27)!

God gives the growth and brings to harvest. We are but
His servants -- seedsowers and harvesters. Let us not mag-
nify our role in the process of conversion. As Paul says,

> I bid every one among you not to think of him-
> self more highly than he ought to think, but
> to think with sober judgment, each according
> to the measure of faith which God has assigned
> him (Rom. 12:3).

In humility and with thanks to God, the faithful witness
bows to his servant role in God's plan of salvation for men.
He plants and waters and harvests, but God gives the increase.
To Him be the glory! Amen.

8

Dialogue

"On what basis can a Christian enter into dialogue with a Muslim? There is none!"

I could hardly believe my ears. I was surprised to be hearing an almost word-for-word repeat of a conversation I had just heard on the other side of the street. It was the same conclusion; only different characters.

About half an hour before this, Muhammadu and Jonathan had been debating the kind of approach the African nations ought to use in dealing with South Africa. The subject was about to come up again on the agenda of the Organization of African Unity Heads of State meeting.

Muhammadu argued it was high time for more people to give support to the idea of dialogue at many different levels with various representatives of the South African Government. Jonathan opposed that idea just as strongly as Muhammadu defended it. Instead he called upon every able-bodied man to offer himself in the service of humanity by becoming part of a mighty united fighting force. When this great army took shape, either South Africa would capitulate and reform its ugly apartheid policies, or this force would move upon South Africa. Once and for all, Africans would right the unfortunate situation which existed there.

Muhammadu felt such a procedure could only result in tre-mendous bloodshed, besides stirring up hatred and bitterness which might take generations to remove. Most certainly, the

worst-affected victims would be the very people they were
interested in trying to help. Muhammadu thought there was
nothing wrong in first trying an approach of dialogue.
"After all, they're human, too," Muhammadu reasoned. "They
must have hearts just like we have."

"That's where you're wrong," Jonathan replied. "Dead
wrong. That's the whole problem. If they had hearts like
the rest of mankind, and brains like the rest of the human
race, then you could talk with them. As it is, they have
rocks where they ought to have brains and stones where they
ought to have hearts. The only language people like that
understand is the language of force. That's why the only
alternative left is war."

The next thing I knew, here was Jonathan outside my
back window saying a similar thing to Ama. The only difference was that this time the subject was not South Africa;
it was Islam.

It all started when Ama mentioned she had just had an
interesting talk with Alihu. She was excited over the new
insights which had come to her while Alihu was telling her
about Muslim sacrifice. She said, "You know, I always
thought Muslims sacrificed in order to make some kind of an
atonement for their sins. I didn't know that it was also a
kind of thanksgiving. Why, that's just like King David
said, 'Offer to God a sacrifice of thanksgiving' (Ps. 50:14).
This makes me wonder if there's a connexion between sacrifice and thanksgiving in the Lord's Supper. What do you
think, Jonathan, is this why some churches call Holy Communion the Eucharist?"

Jonathan ignored her question and responded by asking
another, "What are you doing, Ama, talking about things
like that with Muslims? If you're not careful, the next
thing you'll be a Muslim yourself, and you know what that
means -- eternal damnation. The safest thing is not even
to talk with them."

"I disagree with you, Jonathan. There's no harm in talking with people, whether they're Christians, or Muslims, or
who they are. In fact, our pastor was just telling us this
past Sunday that a faithful Christian witness is ready to
enter into dialogue with anybody and everybody about his
convictions. Don't you think that's a good way for a Christian to communicate the meaning of his faith to others?"

"No," Jonathan replied, "on what basis can a Christian enter into dialogue with a Muslim? There is none!"

"What about the basis of our common humanity, the fact that we together are children of God dependent upon His grace, the fact that we each might have something to offer the other in our search to know God more perfectly and fulfil His will more obediently?"

"That's just where the problem comes in," and I smiled to myself as I heard Jonathan's answer parallel almost exactly the one he had given to Muhammadu. "That's the whole problem. We have nothing in common with Muslims. We have the truth. They are in error. We have everything to offer, but nothing to gain from them. That's why the word 'dialogue' doesn't fit. When you talk about dialogue, it's when two equals are negotiating with each other in hopes of coming up with some kind of agreement, or compromise. But, there's nothing we can compromise. You either accept the truth, or you don't."

"I'm not so sure, Jonathan, that we already have all the truth so neatly wrapped up in such a nice package, or that it's like a bottle of liquid that's filled so full to the top that it can't hold any more. Like today, in my conversation with Alihu. I never thought of sacrifice as being thanksgiving. It took Alihu, a Muslim, to give me that insight. Now that he's mentioned this to me, I've already thought about a lot of things -- besides Holy Communion. There's the place where Paul says, 'By the mercies of God, present your bodies as a living sacrifice' (Rom. 12:1). The main motive behind that offer has to be one of thanksgiving because 'there is now no condemnation for those who are in Christ Jesus' (Rom. 8:1). To be honest, I have to say I gained something from Alihu, even if he is a Muslim."

"I don't know if Alihu learned anything from me. I told him that whenever I saw them sacrificing their animals it reminded me of how Jesus sacrificed Himself for us, and I recited to him that beautiful portion from the Old Testament:

> All we like sheep have gone astray;
>   we have turned every one to his own way;
> and the Lord has laid on Him the iniquity of us all.
>
> He was oppressed, and He was afflicted,
>   yet He opened not His mouth;
> like a lamb that is led to the slaughter,

> *and like a sheep that before its shearers*
> *is dumb,*
> *so He opened not His mouth (Is. 53:6f).*

Then I told Alihu why this sacrifice of Jesus meant so much
to us:

> *Surely He has borne our griefs and carried our*
> *sorrows; yet we esteemed Him stricken, smitten*
> *by God, and afflicted, but He was wounded for*
> *our transgressions, He was bruised for our*
> *iniquities; Upon Him was the chastisement that*
> *made us whole, and with His stripes we are*
> *healed (Is. 53:4f).*

That's why we have so much peace and joy, I told Alihu, and
why we don't worry even when troubles come -- like sickness,
or death, or even why I'm not worried because God hasn't
given me a child. I know it's not because of my sin because
Jesus already sacrificed Himself for my sins.

"I was hoping all along that Alihu might say, 'Tell me
more about Jesus and His sacrifice. Was it for me and my
people also?' But he didn't say that. He just listened
carefully to what I said. Maybe God used me to plant a
seed that sometime when Alihu is in trouble, he'll turn to
Jesus for help."

"Small chance of that," replied Jonathan, as he prepared
to leave. "At least I'll say this much for you, Ama. You
didn't compromise your faith like I thought you probably
meant when you started to talk about dialogue."

Jonathan went on his way, and soon Ama was in the house
talking with my wife. "What an interesting 'dialogue' you
had with Jonathan," I said as I kidded her about her debate
over the usage of that word.

"Yes, I know," she said. "Maybe we have to think as much
about dialogue with other Christians as we do about dialogue
with those outside the Christian faith."

A MISUNDERSTOOD CONCEPT

Some Muslims wonder what Christians are after by talking
"dialogue," interpreting dialogue as simply a new term to
"conceal" Christian efforts to convert the Muslim world.
Some Christians have been just as suspicious. To them, dia-

logue is what takes place in the smoke-filled back rooms of labour-management negotiations and in the temper-torn corridors of international diplomacy. While they concede that dialogue offers an approach for improving human relationships wherever an important technique is the ability to bargain successfully with an opponent, they are hardly ready to utilize this method in discussions on religious matters. They are uncomfortable with the assumption that each contributor in "Christian-Muslim dialogue" has an equally valid case and cause to represent.[60]

These Christians argue that dialogue is a waste of time because Muslims have nothing substantial to offer to Christians. According to them, the dialogue approach represents only a half-hearted, half-way attempt to communicate the Gospel. In other words, the Christian cannot stop with a simple presentation of the Gospel truth in a matter-of-fact conversational form. He must press for a decision and this is more than simple dialogue. He has the Message. He has the Truth. It is his to offer. It is his to give. This is what proclamation is and the idea of dialogue is something else. We are to "preach Christ crucified" (I Cor. 1:23; 2:2) and "Thus says the Lord" (I Kings 21:19; Jer. 1:9). This message is complete in itself. There is nothing to be added.

Furthermore, the message of "Christ crucified" and "Thus says the Lord" cannot be compromised. It cannot be bargained and debated. It can only be accepted or rejected. By its very nature, its true and faithful proclamation cannot be in the form of a dialogue. So say the opponents of dialogue.

There is an unfortunate oversight and oversimplification in this condemnation of dialogue in that it fails to recognize that whenever Christ is proclaimed, there are at least two parties involved. There is the proclaimer and the hearer. The recipient, however, is not an empty tape waiting to receive a message.[61] He is a person, and as such he has absorbed into his being a wide range of experiences, insights, convictions and reflections. The proclaimer, too, is a person, and as such, he has his own personality and character with all of the learned behaviour, emotions, impressions, and interpretations which combine to make a human being. They, in varying measure, have been recipients of the grace of God.

Dialogue is a sharing of that grace. It simply means that the proclaimer is as open to listening and to learning

as he is to speaking and to sharing. It is a recognition
that he is still in a process of learning himself. "Now
we see in a mirror dimly ... Now I know in part" -- Paul's
experience is our experience (I Cor. 13:12), and dialogue
is a way of describing what happens when we invite another
person to join us in the process of growing in discipleship.

DIALOGUE AND DISCIPLESHIP

A prominent question in the missionary thinking of many
Christians is, "Are you saved?" Strangely, this does not
appear to be a significant question either in the ministry
of Jesus, or in that of His disciples. Rather, the important question was one of "following Jesus."

We can get some help at this point from an African word
for disciples, the Twi word, *asuafo*. The proper connotation is in the English "disciple," but the problem is that
English has drawn its vocabulary from so many foreign languages that even many native speakers of English are not
aware of the root meanings of many of the words they use.
That's why *asuafo* is so much more vivid in meaning to Twi-
speakers than is the word disciple to speakers of English.

Perhaps you have heard someone say, *Mesua Twi,*i.e., "I
am studying Twi." The *sua* used there is the same *sua* used
in *asuafo,* but how many of us think of a disciple as being
a student? Yet, that's what he is! He is a student of
Jesus! That's exactly what it meant in the time of Jesus.
To be a follower of Jesus, to be a disciple, was to be someone who walked with Jesus to learn from Him.

It should be pointed out here that we are not talking of
the "ever learning, and never able to come to the knowledge
of the truth" of 2 Timothy 3:7 (KJV). We have available to
us the Truth in Christ, the full truth. We have seen that
He is "the Way, the Truth, and the Life"; we have come to
understand the meaning of His "no one comes to the Father,
but by Me" (John 14:6). We have submitted to the knowledge
that "there is salvation in no one else, for there is no
other name under heaven given among men by which we must be
saved" (Acts 4:12). We have bowed before the fact that "no
other foundation can any one lay than that which is laid,
which is Jesus Christ" (I Cor. 3:11).

We possess the full truth in Christ. Yet, is any one of
us prepared to assert that we have received God's final revelation to ourselves? Just as His mercies are new to us every

morning (Lam. 3:23), so each new day brings new opportunities
to grow in our apprehension, understanding and appreciation
of His truth. To be open to that possibility is part of
what it is to be a disciple, a "learner" among the *asuafo*
of Jesus. To recognize that we are learners is not to deny
that we have received the truth in Jesus, but to admit and
to anticipate that God has even greater blessings of truth
still before us. As Paul expressed it so accurately, "We
can see and understand only a little about God now, as if
we were peering at His reflection in a poor mirror ... now
all that I know is hasty and blurred" (I Cor. 13:12, LB).

We know we have the truth of God in Christ. What about
those to whom we wish to communicate this truth, those who
have not yet received it, those who have not yet met the
real Christ?

The Scriptures picture such people as being "dead through
trespasses and sins" (Eph. 2:1). They are described as
"separated from Christ, alienated from the commonwealth of
Israel, and strangers to the covenants of promise, having
no hope and without God in the world" (Eph. 2:12). They are
spoken of as men who "oppose the truth, men of corrupt mind
and counterfeit faith" (2 Tim. 3:8). They are people who
love darkness more than light, "for every one who does evil
hates the light, and does not come to the light, lest his
deeds should be exposed" (John 3:20).

Given this insight from the Scriptures into man's status
and position before God without Christ, it is not so sur-
prising to find some Christians questioning whether anything
useful can come from dialogue with such people. They quite
honestly puzzle over the idea that something good and edifying can come from people who are in darkness. There is,
however, a false assumption in this kind of scepticism regarding the possibilities of mutual benefit growing out of
a dialogue situation. The mistake rests, as it so often
does, in our limitation of God. We wrongly assume that
there are only two parties in the dialogue -- we who have
the truth, and those who are in error. We overlook the fact
altogether that there is also a third party involved -- the
Holy Spirit.

"No one can say 'Jesus is Lord' except by the Holy Spirit"
(I Cor. 12:3). When a person is a Christian, it means that
at some point in his life, the Holy Spirit took possession
of his being, prompting him to utter that confession. The
process of preparation for that moment of conversion and con-

fession may have been long, or it may have been short, but
whether long or short, it was a time of intense activity on
the part of the Holy Spirit. The channels, events and persons He may have used in His timetable of preparation for
that moment may have varied considerably in each instance.

Prior to that moment, however, even while men are in
darkness, they are not without a witness from Him. As Paul
testifies, "God did not leave Himself without witness, for
He did good and gave you from heaven rains and fruitful sea-
sons, satisfying your hearts with food and gladness" (Acts
14:17). The simple truth of the matter is that God has
borne witness to Himself through His gracious provision for
men's needs. "He makes His sun rise on the evil and on the
good, and sends rain on the just and on the unjust" (Matt.
5:45). He expects men to accept this witness to "His eternal power and Godhead" (Rom. 1:20, KJV), but while there is
every reason for men to turn from their idolatry and fetishes
to seek the living God, there are few who respond. Hence,
the Gospel must be preached to them. It is at this point
we begin to realize that God has been going before us and
preparing the way for our witness to Jesus' saving work. We
cannot but affirm that God has been working in the lives of
Muslims and others with whom we enter into dialogue long before we meet them face to face.[62] Because of His presence,
there is also the possibility of new blessings for us.
There is every possibility that God may speak to us through
them, even as we pray that God will speak to them through us.

There is also, we should note, an important connexion between dialogue and discipleship. Jesus invites people to
"follow" Him, but immediately they enter into this new relationship of discipleship, He instructs them to "go" (Matt.
10:5; Luke 10:3). In the "going," a vital part of discipleship is confession as is emphasized by both Jesus and Paul:

> *Jesus:* If anyone publicly acknowledges Me as
> his friend, I will openly acknowledge him as
> My friend before My Father in heaven. But if
> anyone publicly denies Me, I will openly deny
> him before My Father in heaven (Matt. 10:32, LB).

> *Paul:* If you confess with your lips that Jesus
> is Lord and believe in your heart that God
> raised Him from the dead, you will be saved.
> For man believes with his heart and so is jus-
> tified, and he confesses with his lips and so
> is saved (Rom. 10:9f).

Publicly acknowledging Jesus as Lord can be done in many ways, but one important channel through which a Christian's confession of faith can flow is dialogue.

As a descriptive concept, dialogue is an accurate assessment of one of many things that happens when a person takes his discipleship seriously and confesses his faith to the world. It recognizes that confession is more than a monologue.[63] In fact, in a sense confession before the world is always a kind of dialogue, for it involves the one giving the testimony, the one hearing the testimony, and the Holy Spirit interacting with each.

PETER'S DIALOGUE WITH AN UNBELIEVER

Peter was mystified by the strange vision which came to him about noontime as he was at prayer (Acts 10:9-16). Three times a great sheet with all kinds of animals, reptiles, and birds came to rest upon the earth with the command, "Rise, Peter, kill and eat." Three times Peter resisted the temptation replying, "No, Lord; for I have never eaten anything that is common or unclean." Three times, also, the same response came from God, "What God has cleansed, you must not call common."

Peter was perplexed at what the meaning might be. He couldn't have helped but be reminded once again of his threefold denial of Jesus during His Passion. Remember how Jesus had tormented Peter's conscience with His threefold question, "Simon, son of John, do you love Me" (John 21:15-19)? Now, here again in a different time and circumstance came the same ugly reminder of that moment when his courage had failed him -- not in the palaces of kings and queens and governors, but in the back courtyard with the household servants and nightwatchmen.

As Peter was still mulling over this mystery, there was a call at the gate. Three servants from the household of one Cornelius were there with a message that their master wanted Peter to accompany them to his home. Ordinarily, Peter would have been most hesitant about accepting such an invitation, for just as we recognize a person's origins by his name, so Peter knew that Cornelius was not a Jew, but a Gentile. It was unlawful for Jews to visit Gentiles, but no sooner had the men arrived when the message of the vision began to come through to Peter. In his own words he later testified to Cornelius,

> You yourselves know how unlawful it is for a
> Jew to associate with or to visit any one of
> another nation, but God has shown me that I
> should not call any man common or unclean.
> So when I was sent for, I came without ob-
> jection (Acts 10:28f).

Peter's approach to Cornelius was one of humility and
service. "I ask then why you sent for me," he went on. He
was ready to listen to Cornelius before he demanded a hearing from Cornelius. Cornelius was a person to whom God had
already spoken before Peter arrived. Peter had a message
for Cornelius but he was open to the possibility that God
also had a message for him by way of Cornelius.

Peter recognized that Cornelius had a relationship with
God before he, Peter, entered Cornelius' compound. It was
a relationship which was by no means completed -- that's why
God called upon Peter to step into the situation. The fact
that Cornelius' faith was not completed, however, did not in
any way minimize or degrade his already established relationship with God. It was on that very relationship and experience that Peter was expected to build. What suited him so
well for this appointed role with Cornelius was his readiness
-- with some prompting by the Holy Spirit -- to recognize
that previous relationship and to seek to build upon it,
rather than to destroy it or its foundations. This is why
Peter's dialogue approach to Cornelius was so fitting and
appropriate.

Thus, even before Peter was able to pass on a blessing to
Cornelius, Cornelius was used by God to bring a blessing to
Peter. Cornelius' testimony served to broaden and expand
Peter's understanding of the reaches of God's love and
mercy in ways that none of the sermons of Jesus had ever
done. All of a sudden, the horizons of God's grace were
limitless and the scope of His forgiveness extended across
the whole of mankind. With this new comprehension of the
"breadth and length and height and depth" of "the love of
Christ which surpasses knowledge" (Eph. 3:18f), Peter could
see that the embrace of God's love included also the Gentile
Cornelius and his Gentile family. He said, "Truly I perceive that God shows no partiality, but in every nation any
one who fears Him and does what is right is acceptable to
Him" (Acts 10:34f).

After God used Cornelius to teach Peter, Peter had an opportunity to teach Cornelius. He unfolded before the Roman

centurion the history of the significant events in the life
of Jesus of which he had been a part, concluding with the
statement, "To Him all the prophets bear witness that every
one who believes in Him receives forgiveness of sins through
His Name" (Acts 10:43). To Peter's surprise and to the
amazement of the believing Jews who had accompanied him,
the Holy Spirit fell upon Cornelius and his household. Without further delay, Peter called for water and they were baptized then and there -- the first record of Gentile converts
being received into the visible church without first becoming "Jews."

Now, for an important question: Was Peter "dialoguing"
with a believer, or an unbeliever, when he first went to
visit Cornelius? Was the Roman centurion a believer in
Christ, or an unbeliever, when he shattered Peter's "salva-
tion-for-the-Jews-only" philosophy of missions? Perhaps
you're asking, does it really matter if he was a believer,
or not? It may not matter to some, but it does if you're
one of those who questions whether it's right for a Christian to enter into dialogue with a non-Christian -- since
he is in the darkness and you have the truth. That predis-
position tends to rule out the expectation of there being a
possibility of any value to mutual exchange. The story of
Peter and Cornelius, however, tells us that even if our
neighbour is in the darkness, God may through him give more
light to us who are already in the light.

DIALOGUE, TRUTH, AND LIGHT

Some of the deepest bitterness in and among Christians
is generated because of disputes over the truth. Each
church and each faction within each church openly, or covertly,
lays a claim to having possession of the full truth. That
which often distinguishes one faction or one church from
another is the belief that it has the truth in fuller measure
than the others.

Throughout history the hands of the churches have been
bloody from persecuting those who have challenged the truth
as interpreted by whoever has been in control. The Husses
and the Wycliffes, along with their modern counterparts, join
a long list of saints of whom, the Bible says, "the world was
not worthy" (Heb. 11:38). This was the cause of Jesus' lament over the city whose zest for the "truth" was so strong
that it crucified Him,

> O Jerusalem, Jerusalem, killing the prophets
> and stoning those who are sent to you! How

> often would I have gathered your children
> together as a hen gathers her brood under
> her wings, and you would not (Matt. 23:37).

Conflicts over the truth have again and again erupted into hatred and sometimes even into violence. Families have been torn apart and brothers cast asunder with wounds which linger and fester long after they have been made. From time to time they break open again, spewing forth new venom to repoison whatever atmosphere of understanding may have temporarily prevailed.

Dialogue is an attempt to open a new door to understanding -- whether it is a new door to understanding between Christian and Muslim, or between Christian and Christian. For a Christian, it doesn't have to mean a compromising of principles or a sacrificing of truth. It can rather denote a readiness to discover the truth more fully as one waits upon the Lord, listening for His voice.

Truth, like light, is multi-splendoured. When we look at the light of the sun we say it is white, but we're wrong. Or, rather, we should say we're right and we're wrong, for to all outward appearances, the light is white. But have you looked at that light through a prism? Of, if you haven't looked at it through a prism you've at least looked at it through the mist which in its prism-like effect creates the rainbow. It is through a prism or in the rainbow that we see the true colours of the white light which comes to us from the sun. It really isn't white at all. It turns out, rather, to be violet, indigo, blue, green, yellow, orange and red -- the colours we call the spectrum -- with even yet other colours that we are not able to distinguish with the naked eye. What, then, is the truth about light?[64]

Truth, too, is like the light of the sun. It is multi-splendoured in its beauty. Like a diamond with its many-sided beauty, so is the truth. It is bigger than the doctrines of our individual churches or the comprehension of our feeble minds. It is a drink which God offers to us in its fullness, but after we have drunk deeply, we have still only drunk in part. There is always more, each new draught as exciting, as satisfying, and as fulfilling as was the first.

Perhaps it is not the truth of God which torments men as much as it is the interpretations and applications men draw from that truth. At one time in history, for example, the

church pronounced the earth to be flat, not round. That
glaring misinterpretation ought to warn each one of us in
our various groups to weigh very carefully our apprehension
of the truth, for those who come along tomorrow may disprove
the assertions we have made today.

Dialogue is not only a way of communicating and sharing
the truth; it is a way of testing the truth. Herein lies
the real blessing as people from different religious backgrounds come together to test the validity of their religious convictions and experiences. Under the guidance of
God's Holy Spirit, such an undertaking is bound to bear
fruit, for "when the Spirit of truth comes, He will guide
you into all the truth" (John 16:13).

THE DOOR TO DIALOGUE IS OPEN DAILY

We're often frustrated by coming to the door of a bank or
an office building to meet the sign, "Closed." The door to
dialogue between persons, however, is never closed -- unless
we close that door ourselves.

When we use the word dialogue, we're not talking primarily
about the highly formalized meeting of, for example, three
Muslims and three Christians sitting down at a university
table to exchange ideas on certain questions and debate certain differences. This kind of dialogue does go on and has
its place. What we are referring to, rather, is more the
kind of possibilities which come to people daily in the market places, waiting for buses, walking on the way, chatting
in their living rooms. Sometimes it involves conversation,
but at other times it might only be a smile, a helping hand,
or a word of encouragement. These are ways, too, in which a
Christian shares the truth with his neighbour, for the truth
is not only something we believe; it is something we live!
As we have seen, truth is not simply something intellectual,
but a lived faithfulness.

We know the followers of Jesus were first called Christians at Antioch (Acts 11:26), but we don't really know when
the religion they followed started to be called Christianity.
The only name we know from the early church is that these
disciples were people "belonging to the Way" (Acts 9:2).
That to which they belonged was not thought of as an institution as much as a "walk." These were people who were walking in the "Way" of Jesus.

Paul has a fitting word for those who today are serious
about walking the "Way of Jesus. He said,

> Conduct yourselves wisely toward outsiders,
> making the most of the time. Let your speech
> always be gracious, seasoned with salt, so
> that you may know how you ought to answer
> every one (Col. 4:5f).

What better advice than that for those who are aware that
the door to dialogue is daily open, and who themselves are
ready to walk through!

9

All Things
to All Men

CAN CHRISTIANS EAT SACRIFICED MEAT?

Kwesi and Ama had not faced a problem like this before.

Muhammadu's son had just brought over a sizable piece of mutton. They knew it was the time of a Muslim festival and that Muhammadu had sacrificed a sheep. This was what worried them. Since the sheep had been butchered with all the Muslim ritual, they didn't know if it was right to accept the meat, or not. Ama thought it would appear as though they were approving the idea of sacrifice, even if it were a sacrifice of thanksgiving. She told Kwesi that no matter how you looked at it, it was still a sacrifice, and Christ had taken away the need for sacrifice. She knew her Bible much better than Kwesi, and she reminded him how Hebrews said, "It is impossible that the blood of bulls and goats should take away sins" (Heb. 10:4). Nor was it necessary! Christ had once and for all offered Himself as the Sacrifice for man, Ama said, and now that there was forgiveness of sins, there was no longer any necessity for an offering for sin (Heb. 10:5-18). She thought if they took the meat it would look to Muslims as if Christians felt sacrifice was important, too.

Kwesi argued, "But, what if we don't take it? Won't that look as if we think we're better than our neighbours? Most of them think sacrifices are necessary -- especially for certain occasions. Besides, they brought us this as a gift. If we don't accept it, how will that look?"

"I just wish," Ama said, "that we knew what is going on in Muhammadu's mind. I wonder if he sent over this meat because he knows we're against sacrifice and wants to trick us into denying our faith in one way or another. Is this how Satan is trying to tempt us because he knows how much we need the meat? Since your brother and your two nephews have come to stay with us, we just haven't been able to make ends meet. Your brother has been here four months now -- and still no sign of work. Does he think this can go on forever? And now he wants to bring his wife here. No job, no house, no money. At least the nephews help around the house, and it's good for them to go to school here, but your brother does nothing. He's only a drain on our family income. If we were back in the village, we could always add some extra yam and cassava to the cooking pot. We can't do that in the town. Here we've got to buy every morsel we consume and there's only so much money every month. Kwesi, you've got to tell your brother he either has to find work, or go back to the village. We can't keep this up much longer."

"Maybe that's why Muhammadu sent over the meat," replied Kwesi. "He knows just how much we need it. I don't know why we have to suspect he has sinister motives behind what he's doing. He sees that we're in need. God has provided him with a surplus and in thanksgiving to God he's sharing his surplus with us. Is that so evil?"

"You're just trying to avoid facing the issue of your brother. Kwesi, you've got to talk to him. With the cost of meat today -- that's why we've had less and less meat lately! And that's all the more reason I think we have to be careful with this kind of temptation. Jesus was tempted when He was hungry. But, even then, he didn't compromise His faith and loyalty to God. I don't think we should either -- just because we need the meat."

The meat was still sitting on the table untouched when Ama slipped on a headscarf and walked over to our house. Before she touched the meat she was going to consult with me.

She found Pius and me hovering over my wireless. Pius knew something about radios, and he had come over with his tools, testers, and whatever to try to repair the set. After the usual greetings, Ama told us about the meat. She said she knew it had been sacrificed because one of Kwesi's nephews had watched the slaughter of the animal. "What are we to do," Ama asked? "Is it alright for us to eat the meat, or not?"

"That's an interesting problem" Pius said. "In fact, we just talked about that the other night in our Bible class. Maybe you heard that Father Amissah has started a Bible study group. It's the first time most of us have ever gotten into the Bible, and it's been very exciting. We've been going through I Corinthians because Father says it deals with so many practical problems in the life of the churches of today. We just went through I Corinthians 8 where Paul talks about food offered to idols."

"Is that really the same?" interrupted Ama. "Would you say that Muslim sacrifices are offered to idols?"

"No, I wouldn't exactly say that," Pius responded. "That brings us back to the old question of whether or not Christians and Muslims worship the same God, or whether instead Muslims worship an idol. I'm not sure that I'm ready to say that Muslims are worshipping an idol. But that doesn't matter. It seems to me the principles are the same -- whether it's food sacrificed to idols, or whether it's food sacrificed in error to the true God."

"O.K., then," Ama said, "What conclusions did your Bible study group reach?"

"Well, the main thing is that a Christian can eat anything as long as he gives thanks to God for it, even if that thing is sacrificed to an idol. Christians know that idols have no existence. Therefore, it doesn't make any difference if someone says that a certain food was sacrificed to this idol, or to that. Since the idol has no existence in the first place (even though some people believe that it has), the Christian can simply thank God for the gift of that food and go on and enjoy it all the same, in spite of what other people may think. The only warning is that we should be concerned about weaker Christians. Let's take an example. The Yam Harvest, or the planting season comes. Your neighbour makes a sacrifice to the ancestral spirits out of fear that if he doesn't, misfortune is going to strike him, or his family. You yourself know that this sacrifice is unnecessary and useless. For you to eat of that food, there is no problem. But, your neighbour on the other side of you is a new Christian. He's been told that he's in God's hands, and he believes it, but there still is a lingering doubt. Every time an old festival occasion comes, his faith is put to a new test. Will everything really be alright if he doesn't do the old rites?

"It's at times like that you see a new Christian watching old Christians very carefully. Before he became a Christian,

*he never thought about these things so he never observed
what Christians were doing. Perhaps even, he assumed that
Christians did everything pagans do -- only in a different
way. Now, in Christ, he's entered into a new relationship
with God. He's made a new commitment and he looks at life
through a different set of lenses. He still, however, lives
in the same neighbourhood. He still goes through the same
rhythm of life as far as planting and harvest goes. At the
outset of his Christian pilgrimage he might not have anticipated how far-reaching the consequences of that decision
would be in the events of his everyday life. Almost daily
he's faced with new decisions which grow out of his original decision to follow Christ.*

*"These are the times when he watches his fellow Chris-
tians very closely, not only to observe how they act in
crisis situations, but also to find added assurance that
he's doing the right thing by not following the old ways.
If then, while he's wavering between what is right and what
is wrong as far as participating in the old sacrificial
rites is concerned, and he sees me, an old Christian, eating
'sacrificed' food, it strengthens his fears. From my bad
example, he's encouraged to walk the old path once again for
fear that if he doesn't he'll suffer the consequences. That's
what Paul meant when he said, 'Take care lest this liberty
of yours somehow become a stumbling block to the weak'"
(I Cor. 8:9).*

*"I guess that's what bothers me," Ama replied. "Now,
take Kwesi's brother, for example. He was baptized just
last year so he's still really learning what it is to be a
Christian. Since he's been looking for a job for so long,
he's been getting very discouraged. He's beginning to wonder if something might be wrong. I overheard him telling
Kwesi what Abdullahi had suggested. If you go too long without getting a job, you have to go to the local fetish priest
with a chicken, or some other appropriate gift. He'll make
the right sacrifices and help you get into the right harmony
with the spirits that control this area. So, what happens
if we eat this meat? What will Kwesi's brother think? Will
he think Kwesi and I believe in the power of sacrifice, that
we're eating the meat to get more power, or something? What
will Abdullahi think? I never thought about this until now,
but I wonder what Abdullahi thinks about Muslim sacrifice.
From what he said to Kwesi's brother, my guess is that he
has quite a different idea about its meaning than has either
Alihu, or Muhammadu."*

"If I might interject another idea altogether," I finally
interrupted, "there's one thing I never thought about until
now either. You know, it's a funny thing, but all the meat
we buy in the market place has been slaughtered by Muslim
butchers in a ritual way. We buy it every day and think
nothing about it. Is there any difference between the meat
Muhammadu has given you and the meat we buy every day in
the market?"

"That's an interesting point," said Pius. "You know,
when I first came to town, I didn't know all the butchers
were Muslims.[65] When I found out, I wondered why. Then
somebody told me that Muslims wouldn't buy meat unless a
malam had cut the animal's throat in a certain way and the
name of God was spoken over it. Now with the problem of
the meat Muhammadu's given Ama, is there any difference in
the one ritual over against the other?"

I reached over and picked up a Bible from the table. "It
seems to me there's something else we ought to remember,"
and I paged around searching for a particular reference.
After a little while I found what I was looking for and I
read I Corinthians 10:24-30. I don't know if that helps,
or not," I continued. "We never really ask any questions
when we buy our meat in the market. Why should we now
trouble ourselves with a lot of questions about this particular meat?"

"There is a difference, though, Yakubu," said Ama. "We
don't think of the market meat as sacrificed. We all know,
however, *this meat has been sacrificed*. That makes a difference, doesn't it, even according to what you read?"

"What about this?" I responded? "Listen to these verses:

> Whether you eat or drink, or whatever you do,
> do all to the glory of God. Give no offence
> to Jews or to Greeks or to the church of God,
> just as I try to please all men in everything
> I do, not seeking my own advantage, but that
> of many, that they may be saved (I Cor. 10:31ff).

What happens if you send the meat back to Muhammadu? Won't
that create a bigger offence than eating it?"

Ama smiled as if a load had been lifted off her heart.
"I think that's the best answer yet," she said. "Returning
the meat would probably create more problems than keeping

*the meat. We surely can use the meat, and God knows we're
grateful for it! The market money just doesn't go as far as
it used to with all these extra mouths to feed."*

I turned back to poring over my Bible. Putting my finger
on another verse, I started reading out loud, "I have become all things to all men that I might by all means save
some" (I Cor. 9:22). I paused for a moment, and then
asked, "Doesn't this example of a missionary approach say
something to this matter also? What does it mean to 'become all things to all men,' if not to enjoy their food with
them, respect their values, share in their customs; in short,
to identify with them wherever possible?"

"You know," said Pius. "I've wondered about those words.
We haven't got there, as yet, in our Bible study, but when
we do, there's one question I want to raise. If I hear Paul
correctly, doesn't that make him out to be a sort of two-
faced person? He lives one kind of life with me, and turns
right around and lives another kind of life with you."

"Of course," I answered, "there weren't any Muslims around
when Paul practised that philosophy of mission, but I wonder
if there had been and he had worked among them if he wouldn't
have said, 'To the Jews, I became as a Jew and to the Muslims, I became as a Muslim.' The more I think about it, Ama,
I think that's just what you're doing when you accept
Muhammadu's gift of meat to your family. You don't have to
have a guilty conscience about it. Enjoy it. Thank God for
it. Thank God for Muhammadu as a neighbour. Isn't that
'becoming all things to all men'?"

THE GAP BETWEEN JEWS AND GENTILES

How was it that Peter was so easily identified in the
courtyard of the High Priest? Had one of the servants accompanied the nighttime raiding party which had captured
Jesus, or had one of them seen Peter with Jesus on a prior
occasion? His accent betrayed him, this we know (Matt.
26:73), but were there other distinguishing marks which set
Peter off as a Galilean?

It was no different when Peter and the disciples stood
up to speak on the day of Pentecost. Here were Galileans
speaking in languages whose home bases were far removed from
their Galilee. Yet, they were clearly recognized as Galileans! What was there which so clearly and unmistakably revealed them to be from Galilee (Acts 2:7)? Was it again

a matter of accent, simply because it is so difficult to speak a foreign language without an accent? Or, did their mannerisms or their clothing give them away? Or, was it any one of the multitude of minor similarities and differences which piece themselves together to give us each the particular cultural identity we carry with us throughout life?

Try to put your fingers, for example, on all the intricate details which make it possible for us to say, "He is an African." We can look at the same person on another level with another set of criteria and conclude, "He is a Ghanaian." We can examine him from a third perspective and observe, "He is a Northerner," or we can put him in yet a fourth kind of microscope and find that "He is a Frafra," or "a Fanti," or "a Fulani." What are the similarities and the differences which make it possible to ascertain that a person is from this continent, or that continent, this nation, or that nation, this locality, or that locality, this tribe, or that tribe?

The problem we have in trying to isolate the essential distinguishing marks between nations and tribes in our own time points up the magnitude of the task of trying to do the same with the nations and the tribes of biblical times. With all the information we have about those ancient days, we have surprisingly little about all the intricate details which fit together to make up the cultures Paul speaks of as being Jewish or Gentile. We have seen how obvious to others were the marks of distinction which Peter and the Galilean Apostles bore. They were all Jews. Imagine how much greater must have been the obvious distinctions which separated Jew from Gentile!

While we don't know all the minute details of life in those times, one thing which stands out very clearly from the biblical account is that the gap between Jews and Gentiles was very, very great. Whatever differences existed were accentuated by the fact that for the Jews there was only one race of people -- their own. For them there was only one nation which counted -- the Jewish nation. All other people were outside the Covenant of God's Grace -- unless they were prepared to undergo the requirements which would turn them into "Jews."

Unless we can appreciate the distance which separated Jewish culture from the Gentile cultures of that day, we can hardly appreciate the dramatic significance of Paul's

effort to be a Jew to the Jews and a Gentile to the Gentiles.
Here was a man who was immersed as much as is anyone of us
in his own culture, yet who "because of the surpassing worth
of knowing Christ Jesus" was ready to "count everything" of
his own cultural heritage "as loss" (Phil. 3:8). He was
ready to immerse himself in the strange world of cultures
which belonged to others "for the sake of the Gospel"
(I Cor. 9:23).

PRACTICAL ASPECTS OF IDENTIFICATION

It is extremely difficult to identify with someone who is
totally immersed in a culture which is totally foreign to
ours. Yet, this is what Paul attempted to do "for the sake
of the Gospel." What all did this involve? What does it
mean for us in our concern to be "a Muslim to Muslims?"

One clue from the Scriptures tells us that Paul's cultural identification with the Gentiles meant eating with
them (Gal. 2:11-16). A little step? Maybe. But, also,
maybe a very big step! The ways of cooking and preparing
food are so different, the flavouring and choice of foods
so varied, the tastes we develop so stratified that, in
fact, the simple step of eating with and appreciating the
food of the Gentiles may have been a very big hurdle. No
one who has ever lived in urban Africa and smelled the
exotic and unique fragrances from the thousands of cooking
pots which represent hundreds of different tribal tastes
will challenge the fact that eating another's food may be
a trying obstacle to identification.

The same is true with clothing and with language. The
clothing of others may look as strange to us as their languages sound to us. Yet, this, too, is a part of being
"all things to all men." Which of us, "for the sake of the
Gospel," is ready to undertake the laborious task of learning Dagbani, Gonja, Mampruli, or Wala? Who of us will undertake the study of Hausa or Arabic? Who of us are ready
to exchange our traditional cloths for Northern smocks, or
our *kentes* for *rigas*? To date, we have made so few beginnings toward becoming Muslims to Muslims. This, too, is
part of following Jesus, for following Him is more than
prayers and praises. It is honouring all men (I Pet. 2:17)
and counting others better than ourselves (Phil. 2:3). It
is through love being servants of one another (Gal. 5:13).
It is giving no offence to Jews or to Greeks or the church
of God (I Cor. 10:32). It is being "all things to all men."

THE PROBLEM OF RELIGIOUS ELEMENTS IN CULTURE

Integrating one's life into a foreign culture is not easy.
It isn't just a simple matter of exchanging one cultural
component for another, a toothbrush for a chewing stick, a
kente cloth for a Northern smock, and Coca Cola for kola nut.
These things are certainly a part of cultural identification,
and we cannot emphasize enough their crucial importance for
anyone who is serious about trying to apply Paul's "rule of
thumb" to his own life. There is more, however, and that
has to do with the difficult task of wrestling with those
aspects of culture which have a religious meaning.

This is why Peter had a problem at Antioch. His problem
didn't have to do with the food of the Gentiles, but rather,
with the very fact of eating with them. Peter had grown up
in a culture where even associating with Gentiles was a dese-
cration -- that was why the washing of hands after returning
from the market place was a requirement (Mark 7:3). The
ritual for that purpose was more than a simple rule of clean-
liness; it was a ritual of purification to cleanse Jews from
their contamination by the Gentile world.

In Antioch Peter was torn by the anxiety of trying to
keep loyal to the traditions of his fathers and the pull of
identifying with the Gentiles who were responding to the
Gospel. He followed the latter alternative until some leading Jewish believers from the "circumcision party" came to
Antioch from Jerusalem. Their presence caused Peter and
even Barnabas to withdraw from their previous associations
with the Gentiles.

Paul denounced this kind of inconsistency and two-facedness
(Gal. 2:11), attacking them for not being "straightforward
about the truth of the Gospel" (Gal. 2:14). He saw in this
return to the legalities from which Christ had freed all believers a distortion of the purpose of the Law and a misinterpretation of the character of the Gospel. The Law was
but "our custodian until Christ came" (Gal. 3:24). Now, however, by baptism we have "put on Christ," and so clothed, we
live in a relationship with others in which "there is neither
Jew nor Greek, there is neither slave nor free, there is
neither male nor female; for you are all one in Christ Jesus"
(Gal. 3:28).

Paul accused Peter and the others of not being "straightforward about the truth of the Gospel." We almost find ourselves asking Paul, "Yes, but what about your philosophy of

being 'all things to all men'? Couldn't you say this was
what Peter and Barnabas were trying to do? While the Judaizers
were around, they tried to live according to their standards.
When the Judaizers were not around, then they lived according to a different pattern with the Gentiles. Wasn't that
being 'all things to all men'?"

It's possible that Paul by way of reply might refer us
to his own two separate decisions regarding two of his co-
workers, Timothy and Titus. The one was circumcized after
coming to faith; the other, not. Titus was a Greek, and
Paul indicates a pressure from the Judaizers insisting on
Titus' being circumcized (Gal. 2:3-5). In keeping with his
understanding of the Gospel that we are "justified by faith
in Christ, and not by works of the Law" (Gal. 2:16), Paul
was successful in having Titus accepted as a full-fledged
Christian without being compelled to be circumcized. With
Timothy, the son of a Greek father and a Jewish mother,
Paul followed a different procedure. Since circumcision
was a custom of the Jews, and Timothy was part Jewish, Paul
acquiesced to his circumcision (Acts 16:3). He agreed to
Timothy's circumcision, not on the basis of its necessity
for salvation, but because it was a widely-accepted Jewish
custom.

Paul's philosophy of being "all things to all men" had a
consistency which Peter's actions did not have. Paul expressed it like this: "Though I am free from all men, I have
made myself a slave to all, that I might win the more ...
not being without Law toward God but under the Law of Christ"
(I Cor. 9:19,21). In another place Paul said, "Bear one
another's burdens, and so fulfil the Law of Christ" (Gal.
6:2). It was a concern for the brother, or you might say,
the other, which dictated the direction of Paul's being
"all things to all men." He was "free from all men," but
voluntarily "a slave to all," intent upon winning from all
a hearing for the Gospel.

The same guidelines can give us direction as we seek to
open and walk through a new door of exploration into just
what the "all things to all men" might mean as far as being
a Muslim to the Muslims. Could it mean fasting and Scripture reading during the month of Ramadan?[66] Might it mean
contributing to the building of a mosque or an Arabic school?
Could it mean joining in the celebration of a Muslim feast?
Might it mean meditating quietly in the back of a mosque
while Muslims recite the Friday prayers?

As with so many questions regarding the application of
Christian principles to modern situations, the Bible doesn't
give us all the final answers. It is filled with clues to
help us make decisions which are pleasing to God, but the
final decisions are ours. This procedure seems to be in
keeping with the tremendous freedom God has given us in
Christ. While we may lament the fact that God has not been
more explicit in giving us more specific directions and more
exact in deciding different questions for us, we have been
given this freedom and we know His will. He "desires all
men to be saved and to come to the knowledge of the truth"
(I Tim. 2:4). This truth is that "there is one God, and
there is one Mediator between God and men, the man Christ
Jesus, who gave Himself as a ransom for all" (I Tim. 2:5f).
Jesus, the "one Mediator," has appointed us His "ambassadors" with the freedom to be "all things to all men" as we
try to fulfil our commission to "make disciples of all nations" (Matt. 28:19).

The above questions that deal with the matter of being
all things to all men are very sensitive. They are so because they deal with religious elements in Muslim culture
in which participation on the part of a Christian may be
variously interpreted by Christian and Muslim alike. Even,
there will be a considerable variation among different Christians as to how to respond and react to such questions and
such situations. Each individual and group will look at
them in the light of their own understanding of the Word of
God's voice to them via their consciences in tune with that
Word. If, however, the final decisions are undertaken according to the "Law of Christ," which is love, and in the
freedom which God gives, yet as being slave to all, the Name
of Christ will be glorified and men will be drawn to consider His claim upon their lives. This is what "all things
to all men" can mean in the modern-day context of being a
Muslim to Muslims.

10

Paving New Ground

WHAT -- MUSLIMS JOIN THE CHRISTIAN COUNCIL?

"You can't join the Christian Council -- you're not Christians!"

It was clear that Alihu was somewhat taken aback by Muhammadu's hint that the Ghana Muslim Mission was seriously considering becoming a member body of the Christian Council. His outburst indicated as much!

"Do you really mean," Alihu continued, "that you would join the Christian Council even though you are Muslims? Don't tell me the Muslim Mission has gone that far in its syncretism! How many of your people are really serious about this idea?"

"Well, there's only a few of us at the moment," replied Muhammadu. "But, the idea isn't all that cockeyed, you know. Of course, there would have to be some changes in the Christian Council constitution, but we have every reason to believe the Christian Council would seriously consider such changes."

Alihu shook his head in disbelief, "I don't know what the world is coming to. I never thought I'd see the day when Christians and Muslims would try to work together. That's an impossible proposition, Muhammadu. You people don't know what you're getting yourself into. You know how the Quran warns against taking Christians to be our friends (Q. 5:54). Some of them are good people, but you can't begin to trust them. Didn't you ever read the poem Alhaji

Imoru, our great Ghanaian saint, wrote years ago when the
Europeans first came here?[67] Hold on a minute -- I'll find
it for you. I just had it in my hands last week. Every
word of it rings true."

   Alihu took Muhammadu into his room and rummaged around
through a pile of papers and books on his desk. Finally,
he picked up an old tattered handwritten manuscript, carefully spread it out on the table in front of him, and began
to read and translate. It was in Arabic, of course, and
since Muhammadu couldn't read the Arabic, Alihu had to translate it for his benefit sentence by sentence. It read like
this:

> I've set out this poem in rhyme
> For the profit of intelligent folk...
> Anyone with brains will heed it.
> From our words, He'll grasp our intention.
>
> A sun of disaster has risen in the West,
> Glaring down on people and populated places.
> Poetically speaking, I mean the catastrophe of
>   the Christians.
> The Christian calamity has come upon us
> Like a dust-cloud.
>
> At the start of the affair, they came peacefully,
> With soft sweet talk.
> "We've come to trade," they said,
> "To reform the beliefs of the people,
> To halt oppression here below, and theft,
> To clean up and overthrow corruption."
> Not all of us grasped their motives,
> So now we've become their inferiors
> They deluded us with little gifts
> And fed us tasty foods...
> But recently they've changed their tune
> (Braimah 1967:191f).

Alihu put the manuscript away as carefully as he had taken
it out, and then with a look of quiet triumph, glanced over
to see how the message had hit home to Muhammadu.

   "You're right," Muhammadu said. "Everything that Alhaji
Imoru said has come true. That doesn't mean, though, that
we're not living in a totally different situation today.
There's some Christians who are hypocrites, but you'll have
to admit, there are a lot of Muslims who are hypocrites, too.

Imoru is correct. There were a lot of Christians who came
here to fill their pockets, to lie and to cheat and to deceive, to get everything they could out of this country.
But, there were also a lot of Christians who came here with
a different purpose in mind altogether. I think it's time
we started to make a distinction between Europeans and
Christians. You know, all the Europeans who came here were
not Christians. Besides that, Christianity has taken root
in this country just as has Islam. If European Christians
had their faults -- which they did, is it fair to charge
those faults to our Ghanaian Christian neighbours? These
are the people we're talking about when we're thinking
about the Christian Council."

"Well, all I can say is that it will never work. Look
what they tried to do to us just a few years ago. The
Ghana Government 'Alien Quit Order' was purposely directed
against us Muslims by the Christians in power in order to
get rid of us."[68]

"What do you mean?" interrupted Muhammadu. "I cheered
for that order as much as did the next fellow. It was
high time something was done to control the number of
foreigners coming into this country."

"Yes, but you know the Muslims were the most seriously
affected. You remember how Muslims were openly attacked
on the streets -- even native-born Ghanaians. They were
harassed and questioned as to why they weren't on their
way out of the country."

"That's true," Muhammadu answered, "but you also have to
remember that most Muslims hadn't made much effort to identify with national goals or aspirations. That's one of the
reasons why the Ghana Muslim Mission was founded -- to try
to put Islam more into the heart of the life of this country."

"I've said all along," Alihu argued, "that the Muslim
Mission is only trying to copy the Christians.[69] They
build schools; you want to build schools. They build hospitals; you want to build hospitals. They translate the
Bible; you want to translate the Quran. They pray in their
different languages; you want to leave the Arabic and pray
in any language. There are some things about Islam that
you cannot change. Once you begin to change them, you make
it possible for everything to change. Then it is no longer
Islam. Then it is something else."

"*Don't get me wrong,*" Muhammadu replied, "*I appreciate how the Quran came to us in Arabic, and the prayers, and all. But, let's admit it, Arabic isn't our language. The Christians had the same kind of problem. They looked upon Latin as a sacred language back in the Dark Ages. Then Luther came along and said, 'Why should we worship God in a language we don't even speak. If God created us, then surely God can speak our language,' and Luther went on to translate the Bible into German.[70] This brought a renewal into the church, a whole reformation. That's why we want to see the Quran in our own Ghanaian language so we can find out what Islam is really all about! How can you do your 'Islam' if you don't even know what Islam is all about?*"

"*It was still God's will to give man the Quran and the prayers in Arabic. Let's not forget that the Sacred Text is in heaven. In this modern time is it all of a sudden too great a "submission" for us people to try to learn Arabic? People have done it for centuries, and who are we to say that it should be different? After all, God could have given us the Quran in English, or Twi, or Ga, or Hausa, but He didn't. He gave us an Arabic Quran.*"[71]

"*True, He gave us an Arabic Quran, but He also gave me my language, and He gave you your language. I'm proud of my language just as you're proud of your language, and I believe that God can speak my language just as well as He speaks Arabic. Once we make some progress in this matter of language, we can begin to make progress in other areas as well.*"

"*You mean, like joining the Christian Council,*" Alihu said, and both men laughed. On that note, Muhammadu excused himself and begged to leave. When he reached home, I was there waiting for him.

Muhammadu told me about his discussion with Alihu, and then he asked, "*Yakubu, is it really such a crazy idea for us to think about joining the Christian Council?*"

"*Now, I don't know,*" I replied. "*I've never thought about that before, but just offhand, I don't see why not. It might work in a beneficial way for both you and the Christian Council if you were to come in. I know some Christians would be opposed to the idea and I suppose the same would be true for some Muslims. Might I ask, whatever made you think about wanting to join the Christian Council?*"

"Well, I'll tell you. Lately, I've been doing a lot of thinking, and so have a lot of other people. We're disturbed by the sick things which are happening in public life from the top man to the bottom. Everywhere you drive, you have to bribe the police. Every office you visit, you have to bribe the officer. Bribery, corruption, nepotism -- you see it all around, and you can't avoid it yourself. But, this thing has to end somewhere!

"Then, look around and see what's happening to our children. They're getting a better education than we had, but they don't want to pay attention to God anymore. All they think about is money and fast cars and women and fine clothes. It's like a disease creeping down on our society, and I'm not sure we Muslims can stop it alone, or that you Christians can stop it alone. But, maybe we can stop it together.

"Some of us have read about the things you in the Christian Council have been doing, and the way you're trying to study the cause of some of these evils, expose them, and fight against them. Some of us think we ought to join you in the battle."[72]

"That's a great idea," I said. "It's certainly worth investigating. Why don't you continue to discuss it among yourselves, and in the meantime, let me mention it to our pastor, who, in turn, can bring it before the head of our church? I certainly can't promise a favourable reception to this idea, but at least I'll try to have it get a good hearing."

"I think we'd be grateful for that," Muhammadu replied. And with that, we turned to our other business and soon I was on my way.

When I reached the road, there was Jonathan on his way home with a heavy parcel. Putting it down to catch his breath, he chuckled, "Fraternizing with the Muslims again?"

"Yes," I said, "you have to find out what the 'enemy' camp is thinking every now and again." Jonathan had frequently spoken to me about both Catholics and Muslims being the "enemy." I didn't want to mention my discussion with Muhammadu to Jonathan because I already knew where he would stand on that question. To my surprise, he brought it up himself.

"Guess what I heard in the market place?" he said. "The Muslims want to join the Christian Council. Did you ever hear of such a ridiculous idea? You know what, I'll bet you anything the Christian Council will probably take them in. That's just how dead the Christian Council is."

"Do you really think so?" I asked. "I mean that the Christian Council is so dead, and in the second place, that this is such a ridiculous idea?"[73]

"I can answer that in one sentence," said Jonathan. "If the Christian Council is foolish enough to take the Muslims in, then it is dead."

"In other words," I replied, "if the Christian Council doesn't take them in, you'll still have some hope for the Christian Council?"

"You might put it that way. Apart from this Muslim question the biggest problem, I suppose, is that the Christian Council spends all its time talking about national troubles like bribery and corruption, the ills of society which nobody can heal -- even Jesus said, 'The poor we'll always have with us' -- when, in fact, the Christian Council is dead, or almost dead. It has all its priorities in the wrong places."

"I'll agree with you, Jonathan, we often do get our priorities in the wrong places. I hope, however, I'm not hearing you say that we shouldn't be concerned about bribery, corruption and other national and local evils. One of the things that disturbs me is that we have such a high percentage of Christians in this country, and yet these same problems are continually with us. The very man who sits behind a desk and idles away our time waiting for a bribe turns out to be the steward in next Sunday's church service. The policeman who puts his own private tax on all the cars which travel through his checkpoint sings in the church choir. Shouldn't the churches have something to say to these people, and isn't the kind of joint mouthpiece which the Christian Council offers one of the most effective tools to combat these evils? That's why some of the Muslims feel they ought to join us. Then we can fight these things together. They admire what they've seen the Christian Council doing, and now they want to do their share."

"Well, why don't they become Christians and then they can do their share?" With that, Jonathan picked up his

*parcel and strode on down the road. The road was badly in
need of repair. I wondered if the repair would ever come
since the Local Council was so filled with graft that we
didn't know where any of our monies were going.*

*"Paving new ground," I thought to myself as he strolled
away, "It's just as difficult a proposition whether we're
talking about city streets, or human hearts. I wonder who
will take the lead?"*

YEARNINGS FOR BROTHERHOOD

There are stirrings all over the world today. Feelings
of communality are growing, some superficial and almost
artificial; others serious and strong. Such feelings have
long traversed the boundaries which separate various Christian churches (ecumenism).[74] They are now beginning to
cross the wasteland which has separated Christians from
Muslims.

Some of the deepest yearnings for new attempts at
brotherhood are growing out of the anxiety caused by the
deterioration and demise of traditional extended family
ties. Expanding cities and the new money economy have continued to destroy the cohesiveness of traditional family
structures. Formerly, churches helped stabilize and
strengthen social organization wherever they were represented. Today things have changed. Where previously the
church played a significant social role, today it is only
one of many alternatives in the social life of a community.
With the migration of people to and from the towns, the
introduction and organization of competing clubs and tribal
societies, and the advent of many new denominations, the
strengthening ties of a former day are now in disarray.

Families are asking, "How is it we're drifting so far
apart?" Whereas in a previous generation, family members
were all part of the same church, they now find themselves
divided up in many different denominations. Not only that,
many family members have become totally inactive in the
church, except for festival occasions. This kind of unrest
has fostered a growing interest in the possibilities of
church union. Even while the talk of church union flour-
ishes and spreads, however, churches continue to arise on
the horizon. This, in turn, causes additional frustration
over how everything is changing and seems to be falling
apart.

The question Muhammadu raised is intentionally provoca-
tive, but it is not altogether unrealistic. As Muslim
communities find themselves caught up in the general unrest
and frustration of our time, many Muslims have come to wonder, as does Muhammadu, if joining groups like Christian
Councils might not help resolve at least some of the current problems and difficulties. Their theory and hope is
that if all religious bodies were to join hands in a gigantic effort to correct the ills of society, it would have
much more chance of success than the feeble efforts of any
single group.

What is happening today in the world has come to many
people by surprise, but it does not come as unexpected to
students of the Word of God. Centuries ago already, Paul
anticipated these intense disturbances in the family of
man (2 Tim. 3:1-5), and before him, Jesus had spoken in
similar terms of the unrest to come (Matt. 24:7-12). He
pictured it as a time of nation rising against nation and
kingdom against kingdom. Along with famines and earthquakes,
these confrontations would be "but the beginning of the suf-
ferings." In the greater stress yet to come, even more
severe tests of faith would be put upon those who follow in
His train.

The unrest in Africa, as elsewhere, is just one more
indicator that these prophecies are being fulfilled. The
world is hastening to its impending doom and man, left to
his own resources, feels very much alone as he observes,
contemplates, and unwillingly, but automatically gets caught
up in a swirl of evil and uncertainty. As the end draws
near, it is this aloneness which increases yearnings for
stability, certainty and brotherhood.

WEIGHING THE ALTERNATIVES FOR BROTHERHOOD

Islam and Christianity represent different attempts to
resolve the tensions of man's inner being. They are not
the only alternatives open to him, however, for there are,
besides these, the other great institutionalized world
religions -- Buddhism, Hinduism, Shintoism, Communism, and
others. In addition, there are the institutionally unor-
ganized, but nevertheless widely followed, religious expressions like African animism and the now rapidly spread-
ing secularism of twentieth century man. Finally, there is
the "mother" religion of both Islam and Christianity --
Judaism. Each of these in its own distinctive way offers
man some kind of relief from his anxieties.

From birth on, each of us lives with a feeling of great helplessness as we struggle for survival against the forces of environment which we cannot control. In searching for security we opt for one or another religious expression, each of which attempts to achieve some measure of harmony with the forces which limit and control our existence. Who and what these forces are is variously interpreted, but for Christians and Muslims there is no question as to what the major disruptive force is. It is that of Satan and his army of evil angels. By various deceits, he and the "principalities and powers" in his service seek to destroy our confidence in God. By filling us with lies and doubts in efforts to cause us to forget God, he succeeds in disrupting the harmony which God had intended for His creation.

In addition to recognizing Satan's power among men, Christians have isolated man's own sinfulness as the immediate cause of his disharmony with God. Our natural response to Satan's lies and deceptions is to disobey God's will and live in disloyalty to Him. The signs of this disobedience and disloyalty are everywhere evident, surfacing among other ways as "Immorality, impurity, licentiousness, idolatry, sorcery, enmity, strife, jealousy, anger, selfishness, dissension, party spirit, envy, drunkenness, carousing, and the like" (Gal. 5:19ff). Unredeemed man, caught in the bind and grasp of sin, lives in misery and uncertainty from cradle to grave.

To ease the pain, the anguish, and the uncertainty with which he daily lives, man invents all kinds of alternatives for relief. He chooses idolatry in a great variety of forms, putting his trust in beings and things which have no existence (I Cor. 8:4). He tries to forget about his anguish by amassing all kinds of worldly goods in spite of the fact that it profits him nothing to gain the whole world and lose his own soul (Matt. 16:26). He turns to efforts of piety, even though no one will be justified by works of the Law (Gal. 2:16). He cleverly welds together into religious systems standards of ethics and morality which seek to control and channel his wayward energies into pathways of righteousness. Out of these varied efforts grow the religious brotherhoods men bring into existence to satisfy their deepest yearnings for security.

If any of us were in a situation where the two choices for satisfying those deep yearnings would be Islam, or idolatry, perhaps the majority of us would choose Islam. The Quran is filled with denunciations of idolatry, and during

Muhammad's ministry, this was a distinctive emphasis. Over and over again, he called upon people to renounce their idols and to reorder their lives by bowing in worship to "God, the Merciful, the Compassionate." Responding to his preaching, people destroyed idol after idol, turning in "submission" to God, the Creator of the universe. Whatever we think of Muhammad, we have to acknowledge that God used him in a powerful way to virtually destroy gross idolatry in what is today a major part of the Muslim world.[75] It was from those beginnings that Islam has gone on to become a highly significant and notably successful attempt at human brotherhood.

ISLAM, AN ATTEMPT AT BROTHERHOOD

The concept of *Umma* is almost as important to Islam as is the concept of *Shari'a*. *Umma* is "the Community" and is comparable in meaning to "the Church, the Communion of Saints." When one becomes a Muslim, he leaves the *Dar al-Harb* ("The World of War") and becomes part of the *Dar al-Islam* ("The World of Islam").[76]

The boundaries of *Dar al-Islam* and *Dar al-Harb* have varied according to the definition employed by various Muslim theorists and legal experts. At times, as in early Islam, Christians were part of the *Dar al-Islam* by virtue of their being "People of the Book." When Muslim animosities turned against Christians, they became part of the *Dar al-Harb*. There have even been times when Muslims have been part of the *Dar al-Harb*, as during the wars initiated by Uthman dan Fodio in Northern Nigeria. There is extant, by way of illustration, a most interesting correspondence between Uthman dan Fodio and Al-Kanemi, the ruler of Kanem-Bornu. Al-Kanemi asked dan Fodio why his people -- the Beri-Beri, as they are known in Ghana today, or Kanuri, as they are known in Nigeria -- were part of the *Dar al-Harb*, and not part of the *Dar al-Islam*. Dan Fodio wrote back to insist that Al-Kanemi was wrong. He told them that people were not part of the *Dar al-Islam* just because they called themselves Muslim. They had to live like Muslims, which meant putting away pagan practices. He charged them with syncretism, and the mixing of Islam with paganism. Having done this, dan Fodio said, they could no longer properly be called Muslim. They were no longer part of the *Dar al-Islam*, and for that reason, his armies would continue their onslaught.

Umma is sometimes translated as "nation." The idea is similar to Peter's "You are a chosen race ... a holy nation,

God's own people" (I Pet. 2:9). It is a transcultural,
transnational, transracial "nation," the uniting factor of
which is the *islam* (submission) of all who are thus united
together. From this aspect of the *Umma* you can see why
groups which emphasize race, nationality, or culture have
difficulty being accepted by the greater majority of Muslims (This, for example, is the dilemma of the Black Muslims in America).[77] As in ideal Christianity, so in ideal
Islam, once a man comes to obey the truth, there is no
race, culture, or nation except the new nation which has
come into being as the creation of God Almighty. In Islam
this new nation is the *Umma* which ideally breaks down all
barriers and unites into one family all who confess "there
is no God but God and Muhammad is His Prophet." In the
brotherhood which has united around that confession there
has emerged a significant attempt at meeting man's deepest
yearnings for acceptance and fellowship.

THE BROTHERHOOD WHICH CHRIST BRINGS

On the basis of Islam's and Christianity's contribution
to brotherhood, we might be encouraged to endorse Muhammadu's
idea that these two forces working together could bring
peace and harmony into the world. We might expect that together they could resolve the problems of modern man,
stamping out dishonesty, corruption, and all the other ills
which torment the world of today. Contrary to such antici-
pations, however, neither Muslims joining Christian Councils, nor church union, will automatically relieve the deeply
felt tensions and human yearnings for brotherhood. Something
more is needed and that something has to do with a crushing
of the human ego and a total reorientation of the human
heart. This, as we have seen, is not man's act; it is God's,
and it comes at His initiative. It has to do with what happens when God confronts men in the person of Jesus Christ.

God's sending of Jesus into the world was His way of
speaking to the deepest yearnings of man. His coming was
the fulfilment of the Word spoken centuries before:

> The Spirit of the Lord God is upon Me,
>   because the Lord has anointed Me
> to bring good tidings to the afflicted,
>   He has sent Me to bind up the brokenhearted,
> to proclaim liberty to the captives,
>   and the opening of the prison
>   to those who are bound (Is. 61:1).

When Jesus announced, "Today this Scripture has been fulfilled in your hearing" (Luke 4:21), he publicly proclaimed
that He was that Anointed One, the "Christ." "I came that
they may have life," He said, "and have it abundantly"
(John 10:10).

Jesus, the "Sent One," sent "not to condemn the world,
but that the world might be saved through Him" (John 3:17),
commissioned us who follow Him to carry on His work in the
world. His is the work of reconciliation, and in the words
of His prayer to the Father He said, "As Thou didst send Me
into the world, so I have sent them into the world" (John
17:18). Everywhere around us the world is in turmoil, men
yearning for brotherhood, for acceptance, for freedom from
anxiety, for peace of mind and soul and body. God has given
us all that in Christ, and even more! Now comes this Word,
"Freely ye have received; freely give" (Matt. 10:8, KJV).

How beautifully Paul captured the excitement of that
motivation when he wrote so simply and with such warm appeal:

> God has given us the privilege of urging
> everyone to come into His favour and be re-
> conciled to Him. For God was in Christ,
> restoring the world to Himself, no longer
> counting men's sins against them but blot-
> ting them out. This is the wonderful mes-
> sage He has given us to tell others. We
> are Christ's ambassadors. God is using us
> to speak to you; we beg you, as though Christ
> Himself were here pleading with you, receive
> the love He offers you -- be reconciled to
> God. For God took the sinless Christ and
> poured into Him our sins. Then, in exchange,
> he poured God's goodness into us.
>
> As God's partners we beg you not to toss aside
> this marvelous message of God's great kindness
> ... Right now God is ready to welcome you.
> Today He is ready to save you (2 Cor. 5:18-21,
> 6:1f, LB).

How different this picture is from the one we regularly see
of Christians and Muslims being in a fierce competition with
each other. The picture here is one of Christians engaged
in a work of reconciliation. It is one of Christians ex-
tending a hand of "welcome" to Muslims, the same hand of
"welcome" which God has extended to them. It is offering a

new "kindness" to Muslims, the same "kindness" which God
has offered to them. It is pleading with Muslims to receive the same "love" by which "God took the sinless Christ
and poured into Him our sins," and "in exchange, poured
God's goodness into us." It is striving to be at peace
with all men, including Muslims (Heb. 12:14f), for Christ
has given us His peace (John 14:27).

Now, commissioned by His love, for "the love of Christ
controls us" (2 Cor. 5:14), "we are ambassadors for Christ,
God making His appeal through us." "His" is the appeal
that men might "Believe that Jesus is the Christ, the Son
of God, and that believing they may have life in His Name"
(John 20:31). "God gave us eternal life, and this life is
in His Son. He who has the Son has life; he who has not
the Son of God has not life" (I John 5:11f).

Thus, in Christ a new alternative comes to the Muslim
world. It is not an alternative which condemns as much as
it is an alternative which offers every person a new kind
of relationship with God, a relationship based not upon
works, but upon faith. It offers the alternative of a
"submission" based not upon one's own efforts, but upon
Christ's. The certainty of God's accepting this submission is as sure as Jesus is risen from the dead! Obedience to this "submission" is to enter into a perfect brotherhood relationship with Jesus for, as He said, "Whoever
does the will of My Father in heaven is My brother, and
sister, and mother" (Matt. 12:50). In Christ, a totally
different kind of religious brotherhood has been created
and offered to man. This is how God has spoken to man's
deepest yearnings for acceptance and for perfect brotherhood.

The members of this new family, the brotherhood of Christ
are representatives of a different Way, unique from all the
religious alternatives devised by man. In the midst of all
the religious traditions put together and developed by man,
there is this distinctive alternative designed by God. As
we have seen, those who represent this Way to the world have
an appointment from Christ Himself. They are His ambassadors!

AMBASSADORS

One of the exciting attractions of life in a capital city
like Accra is to see ambassadors and high commissioners
from all over the world. They travel to and from their of-

fices in fine cars and sit in the front rows at public ceremonies. Honour and prestige accompany their work as liai-
sons between their homelands and the Government and people
of Ghana. The more warmth, diplomacy, and understanding
they are capable of generating, the more potentially successful is their mission of creating an atmosphere of harmony
and healthy rapport between their people and the people of
Ghana.

At the same time, for all the glitter and glow that comes
with their office, ambassadors are in extremely vulnerable
positions. If, for example, the Government of Ghana wanted
to order every diplomat out of the country within twenty-
four hours, it could do so. Each ambassador is in Ghana
purely and solely as a guest of the Government and people of
Ghana. If, for any reason, he, or his country, falls into
disfavour, he can be declared *persona non grata* and asked to
make an immediate exit.

It is the same with Christ's ambassadors. They come from
many nationalities, but their real "commonwealth is in
heaven" (Phil. 3:20). Like Abraham, Isaac, and Jacob before
them, they are "strangers and exiles on the earth ... seeking a homeland." God "has prepared for them a city" and
they, thus, "have no lasting city" here, but they "seek the
city which is to come" (Heb. 11:13-16; 13:14). They are
those for whom Christ prayed as He prepared to leave them:

> I do not pray that Thou shouldst take them
> out of the world, but that Thou shouldst
> keep them from the evil one. They are not
> of the world, even as I am not of the world
> ... As Thou didst send Me into the world,
> so I have sent them into the world (John
> 17:15f, 18).

As Christ's ambassadors, these disciples of all time are
just as open to insult, attack, and humiliation as are the
ambassadors from any one country to another. Even though
they carry higher credentials than any diplomat in the world,
they are as vulnerable to the hatred of the world as was the
Master who sent them forth. This kind of treatment is not
unexpected for Jesus had told them to anticipate just that
(John 15:18ff).

Jesus spoke again and again of the cross His ambassadors
would have to shoulder. He warned them of the unpleasant
receptions they would receive. He spoke of rejection and

reviling, but he also spoke of promise, "Lo, I am with you
always" (Matt. 28:20). It is this promise that gives them
such a unique position among all the ambassadors in the
world. Even when under attack, they have an attitude, a
life-style, a manner of living that glorifies Christ and
reaches out with a warm forgiving appeal of welcome to
others. It was Peter who summed up their peculiarly difficult role in such a challenging way:

> Do not return evil for evil or reviling for
> reviling; but *on the contrary bless, for to
> this you have been called* ... Always be pre-
> pared to make a defence to any one who calls
> you to account for the hope that is in you,
> yet do it *with gentleness and reverence,* and
> keep your conscience clear, so that, when you
> are abused, those who revile your good be-
> haviour in Christ may be put to shame
> (I Pet. 3:9, 15f).

These diplomats, even in their torment, carry with them a
special glory for it was Christ who said to the Father,
"The glory which Thou hast given Me I have given to them"
(John 17:22). Often beaten and bruised, often battered and
bleeding, but always blessed and blessing, they are God's
representatives in the world. It is His glory they bear.
It is His glory they share.

If the idea of "paving new ground" catches our imaginations in any way, one of the first challenges before us is
to begin removing the debris of centuries of misunderstanding between Christians and Muslims. The rubble of misrepresentation and overgeneralization stands as a mighty obstacle
to any open and frank communication. Peter suggests the
tone with which we might approach such a situation by calling our attention to two essential qualities for good diplomacy -- "gentleness and reverence." This is how we are to
answer those who ask us about the hope within us.

Several questions come to mind as we ponder the implications of employing such an approach in our conversations
with Muslims. How far, for example, does God expect us to
go in our exercise of these qualities? Are we to be gentle
and reverent only as we answer those who ask us about our
faith, or is Peter telling us of a quality of life which is
to be as much a part of our initiative as it is a part of
our defence? Let's not forget that God took the initiative
in our behalf; isn't it in order that now as Christ's ambassadors we take the initiative in His?

When Christians talk with, or about, Muslims, the temptation is to point accusing fingers at them, charging them with
being at fault for the present communication impasse because
of their stubbornness and hardheartedness. Peter's advice
reminds us to look first to ourselves. We can hardly begin
to remove the rubble or to destroy the debris unless we are
filled with a generous measure of gentleness and reverence
-- gentleness and reverence not only for the Muslim, but an
attitude of kindliness and respect also for the persons and
things he holds sacred. It is exactly at this point that a
peculiar difficulty enters into the picture for the Christian. His problem has to do with the person of Muhammad and
the status of the Quran. His primary question is: What does
gentleness and reverence mean in this context? Does it mean
gentleness and reverence for the Muslim only, or does it mean
gentleness and reverence also for Muhammad and the Quran?

In other words, how are we Christians to approach Muslims
on the subject of Muhammad and the Quran? Can we in good
conscience cultivate a sincere respect for him and the "revelation" he brought, or must we denounce him as a false prophet and his revelation as a work of Satan? Is it possible
for our attitudes toward Muhammad and the Quran to reflect
the same gentleness and reverence with which we are to answer
the Muslim regarding our own faith? What is our Master's
will in this matter? What kind of initiative and innovation
can we through the Holy Spirit bring to bear upon this problem? These are some of the questions which cry for answers
as we try to fulfil our callings as ambassadors for Christ.
We shall look for those answers as we continue to explore
how and in what ways to pave new ground for a faithful witness to our risen Lord Christ among our Muslim neighbours.

11

Muhammad
and the Quran

"THE WORDS OF ETERNAL LIFE"

*Matthew was really worked up about something. I was sur-
prised when I found out he was all wound up from trying to
convince his son Kweku that the Bible was the truth and the
Quran was false. One of the amusing aspects of this situation had to do with the fact that neither Matthew, nor his
son, had ever seemed overly concerned about religious matters.*

*You remember how disturbed people had been when Kweku
married Muhammadu's daughter. Usually such marriages are
turned around. Muslims permit their sons to marry non-
Muslim wives, but rarely permit their daughters to marry
non-Muslim husbands. Alihu, for one, could not begin to
understand how Muhammadu had ever allowed this thing to
happen.*

*Everyone had assumed that Muhammadu's daughter would be-
come a Christian, although she hadn't started attending
church yet. She had become pregnant soon after they were
married and everybody knew that she was having a hard time
with her pregnancy. That's why it was understandable that
she didn't become active in the church right away. Of course,
you couldn't tell either if she was practising her Islam, or
not. You know, you never can tell about a woman. You never
see them going to the mosque, or praying in the open squares
-- unless, of course, they're older women.*

*Now that the baby had come, Matthew and his wife were
pushing Kweku that it was time to have the baby baptized.*

It was in that situation that the argument over the Bible
and the Quran arose.

It was clear from Matthew's report to me that the most
upsetting thing to him and his wife was that it looked like
instead of their daughter-in-law, Maryamu, investigating
Christianity, it was their son who was seriously considering
Islam. It was clear that he had been doing a lot of reading, or having a lot of discussions with somebody about the
relative merits of the Bible over against the Quran. Matthew
couldn't tell if Kweku himself believed the things he was
saying, or if he was just raising the questions in his own
search to try to find answers to challenges others were
raising. What Matthew wanted me to do was to talk with
Kweku and try to convince him that the Bible was the truth
and the Quran was in error. He could see that Kweku was
filled with all kinds of doubts, but he didn't quite know
how to respond to them.

The chance arrived for me to talk with Kweku two days
later. He returned a set of tools which Matthew had borrowed and I invited him to sit down and relax for awhile.
I mentioned that his father had been over and we had talked
about the Bible and the Quran.

"Yes," Kweku said, "we had what you might call some big
disagreements over several things. You know, in some ways
my father is real progressive in his thinking; in other
ways, he's got a closed mind and a 'colonial mentality' --
like when it comes to his ideas about the Bible."

"What exactly do you mean when you talk about a 'colonial
mentality' as far as the Bible is concerned?"

"What I mean is that the scholarship of the last hundred
years, or so, has only helped to prove what Muslims have
said all along. The Bible is filled with mistakes."

"On what grounds," I interrupted, "do you conclude that
the Quran doesn't have any mistakes?"

"That's easy," he said, "there's only one authorship to
the Quran and that is God's. Unlike the Bible, the Quran
has been handed down in its original Arabic text and it
doesn't have all the variant readings which go along with
the Hebrew and Greek manuscripts of the Bible. To me, this
says a lot! Besides, the whole original Gospel which Jesus
brought has been lost. All we have is what other people re-

membered about it. It's different with the Quran where you
have the exact revelation from God to Muhammad."

"I follow what you say, Kweku, but there are several
things you need to keep in mind. For one, I wonder if you
know that there actually were different versions of the
Quran, but Uthman, the Fourth Caliph, ordered that all versions of the Quran except one be destroyed. Even then, he
wasn't totally successful because I understand some variant
texts are still in circulation, although they don't have
nearly the wide circulation, nor the open discussion, which
goes along with the biblical texts. I think it's only a
matter of time and Muslims will begin looking as critically
at the text of the Quran as Christians have done with the
Bible.

"Another thing we shouldn't forget is that the Quran and
Quranic scholarship have a way of dealing with contradictions
which has never been a part of biblical scholarship. You've
heard of the Doctrine of Abrogation, haven't you?[78] If there
are two verses which contradict each other, and if Muslims
can determine the order in which those verses were announced,
they conclude that the later verse 'abrogates,' or replaces,
the earlier verse. This kind of technique can solve a lot
of textual problems.

"Then, this business about the Gospel. Of course, we
don't have the actual words which Jesus brought in the sense
in which the Quran is supposedly the actual word of God delivered through Muhammad. To me, this doesn't in any way
negate the validity of the words of Jesus as reported by
Matthew, Mark, Luke and John. I don't know how I'd begin
to prove this. In fact, I don't think there's any way we
can prove matters like this. In the final analysis, it
ends up being a matter of faith. I know that the words of
Jesus were not directly written by Him, but at the same time
I trust fully that they are His words, and in that trust I
draw strength, help, and guidance from them, and of course,
ultimately from Jesus Himself.

"I have to admit that how this whole process of faith
happens is to me, and perhaps to every Christian, a mystery.
The fact that Jesus didn't directly write any of these
words himself, or dictate them to a secretary, doesn't particularly disturb me because of what the Bible says about
the work of the Holy Spirit. It was Jesus Himself who said,

            These things I have spoken to you, while I am
            still with you. But the Counsellor, the Holy

> *Spirit, whom the Father will send in My Name,*
> *He will teach you all things, and bring to*
> *your remembrance all that I have said to you*
> *(John 14:25f).*

Matthew and the other Gospel writers could not have written
what they did if it had not been for the work of the Holy
Spirit. In fact, it wasn't only the Gospels which took form
in this fashion, but this is how the whole Bible gradually
came to be. As Peter said, 'Men moved by the Holy Spirit
spoke from God' (2 Pet. 1:21), to which Paul added, 'All
scripture is inspired by God' (2 Tim. 3:16).

"What is deceptive, Kweku," I continued, "is how our
Bibles are put together in such handy volumes, indexed and
all. I sometimes think we might have more respect for the
Bible's timeless truth if we could pick up each biblical
document in its near original form. This means we'd handle
a several thousand year old crumbling manuscript of Moses
telling us about the creation of the world and the giving
of the Law. Putting that aside, we'd pick up another ancient
faded and falling apart document, the scrolls of Isaiah, and
finally, we'd move into the various writings of the New
Testament. What we miss with our neatly printed texts is a
sense of how the Bible is not one book, but many. That's
what Bible means, a collection of books. The marvellous
thing is that this collection of books spans a period of
some 1500 to 2000 years, and yet there is one theme that
holds them all together, the theme of God's covenanting with
man. To me, it's a wonderful miracle how God has inspired
men to write these books, gather them together, preserve
them, and finally, hand them down to us as a record of His
dealings with mankind. As Paul says, 'Whatever was written
in former days was written for our instruction, that by
steadfastness and by the encouragement of the scriptures we
might have hope'" (Rom. 15:4).

"But what about the Quran, Yakubu" Kweku interjected,
"have you read it?"

"As a matter of fact, I've been reading a lot in the
Quran lately. I've almost read it through -- I suppose you
know it's a little shorter than our New Testament. It took
me a while to get into it -- I guess because it's more like
a book of sermons than a collection of letters as is the
New Testament. It has a lot of repetition, and yet, it is
extremely interesting and very informative, if for no other
reason than that it incorporates some highly useful histori-

*cal material regarding the period of time in history some
five hundred to six hundred years after Christ. It offers
valuable insights into the church of that time as it was
represented in Saudi Arabia, as well as into the Jewish and
pagan communities.*

*"At the same time, to be honest, the words of the Quran
do not speak to me as do the words of the Bible. I don't
quite know how to put my fingers upon this feeling of mine,
or how exactly it has come about that I put my faith in the
words of the Bible. It seems to me that it's happened with
me something like what happened with Peter and the other
disciples. Do you remember how after Jesus fed the five
thousand, the multitudes kept coming, apparently for more
free food, and how Jesus rebuked them (John 6:26f)? After
that, there were more and more people who deserted Jesus
when they saw the free food was finished. Finally, Jesus
asked the handful who were left, 'Will you also go away?'
It was Peter who responded, 'Lord, to whom shall we go?
You have the words of eternal life' (John 6:67f). That's
exactly how I feel about the Bible after having read both
from the Bible and the Quran."*

*Kweku seemed somewhat relieved and appreciative. I could
tell he was going through a great struggle within himself.
As he strolled back home, I breathed a prayer for Kweku and
Maryamu that the Word of Jesus to His disciples would come
true to them: "When the Spirit of truth comes, He will
guide you into all the truth" (John 16:13). How much Kweku
was longing and searching for that guidance!*

CHRISTIANS, MUHAMMAD, AND THE QURAN

Christians have had a very difficult problem knowing how
to relate to Muhammad and the Quran. By and large, their
conclusions have been negative, shaped very much by the
various warnings Jesus and the Apostles gave about false
prophets (Matt. 7:15; 24:9-12,23f). The warnings of Jesus
are not the only ones in Scripture. Paul spoke of the "man
of lawlessness, the son of perdition," and John spoke of
the "antichrist."[79]

As with all prophecy in Scripture, these prophecies and
their meanings need to be carefully studied and restudied
again and again. In the past, various interpretations have
identified Muhammad as one among those who brought these
prophecies to fulfilment. Unfortunately, these interpretations have not always been fair either to Muhammad, or the

biblical text. Take, for instance, Paul's announcement to
the Thessalonians,

> The coming of *the lawless one* by the activity
> of Satan will be with all power and with pre-
> tended signs and wonders, and with all wicked
> deception for those who are to perish, because
> they refused to love the truth, and so be saved.
> Therefore God sends upon them a strong delusion,
> to make them believe what is false, so that all
> may be condemned who did not believe the truth
> but had pleasure in unrighteousness (2 Thess.
> 2:9-12).

While some Christians have seen the coming of Muhammad and
the spread of Islam in this prophecy, there is some difficulty in attempting to identify the "lawless one" with
Muhammad. The problem has to do with an earlier part of
Paul's description of "the man of lawlessness." He spoke
of him as one

> who opposes and exalts himself against every
> so-called god or object of worship, so that
> he takes his seat in the temple of God, pro-
> claiming himself to be God (2 Thess. 2:4).

It is hardly accurate, or fair, to apply that description to
Muhammad. Muhammad never took his place in the "temple of
God, proclaiming himself to be God." Furthermore, he never
claimed to himself any special "power" of any kind. The
only miracle to which he is connected is the miracle of the
Quran, but even for that he claimed no credit. He saw himself only as the mouthpiece of God, a channel for the divine
message.[80]

When we get into John, the special verses which trouble
Christians are these:

> This is the antichrist ... who denies the Father
> and the Son ... Every spirit which does not
> confess Jesus is not of God. This is the spirit
> of the antichrist ... Many deceivers have gone
> out into the world, men who will not acknowledge
> the coming of Jesus Christ in the flesh; such
> a one is the deceiver and the antichrist
> (I John 2:22, 4:3; 2 John 7).

If you put these verses from the Bible alongside the verses
from the Quran which speak to the subject of Jesus' relationship to God, you can see why many Christians conclude
that Muhammad is "the antichrist." Take, for example,
Sura 112. It is one of the shortest of all the chapters in
the Quran, and so it is placed as third to the last, but it
is one of the most popular and oft-recited sentences among
Muslims. It reads:

> Say: "He is God, One
>   God, the Everlasting Refuge,
> who has not begotten, and has not been begotten,
>   and equal to Him is not any one."

The content of that Sura is repeated in another form at
several different places in the Quran. One of the longest
chapters, "The Table," refers to this general subject
several times.[81] It announces more than once that "they
are unbelievers who say, 'God is the Messiah, Mary's son'"
(Q. 5:19,75). Added to this is the frequent theme which
denies the Trinity:

> They are unbelievers
>   who say, "God is the Third of Three."
> No god is there but
>   One God (Q. 5:76).

The same charge of unbelief is advanced in Sura 9, the
only Sura which begins without the *Bismillah.* There
Muhammad is set forth as the "Messenger with the guidance
and the religion of truth" in opposition to the Christians
and Jews who "associate" someone with God (Q. 9:30ff). As
we've already seen, associating someone or something with
God is called *shirk,* the most grievous of all sins in the
mind of a Muslim. While Muslims are bothered with that
kind of a question, Christians are bothered with quite
another altogether: Are not these the proofs that Muhammad
is the antichrist?

The most serious problem in marking Muhammad as Paul's
"man of lawlessness" or John's "antichrist" lies in the
textual evidence which describes these historical figures
as originating from within the church of God. While some
scholars have tried to depict Islam as a "Christian sect,"
or a "Christian heresy," the historical proof for such an
assertion is just as weak as is that which attempts to link
Muhammad with the "antichrist" of John or Paul's "man of
lawlessness." We simply don't know what Muhammad's rela-

tionship to the Christian church of his day was, or for that
matter, how he received his "revelations." While some information would be extremely interesting, a more important
immediate concern is how we should answer Muslims concerning
the "hope" that is in us with "gentleness and reverence."
We must emphasize that we are not calling upon Christians to
be dishonest with themselves, but we are suggesting that
they be extremely careful in their judgments. Careless mis-
judgments and opinions have a way of prejudicing our relationships with others for months and years after an original
misjudgment has been made.[82]

Christians have not only had problems deciding how to
relate to Muhammad and things Islamic; they have had similar
problems relating to native doctors. Although native healing techniques and medicinal herbs have brought relief to
countless numbers of people, Christians have generally looked
down upon everything which has to do with native doctors as
evil. For example, many Christians today feel uncomfortable
with drum beats during a church service. Since drumming has
been part of the symbol and ritual that accompanies native
healing, and since much native healing is intertwined with
heathen ritual and sacrifice, the beating of drums has been
frowned upon as something with which Christians should not
be associated. The feeling is that everything to do with
native healing must be denounced as evil and cast aside as
such.

Many Christians want to do the same with Muhammad and
the Quran. Admittedly, there are difficulties for the Christian with the person of Muhammad and the Quran, but this
does not mean that the Christian has to castigate Muhammad
as a false prophet and the Quran as a work of Satan. The
least a Christian can do is to try to reserve judgment upon
Muhammad. Jesus "came not to condemn the world, but that
the world might be saved through Him" (John 3:17). Our task
as ambassadors for Christ is not to "condemn," but to preach
the Gospel with the same positive, inviting welcome which
was so much a part of the ministry of Jesus.

God used Muhammad to say some important things to the
world of his time. Should we not give God the praise that
such an ethically motivated person exercised so much influence for good in his day? Many of the emphases in his instruction are as valid for our world of today as they were
for the world of his time. Is it not possible that Christians, too, may benefit from some of those profound insights?
Cannot we also perhaps hear God speaking to us through the
Quran?

As we struggle with this new idea of hearing God speak
to us through the voice of the Quran, a suggestion that
Paul gave the Philippians may be very helpful. He said:

> Finally, brethren, whatever is true, whatever
> is honourable, whatever is just, whatever is
> pure, whatever is lovely, whatever is gracious,
> if there is any excellence, if there is any-
> thing worthy of praise, think about these
> things (Phil. 4:8).

The Quran has much which is "true, honourable, just, pure,
lovely, gracious, excellent, and worthy of praise ... Brethren ... think about these things."

THE HOLY BOOKS AS POINTS OF CONTACT

While there is a growing movement for a dialogue between
Christians and Muslims, there have been few suggestions that
Christians and Muslims approach each other with an openness
to God's speaking anew to each through His Holy Word. Inas-
much as both Christians and Muslims regard themselves as
possessing a revealed faith that is inscripturated, their
separate Holy Books offer just the points of contact which
are needed, and yet how rarely these points of contact are
really used. Christians need not fear this kind of exchange.
The Bible is self-authenticating. Furthermore, it will be
to the Christian's advantage to listen to the Muslim as he
expounds the content of the Quran. The tragedy is that, by
and large, Christians know very little about the Quran, and
Muslims know very little about the Bible.

This unfortunate situation means that when Christians
and Muslims talk with each other, they more often talk
about the Bible and the Quran than endeavour to hear what
God is trying to say to them through the Bible and the Quran.
In other words, they talk more about the Speech of God than
they really attempt to listen to His Speech.[83] Since this
is the case, Christians and Muslims seldom, if ever, hear
the Holy Word speaking directly to each other through each
other. The Word comes, instead, by way of interpretations
and colourations which are largely reflections of inherited
conclusions from the remote past. No wonder the Word is
sometimes almost powerless to act, but even then, there have
been blessings. Is it possible now that a totally new and
fresh look at the Scriptures will yield even greater and
more abundant blessings, even unexpected ones, for both
Christian and Muslim?

While this idea of how to proceed in "paving new
ground" has much to commend itself, beginning to experiment
with it in a realistic way on even a small scale has many
problems. One of the most obvious has to do with the precious heritage that is cherished by evangelical Christians
of all denominations -- the Reformation principle of Scripture Alone (*Sola Scriptura*). This principle not only recognizes the Bible to be the *definitive* source and norm of all
Christian doctrine and practice, but the *only* source and
norm. Closely associated with this principle is the conviction that the canon of the Bible has been closed, and
that any other writings such as the Quran cannot be regarded
as authoritative in the same sense as are the words of the
Bible. There is no harm in the Christian being perfectly
honest with his Muslim neighbour at this point -- in fact,
it is very necessary that he be as honest as he can at all
times. His frankness need not be abrasive, however, nor
should it close his mind to the fact that with the Bible
serving as his guide and norm, he can also be open to God's
speaking to him from many different directions-- from nature,
history, and a whole host of persons past and present, as
well as from a vast array of writings ancient and modern.

Another problem -- should the Christian witness be ready
to experiment with the Quran as a helpful point of contact
-- is that Qurans are surprisingly difficult to obtain.
Muslims, except for the Ahmadiyya, have taken little lead in
distributing copies, and Christian bookstores are reluctant
to handle them due to the kind of inhibitions discussed
above. Even when and where they are available, there still
exists a persistent language problem. In Ghana, for example,
the Quran is unavailable in any Ghanaian languages, except
English. This doesn't really relieve the communication
problem in that only a few of the Muslims who are well-
versed in the Quran can read English, and of those, few have
little, if any, respect for the Quran in translation.

Similar difficulties arise relative to Muslims making
use of the Bible. While the number of Muslims who can read
English is growing, the majority of them cannot read at all,
or can only read Arabic script, and that but poorly. In
some ways, as far as West Africa is concerned, the *Ajami*
text is the most useful for the average Muslim reader.[84]
This is the Hausa language written in an Arabic script, but
here again, the communication problem arises as far as useful dialogue goes. Few Christians can speak Hausa; even
fewer, if any, can read either Arabic, or Ajami.

Christians can hardly fault Muslims for not knowing
English, or being able to read and understand any other
language, or script. It is the ambassador who seeks to
learn the language of the country he is visiting, not the
other way around. The initiative necessarily lies with
those who are serious about following Christ. God took the
initiative with us; it is now for us to take the initiative
with others!

We have talked about the kind of difficulties Christians
have with the Quran. Some Muslims have similar difficulties with the Bible. The most common, perhaps, is a distrust of the biblical text. Taking a cue from certain
quranic passages (Q. 2:211; 5:16), many Muslims look upon
the Bible as a corrupted text, the Jews having changed the
Old Testament to suit their purposes; Christians, having
altered the New. Other Muslims are open to using the Bible
and profiting from it. They even find support for this attitude in the Quran:

> We sent ... Jesus
> Son of Mary, confirming
> the Torah before Him;
> and We gave to Him
> the Gospel, wherein
> is guidance and light,
> and confirming the Torah
> before it, as a guidance
> and an admonition unto the godfearing ...
>
> And We have sent down to thee the Book
> with the truth, confirming the Book
> that was before it, and assuring it (Q. 5:47,49,51).

While some Muslims find in these verses an encouragement to
study the Bible, there are others who interpret these verses
differently. They conclude that since the Quran confirms
the Gospel and the Torah before it, there is no need for any
further study of the Torah and the Gospel. The Quran, dupli-
cating and confirming the contents of the earlier revelations, is in itself all sufficient for man.

Once the door to a dialogue of free ideas based upon the
revelation of God to man is open, however, all kinds of exciting themes emerge for further exploration. They spring forth
from almost every page of the Quran, even as they leap forward from almost every page of the Bible. The Christian is
not afraid for the truth God has given him in Christ; the

truth will protect itself. Neither does he see the truth
as something neatly boxed up and self-contained and final;
it is rather something gloriously open-ended, a blessing of
God in which he can grow, and grow, and grow.[85]

Remember, we are looking at this whole subject of dialogue from man's perspective, not from God's. God's truth
is final and complete; we, however, are still growing in
our understanding of it. His Word is all we need to know
for our salvation and a full and perfect relationship with
Him; we are still learning to apply the meaning of that
relationship to our relationships with others. His mercy
in Christ is all-sufficient and fully satisfying in every
way; we are still discovering how to share the great gift
of mercy with our neighbours. This is why a Christian is
interested in living in dialogue with his neighbours because God interacts with him through them, and with them
through him.

D.T. Niles, the Indian Christian whose writings are
well-known in Africa, vividly described this phenomenon of
how Christ is in us, while at the same time He is before
us. In defining Christian service, he asked, "What is
the content of this service?" He answered,

> The content is defined by the command under
> which it is performed; Love thy neighbour
> as thyself (Luke 10:27). There are two per-
> sons in whom God meets men -- Jesus Christ
> and one's neighbour. And both challenge us
> to serve. Jesus Christ demands that we ac-
> cept Him as Master and serve him; our neigh-
> bour becomes the person whom we serve. This
> is because Jesus is involved in both situa-
> tions. He is my Master and my neighbour, too.
>
> "I was hungry, I was thirsty, I was naked, I
> was in prison, I was a stranger" (Matt. 25:31ff).
> It is Jesus Christ who is speaking, but it is
> my neighbour He is describing. Both are one.
>
> This does not, however, exhaust the application
> of the command to love -- for not only do I
> meet Jesus Christ in my neighbour, but my neigh-
> bour meets Jesus Christ in me. *I am the arm of
> the Church stretched out to my neighbour with
> the love with which Christ has loved him.* In
> other words, I must serve my neighbour as if

he was Jesus Christ. I must also serve him
as if I was Jesus Christ (1959:85).

It is the aspect of service which adds a dimension to the
dialogue without which the whole effort might turn out to
be only an intellectual exercise. It is this element of
service which helps give us the needed balance between our
head in the clouds and our feet on the ground -- our head
in clouds of glory, our feet on avenues of human need.

   Christ is the bridge who brings us down from the heavenly
rapture of being one with God to the reality of being one
with our neighbour in the everyday service which is part of
our dialogue with men.[86] If He were not at the heart and
the centre of this dialogue, there would be no possibility
of expecting lasting fruit. As is, there is before us not
only an expectation for fruit that endures, but also the
assurance of an unlimited response to all our prayers (John
15:16, 5-9). The love that generates this fruit in us
reaches out to embrace people wherever they are. If their
lives are centred in the Quran, that love meets them there,
and seeks to draw them from that starting point into a new,
beautiful and dynamic relationship with God. What happens
here is something very wonderful, this interacting of God
with men, His meeting them where they are, His raising them
up from where they were. It is Christ's Spirit, the Holy
Spirit, who mediates this new relationship of love between
God and man.

   While rejoicing in His mercy, we often try to limit His
mediation for others as something which happens only through
the Holy Word, the Bible. Can we really put such a limitation upon Him who has been given "all authority in heaven
and on earth" (Matt. 28:18)? True, His call to accept God's
mercy reaches men through the written and the spoken Word,
but His ways of preparing men for that moment of truth are
multiple and varied. "What is impossible with men is possible with God" (Luke 18:27). Doesn't this mean that Jesus
can use even the Quran to cause men to yearn for His mercy,
forcing them to agonize over how to receive that mercy?
After all, He is the One through whom and for whom "all
things were created, in heaven and on earth, visible and invisible, whether thrones or dominions or principalities or
authorities" (Col. 1:16). He created the world! Can He not
now take the Quran and through it create the hunger and the
thirst for righteousness, the necessary prelude to apprehend-
ing God's mercy (Matt 5:6)? Whereas we would rightly contend
that the Bible brings illumination to man (Ps 119:130), we

should also be prepared to expect God's truth to surface in
the most unexpected quarters.

God meets men where they are.[87] Few Christians, if any,
will dispute this fact. Now, if God meets people where they
are, this means that He draws upon their past experiences,
their thought forms, their vocabularies, their ambitions,
and their hopes in communicating with them. If these experiences, thought forms, vocabularies, ambitions and hopes
have been shaped by the Quran, than God uses these quranically-
shaped cultural perceptions in the process of preparing these
very people for the reception of His Gospel through the revelation of Jesus Christ. The one thing missing is the bridge
to make all this possible. The necessary bridge by which
God embraces His creatures in love is not found in the Quran.

Here, again, is what ambassadorship is all about. It is
being to others what God in Christ has been to us. The bridge
between the diverse elements of the earth's populations and
the Lord God Almighty is found in those whom Christ has chosen as His disciples and appointed to be His ambassadors.

The ambassador whose heart has been touched by the challenge of communicating the Gospel to his Muslim neighbour is
like a Southern Ghanaian going to work for the first time in
the North. The languages are as foreign to him as is the
food and as are the customs. If at all he wants to try to
feel at home, he has to make a beginning somewhere -- bit by
bit learning some new vocabulary, little by little observing
and experimenting with new customs and venturing forward to
try new tastes. The more successfully he adapts himself to
the ways of the North, the more at home he will feel in the
North.

The contrast between the adaptation of Southern businessmen to the ways and customs of the North over against that
of civil servants and even pastors and evangelists is often
striking. The businessmen who are on their own, as opposed
to those who are connected to major companies, continually
struggle with the problems of mastering new languages and
customs so as to succeed in their businesses. How much more
the ambassadors for Christ who are engaged in the "Father's
business"!

The Quran offers the ambassador for Christ not only a
source of personal spiritual stimulation, but an introduction to the mind of the Muslim. It is only an introduction,
for what Islam has taken and made of the Quran may be some-

thing quite different from what we and our Christian perspective might do. Nevertheless, the Quran is an exciting
place from which a Christian can draw many points of contact with which to begin his witness to the Muslim. From
its numerous references to Abraham, Moses, and Noah to its
unique and interesting accounts of Christ, there are open
doors to dialogue and witness just waiting for Christ's
ambassadors to walk through.

Many of us who by God's grace have met the real Christ,
"the Door of the sheep" (John 10:7), have been fed and nurtured and lingering too long inside the comfort and warmth
of the fold. The same Jesus who invited us, "Come ... rest"
(Matt. 11:28), also commanded, "Go ... make disciples"
(Matt. 28:19). "I have other sheep," he said, "that are not
of this fold; I must bring them also, and they will heed My
voice. So there shall be one flock, one shepherd" (John
10:16). His "other sheep" hear His voice through us, His
ambassadors, for "he who hears you hears Me, and he who rejects you rejects Me, and he who rejects Me rejects Him who
sent Me" (Luke 10:16).

This is what is at stake in our witness -- the acceptance, or rejection of the risen Lord Christ. He has "the
words of eternal life." The readiness with which a Muslim
listens to our message may quite conceivably be determined
in part by reactions to what attitudes we reflect towards
Muhammad and the Quran.

12

A Day of Good News

Kweku and Maryamu were all excited. They burst into our home after a hurried *agoo* without even waiting for an *amoo*. Apparently, the message was one of such urgency it could hardly await the delay of the usual courtesies.

"Guess what?" Kweku asked as my wife and I came rushing into the hall. "Maryamu wants the baby to be baptized and she wants to be baptized herself."

"This day is a day of good news," my wife and I chimed together as she embraced Maryamu and I went over to congratulate Kweku. "We're so happy for all of you!"

"Yes," Kweku said, "it's been a long struggle. We've read the Bible and we've read the Quran. We've studied and compared and prayed and talked with many people, both Christians and Muslims, and we finally feel that God has spoken to us and given us the direction we were looking for. We're convinced that we've made the right decision."

"This is a joyful day for us as well as it is for you," I said. "We see it as the answer to many prayers. Tell us, if you can, how you finally came to see the Lord's leading."

"It's a long story," Kweku said. "It would take all day and then some, to tell you about all the various comments, insights, and influences which went into our wrestlings with this question. Maryamu was searching and I couldn't be of any help to her because I was searching, too."

"You probably wouldn't guess it," Maryamu said, "but one person who has been such a help to me is Kweku's mother. She's so quiet and unassuming, and yet she's such a beautiful woman. In some ways, she's such a different person from Kweku's father. Her faith is there for everybody to see, so deep and expressive in a thousand different little ways. Everything is so obvious to me now, but it's funny, I never began to understand her until I read what the Apostle Peter had to say about wives (I Pet. 3:1-4). Then I came to understand her, to know her and to admire her, for there she is, pictured as clear as can be in the New Testament. I could also begin to see why she puts up with some of the things she does, and how she carries on day after day with a kind of inner glow illuminating her every moment. She seems to me to be so much like what Jesus' mother must have been like, which makes me all the happier that I was named Maryamu."

"Speaking of names," Kweku said, "do you think Maryamu should change her name to Mary when she is baptized?"

"Why, I don't know," I said. "I think Maryamu is a beautiful name, and you can glorify Christ with that name as much as you can with the name Mary. I don't think you have to turn your back upon your whole past because you've become a Christian. What concerns me more is how you're going to present this to your parents. I wish they could be as happy over your decision as we are, but even though your father is quite open-minded, I don't think it will be easy for him to accept this. Everyone will ask him how it came about that his own daughter has forsaken the family faith."

"Actually," Kweku interjected, "Maryamu doesn't feel as if she's rejected the family faith as much as she's found a missing dimension to it. There are so many aspects of her faith which have a newer and fuller meaning. You might even say, a completed meaning. Take, for example, the Bismillah. You know, the Bismillah is for Muslims like the sign of the cross is for Christians. We feel we'd like to continue using it at mealtimes. We now understand more fully why God is the Merciful and the Compassionate One. But, like you say, it's not going to be easy to communicate this to Maryamu's family. It wouldn't be so bad if it was just Maryamu's mother and father -- what has us more worried are all the relatives. They'll come over and make it sound as if all this is a shame upon Muhammadu and his wife without ever thinking about how God has been working upon Maryamu."

"That's always the problem isn't it?" I commented.
"Each one of our communities -- whether it's national, or
tribal, or family, tries to put some kind of restriction
around the kind of freedom we have. That's why it would be
so much easier if not only Maryamu, but her family, and the
rest of the relatives could all come to know and worship
the Lord Jesus at one time. Since that hasn't happened,
however, there may be some difficult days ahead for not only
you, Maryamu, but also for your parents, and for you, too,
Kweku. I think we should be prepared for this. The best
we can do now is remind you of how Jesus told us to take up
our cross and follow Him, and at the same time, we can assure you that we're ready to stand by your sides. If ever
either one of you needs a shoulder to cry upon, or someone
to reassure you that you've made the right decision, or
someone to kneel with you in prayer, don't hesitate at all
to come over, or to call us to your house."

"Somehow we got sidetracked from what you were going to
tell us, Kweku," said my wife. "Remember, you started to
tell us how this all came about."

"Well, like I said, it's a long story involving a lot
of people and many different discussions and experiences
and much reading. We can't tell you all that now, but
just to shorten everything, it seems like all of our doubts
and fears came to a head in the early hours this morning.
Maryamu woke up somewhat frightened. She doesn't remember
if she had a dream, or a vision, but all of a sudden she
had a clear picture in her mind as if we were standing at a
crossroads.[88] She woke me and she said, 'Kweku, we can't go
on like this not knowing whether we're on one path or another.
There must be only one way that is really God's way. The
picture which came to me so clearly just now was to look
down the paths beyond the "Y" in the road. There were two
figures beckoning to us. We looked more closely and we
could see that they each were standing alongside a grave.
Not knowing which person to follow, we stood there peering
into the dim light and then we saw that the one was the
figure of Muhammad. It was a statue standing next to his
grave at Medina. We were startled when we looked more
closely at the other. There was also a grave, but we could
see the grave was empty and next to it was Jesus. He was
not dead, but alive!' When Maryamu told me this, she asked,
'Kweku, if it were you alone, whom would you follow?' I
told her that I would follow the living person, and she said,
'That's what we have to do. We can't delay any longer.' We
found out that we both felt the very same."

"That's a perfect testimony." I said, "If you just
tell it as it happened, God is going to use you both to
touch many hearts with your sincerity and your faith. Why,
just now you've helped me look at the resurrection in a way
I'd never thought about before, but what you say is so true.
We're following Christ because He's alive. That conviction
is revolutionizing your lives; it's already revolutionized
ours. Once the word gets around what's happened to you,
there's going to be a lot of criticism from family, friends,
and strangers, but there will also be many who rejoice with
you. Above all, there will be many who are going to be
moved by your testimony just as we have. It may just be
that God has a wonderful purpose for the two of you when it
comes to introducing Maryamu's family to the risen Jesus.
He was meant to be their Saviour as much as He is ours. My
wife and I have been praying for just that -- that someone
would come forward to serve as an effective bridge between
them and the Gospel. You may be just the ones the Lord has
appointed for that task."

"We thank you for that encouragement," Kweku replied,
"and we wish we could stay longer, but we've got some things
to do at my father's before we go over to see Maryamu's
folks this afternoon. Please ask God to go with us. We'll
need more than our own strength, or wisdom."

"Why don't we have a word of prayer right now?" I asked.
All four of us got down on our knees and I tried to put into
words the mingled emotions we all felt, feelings of joy,
relief, confidence, and faint trepidation as Kweku and
Maryamu faced together their new life in Christ. I prayed
especially that God would prepare the way for their meeting
with Maryamu's mother and father. I asked that God would
give them not only a deep and sympathetic understanding,
but also strength and encouragement for the days ahead. They
needed these blessings as much as would Kweku and Maryamu.

No sooner had the young couple taken their leave when
Pius was at the door. He just didn't believe that Maryamu
had really become a Christian. "I didn't know it was possible," he said, "for a Muslim to become a Christian. Have
you ever heard of it happening before, Yakubu?"

Before I had a chance to reply, my wife said, "But, Pius,
surely you've heard of the big movement into Christianity in
Indonesia, haven't you? I've read that thousands upon
thousands of Muslims have become Christians."[89]

"That's true, Pius," I continued, "and the same is happening in other parts of Africa -- except the numbers are not so large. It seems it's only here in Ghana and other parts of West Africa that we've seen Muslims coming into the churches just one by one. I wonder what it would take to start a whole movement of Muslims into the Church as was the case in Indonesia."

"Maybe we ought to be making some kind of plans in that direction," volunteered Pius. "A question that intrigues me as far as the work of evangelism is concerned is this: Where is the dividing line between human efforts and plans and God's initiative? We talked about a similar question yesterday in our Bible class. Did you ever read that verse in Proverbs (21:31): 'The horse is made ready for the day of battle, but the victory belongs to the Lord'? We discussed our role over against God's role in evangelism, and it seemed to us that those words contain some great insight. Only now after this I can see we were too limited in our outlook. We only thought of evangelizing pagans. No one even mentioned that we had any obligations toward Muslims."

"I like that Bible passage, Pius," I responded. "You know what would be really great? If we could get all of our Christian neighbours around here to be seriously concerned about a faithful witness of the Gospel to our Muslim neighbours. I suspect some will say we've got enough problems relating to one another as Christians to say nothing about how we might relate in a more beautiful way to Muslims. I do like that proverb, though: 'The horse is made ready for the day of battle, but the victory belongs to the Lord.' That tells us something really important about preparation for evangelism. Would you be willing one night, if it can be arranged, to talk about some of these things with a few of us? Maybe we could get Kweku and Maryamu, Matthew and his wife, Kwesi and Ama, even Jonathan, if we can talk him into coming. I know the rest of you will really thrill to Kweku and Maryamu's story just as we did. They may even have some suggestions as to how we might more effectively witness to our Muslim neighbours. I won't tell you the story now, but I know you will be deeply moved when they ask the question: 'Who would you follow?'"

"Why wait?" Pius asked. "Let's set a date. How about next Thursday evening at my house?"

A HIGHWAY -- THE HOLY WAY

Is it just a coincidence that the early church was called
the Way (Acts 9:2; 19:9,23; 22:4; 24:14,22), and that the
cry of John the Baptist was "Prepare the way of the Lord"
(Luke 3:4)?[90] John's coming and the dramatic announcement
he made actually foreshadowed the second fulfilment of the
prophecy spoken centuries before by Isaiah. The first had
come at the end of the second great Exodus when King Cyrus
of Persia freed the captive nation Israel for its long trek
home across the desert. That happened around 536 B.C.

Isaiah's words, written in anticipation of that great
homecoming, helped create and maintain an air of expectation
for the faithful remnant who trusted in the promises of God.
"A highway shall be there," Isaiah (35:8) had said, "and it
shall be called the Holy Way." That verse is but one of
many verses detailing the joyful expectations which lie before the people who patiently wait upon the Lord. Similar
descriptions of what lies ahead are given in the great
promises of Joel 2 and Micah 4. A final expectation is expressed in the short prayer of Revelation 22:20, "Amen.
Come, Lord Jesus."

As Christians await that glorious Day, there is another
expectation -- the joyful anticipation of many others coming
to know the Lord. That expectation adds a dimension of
promise and urgency to our missionary concerns for "The
Lord ... is forbearing ... *not wishing that any should perish, but that all should reach repentance*" (2 Pet. 3:9).
Each new day is yet another day of God's grace! He is
waiting ... watching ... yearning: "Ho, every one who thirsts,
come to the waters; and he who has no money, come buy and eat!
Come, buy wine and milk without money and without price"(Is.
55:1). Alongside that invitation is a key question: "Whom
shall I send, and who will go for us" (Is. 6:8)? It is the
Lord of the Church who is speaking, and it is we who have
tasted the "wine and milk" of His goodness who are to respond.

For those who are ready to answer "Here am I! Send me"
with a special burden on their hearts for Muslims, there may
be a feeling that we have said more about Christians in this
book than we have about Muslims. They may be disappointed
that we have not done more to point out the Muslim's strong
points and his weak points. They may have wanted to discover
the arguments which will "defeat" Muslims and the quickest
and simplest way to convert them. We trust that earlier
chapters have raised serious question marks over such an approach to Muslims.

There are several reasons why we have not dealt at greater length and depth with Muslim history, doctrine, and practice. For one thing, the inclusion of even a small amount of such additional material would have served to make this book unwieldy for its purpose. Even more, however, we have been talking about "paving a new way" to understanding, faithful witness, and growth in the Lord.

If we are serious about "paving a new way," there is a great advantage in approaching our Muslim neighbours without a great deal of mental baggage as to what they are supposed to believe and practise. They themselves are our best re- source people as to what they believe and practise. They will be interested in "dialoguing" with us, if we first be- gin to show an interest in them. They are very precious persons, our neighbours -- our Muhammadus, our Alihus, and our Jonathans. They've been redeemed by the precious blood of Christ, our Lord. This means that we no longer regard them from a human point of view (2 Cor. 5:16). We regard them from God's point of view as people who are very spe- cial -- special enough to have taken Jesus the way of the cross. We don't know what plans God has for all these special people -- the Dagomba, Gonja, and Wala Muslims of the North of Ghana and the Fanti Muslims of the South. We don't know in what ways His love will embrace Hausas, Yoru- bas, Wangaras, and Mossis. What we are sure of is that God has called us to be His witnesses and that HIS GLORY SHALL BE REVEALED (Is. 40:5)!

A NEW DAY OF PENTECOST?

How that glory was to be revealed was announced at many places in the Scriptures (e.g. Joel 2:28f). Were those pro- phecies once and for all fulfilled on Pentecost, or can we still expect to see new manifestations of them in our time?[91] If we're open to the latter possibility, none of us can anti- cipate in what glorious manner and with what great contribu- tion from their own religious experience, God may bring a mighty harvest of Muslims into His Kingdom of Grace. When that happens, let us pray that we with our rules and regula- tions, our patterns and our premises, shall not be the ones to stand in the way of His grace. It was only after the might of the Holy Spirit took hold of the imaginations of the early Church that their vision could be extended beyond the borders of the Jewish race to the Gentile world around about them. How much we need that same miracle and might to open our eyes to see the multitudes of Muslims standing right now so close, and yet, so far away. Surely, it is His will

to pour out His Spirit upon them also. But how will God do
it? Is it His plan to pour out His Spirit upon them one by
one? Or, is it His plan to bless them by bringing them into His family of redeemed by families, by villages, and
even by tribes?

The lesson of comprehending the limitless boundaries of
God's outreach of love came slowly to the early church. The
problem of grasping the dimensions of that love showed itself in the difficulties of integrating Gentiles into the
life and missionary vision of the Church. The nature of the
problem and its seriousness grew into the awareness of the
church only slowly. When Cornelius came into the church,
for example, there was no Gentile problem. He was only one
Gentile among many Jewish Christians. During that time, or
prior to it, the persecution of Christians in Jerusalem had
caused many Christians to flee for their lives from that
city. Even under those difficult circumstances, however,
wherever these persecuted disciples went, people were won
for Christ. The influx of new believers seems to have been
a steady phenomenon, and yet there was still no Gentile
problem. All who ventured forth to join the early believers
on this new and exciting path of discipleship were members
of the Jewish race, or proselytes (Acts 11:19). It isn't
until we get to Acts 13 that the Gentile problem really comes
in. When it did, it revolutionized the church!

It may be that if Muslims come in numbers into the Church
of God, their presence will revolutionize the church as we
know it today. It could change the day of worship for many
-- from Sunday to Friday. It could mean a return to serious
fasting. It could reintroduce an emphasis upon pilgrimage.
It could put a new mark of approval upon having regular
times of prayer, for it is not in the keeping of traditions
that an obstacle to the free expression of the Gospel lies;
it is, rather, in what use we make of those traditions and
the meaning we read into them. The door is wide open to all
kinds of possibilities when God's people seek to live in the
total freedom of the Spirit in the service of Him who died
for them and rose again.[92]

Pentecost, scheduled on the Jewish calendar fifty days
after the Passover, was the great Harvest Festival and Homecoming of the people of Israel. Little did people know as
they gathered in Jerusalem that year of the outpouring of
the Spirit what a truly memorable occasion that day was to
become. There turned out to be much more to celebrate than
a harvest of crops; it was a tremendous "harvest" of people

for the Lord (Acts 2:41,47). How the halls of heaven must
have reverberated with the shouts of angels' praises!

Is Pentecost once and for all past, or does each new day
hold the promise of being yet another Pentecost? It does,
if we look upon the work of the Holy Spirit as being continuous and not completed (John 14:16; 15:26; 16:7-15). Then,
we are poised each day for the dawn of an exciting new day.
When we are serious about opening a new door to dialogue between Christians and Muslims, we are living in the expectation that *today* could be another Pentecost. The stirrings
among Muslims represented by Muhammadu (Can Muslims join
the Christian Council?) can either be interpreted as the
voice of Satan trying to lead Christians astray, or it can
be interpreted as a new stirring by the Holy Spirit to herald the approach of another great day of Pentecost. "This
is the day which the Lord has made; let us rejoice and be
glad in it" (Ps. 118:24). Be careful before you pass judgment upon how Christians should react to such stirrings. As
Paul advised, "Do not quench the Spirit" (I Thess. 5:19).
Too often, perhaps, in our zeal for purity and piety and
good order, we have been too ready to do just that.[93]

Too often, too, we have been not only in competition with
Muslims for souls, but in competition with each other. The
Word tells us that the seed we sow today, another may water
tomorrow, and yet a third may bring into harvest (John
4:35,37f). It is not we who give the increase; it is God,
the Lord of the Harvest. "Not by might, nor by power, but
by My Spirit, says the Lord of hosts" (Zech. 4:6). "What is
impossible with men is possible with God" (Luke 18:27).
Doesn't this pattern put into ridicule our denominational
jealousies over the gains of others? Actually, there should
be no cause for jealousy; only rather, room for common rejoicing because we -- all of us who call upon the Name of
the Lord Jesus -- are in this thing of Christian witness together. Together we strengthen each other in the cause of
Christ; together, we weaken each other (Mark 10:38ff, I Cor.
12:26). And, in weakening each other, we bring dishonour to
His Name.[94]

We noted earlier the kinds of yearnings for brotherhood
which are felt in so many places in the word today. Some
even feel strongly that the Christian churches will not be
able to make their faithful and full witness to Christ unless long talked-about church union plans blossom into fulfilment. Our witness to the Resurrection, however, cannot
be held back waiting for new arrangements to unite Chris-

tians into new kinds of family clusters. On a closer look,
that's just what the visible church is -- a large cluster of
families gathered around the Risen Lord. The fact is that
there is a unique unity in the midst of all the diversity
-- if we will only recognize it and praise the Lord for it
(Eph. 4:1-16). This does not mean that we should not lament
and repent over many of our divisions and pray that God would
heal them. What it does mean, however, is that when we take
an honest look at what the Church really is, we can see how
beautifully we complement each other. Yes, with all our
different emphases, worship forms, and interpretations --
Catholic, Protestant, Pentecostal, and new Spiritual church
-- we complement each other wonderfully well as we reach out
to embrace God's world with His love (Rom. 12; I Cor. 12;
I Pet. 4:8-11).

HERALDS OF GOOD TIDINGS

The Bible contains several fascinating accounts of people
who spontaneously responded to an act of God to step out of
their normal role in society to give a dynamic testimony to
God's movement among men. One such was the Samaritan woman
whose lifestyle was hardly one for which she wanted to call
any more public attention than was necessary. Yet, the
shame and humiliation of reminding people of her questionable
sexual connexions did not keep her from hastening into the
village to tell her people of how Jesus had convinced her
that He was a prophet and the Christ.

In the time of Elisha, there were four lepers caught in
a similar totally unexpected situation. Being outcasts of
society, they were forced to live outside the walls of
Samaria, the capital of the Northern Kingdom. During a
period of great famine caused by a Syrian army seige, they
concluded that the death they had to face outside the gates
of the city of Israel could hardly be any worse than the
death they might have to face at the hand of the Syrians.
At least, there was food in the camp of the Syrians, and
there was a remote possibility that the Syrians might throw
them some of their leftover food.

Upon arriving at the edge of the Syrian camp, the lepers
were shocked to find everything deserted. They ate their
fill from the still-simmering cooking pots and began plunder-
ing the tents. It was evident that the Syrians had left in
great haste. All of a sudden, the lepers came to realize
that this news was too important to keep to themselves. "We
are not doing right," they said, "This day is a day of good

news ... now therefore come, let us go and tell the king's
household" (2 Kings 7:9). In spite of their station in
society -- abused, misused, maltreated and hurt, they yet
returned to the people who had cast them out to pass on to
them the "good news" of that day.

The four lepers and the Samaritan woman were "heralds of
good tidings" to their people. Unfortunately, this dimension of a Christian's witness is often hidden, especially
when Christians talk with Muslims. What so easily surfaces
is a tendency to bury the urgency and the joy and the freshness of the Gospel message in an all too hastily dug grave
of loveless argument and futile debate. When that happens,
something very precious is lost, and frequently, doors which
had edged open are closed, only to open with difficulty ever
again.

There is an important place for the kind of witness which
grew out of the spontaneous joy and excitement of these five
people, but there is also a place for another kind of witness
-- a studied, reasoned, and yet, warmly loving testimony of
our faith to others. Indeed, there is room for both kinds
of witness in a Christian approach to Muslims.

There is a feeling of ecstasy which comes with being a
"herald of good tidings"; there is also a sensation of agony.
The agony grows out of the concerns heralds of the Kingdom
have that their message be heard, and that it be heard clearly
and understood. This kind of presentation calls for faith
and it calls for courage. It calls for imagination and it
calls for perseverance. It calls for study and it calls for
prayer.

Paul reminded young Timothy, "Do your best to present
yourself to God as one approved, a workman who has no need
to be ashamed, rightly handling the word of truth" (2 Tim.
2:15). Paul set these words in a context which reminds us
so much of what frequently happens when Christians and Muslims talk with each other. Their discussions often become
a "disputing about words, which does no good, but only ruins
the hearers" (2 Tim. 2:14). The danger with "such godless
chatter" is that "it will lead people into more and more
ungodliness, and their talk will eat its way like gangrene"
(2 Tim. 2:16f). Paul gave a similar warning to Titus: "Avoid
stupid controversies, genealogies, dissensions, and quarrels
over the law, for they are unprofitable and futile" (Tit.
3:9). All of this emphasizes the crucial need for diligent
study and conscious efforts to try to understand those for

whom Christ died that the Word of Christ we speak to them
might speak clearly and powerfully to their deepest needs.

Yakubu and Pius came up with an idea which offers some
excellent possibilities for just such study and conscious
efforts to try to understand Muslims and how to present the
Gospel to them. How workable is their idea? Would it work
in your neighbourhood? The Christians of their neighbourhood come out of different Christian traditions. Would such
different denominational backgrounds enrich such a meeting,
or would they so divide the common ground that nothing healthy could be accomplished?

What works well in Yakubu and Pius' neighbourhood may not
work well in another where people have difficulty communicating with each other because of language. In those areas,
the natural flow of ideas moves along linguistic lines rather
than along the lines of neighbourhood proximity. Where such
conditions prevail, the logical procedure would be to encourage the formation of prayer and study cells along the
lines of easiest communication.

What might such prayer and study cells accomplish? They
might explore more fully the privilege and responsibility
which comes with being "heralds of good tidings." They
could examine the role of "ambassadors" in God's plan for
mankind. They could study the implications of the Great
Commission for their local circumstance. They could wrestle
with the meaning of Christ's "You are My witnesses," seeking
to discover why "witness" and "resurrection" are so intimately
connected in the Scriptures. All this means that their programme would be centred in rich measure in Bible study.

Another aspect of their study would focus on areas other
than the Bible. It would have to do with the Muslims with
whom they are concerned. What comprises Muslim belief and
practice? What is there which Christ has to offer them which
they have not yet found? What stands in the way of their
discovering "the one thing needful" (Luke 10:42)? Is there
anything in their experience which might draw us Christians
even closer to God and help us glorify Him even more? The
source materials for this phase of study would come from the
Quran and from discussions with Muslim friends and neighbours.
There is also another source -- attending and observing Muslim functions, including the Friday service of prayer. Few
Christians have stepped inside a mosque and equally few Muslims have stepped inside a church. We could understand each
other better if we'd closely observe each other in worship.

Of course, prayer ought to be an important part of any
such neighbourhood study programme. The example of Jesus
being diligent in prayer simply undergirds what Paul urges,
"that supplications, prayers, intercessions, and thanksgiv-
ings be made for *all* men" (I Tim. 2:1), including our neighbours. When is the last time you prayed for your neighbours?
Your Abdullahs and your Muhammadus, your Amas and your
Jonathans? We were talking about approaching your Muslim
neighbours; we end up including the names of your Christian
neighbours. This is because Christian concern is not like a
torchlight which is directed first towards this person, then
towards that. If it meets a response here, it continues to
glow; if it meets a rejection there, it turns to a different
direction. This, you may recall, was the criticism which
Muhammadu leveled at Christian witness. He called it a love
which was no different from the love of the world. It loves
what it gets something out of; it loves in order to gain.

If we have given Muhammadu that impression, it is not for
us to become angry at Muhammadu, but rather for us to eval-
uate our love. Perhaps Muhammadu has helped us to see a
failure in our love for the love of Christ which we are to
"herald" to the world is not like a torchlight which zeros
in first on one target and then leaves that target to find
another. It is, rather, like a light which is set on a hill
(Matt. 5:14ff LB). Christian love, like light, reaches out
and radiates in every direction. And so with our prayer concerns.

What a tremendous thing could begin happening if literally
thousands of little prayer and study cells would begin gathering together once a week, or once a month, to pray together
for their Muslim neighbours. But perhaps we cannot start with
a thousand. Perhaps we can start with only ten, or maybe even
only one. Who will step forward with the initiative to make
a beginning? Who will offer their homes?

THE FOG WILL LIFT SLOWLY

Such diligent prayer and study is bound to begin lifting
the fog which grievously distorts and restricts Christian
witness among Muslims today.[95] Many Christians are discouraged from witnessing to Muslims because, like Pius, they believe Muslims will never respond to the Gospel. They have
been misled by erronious assessments like the following from
scholars of considerable repute: "The trend is undeniable;
for every convert to Christianity in Africa today, there are,
it has been estimated, nine or ten converts to Islam"
(Kritzeck 1969:2). Another calculates that two out of every

five people in Ghana are Muslim, the figures rising to eight
out of ten in the Northern Territories" (Brelvi 1964:357).
A third predicts that "by the year 2000 most of Africa is
likely to be under Islam's sway" (Watt 1968:5). These figures are simply untrue. They are part of the fog which
blankets the horizon so that we do not see the "fields white
unto harvest."

When the fog lifts a little bit, we shall perceive that
the people of the "Northern Territories" are not Muslim, nor
are they Christian.[96] They can hardly be classified as one
people either, for they come from many, many different tribes.
Their languages and their cultures are related, but they are
not the same. In almost every one of these tribes there is
a great deal of movement these days -- physical movement to
and from the cities; ideological movement as the animistic
ideas they bring to the towns from their home villages are
tested in the urban milieu and found wanting.[97] Like
Abdullahi, they are people who are searching for new roots
that are firm, security, and companionship. For too long
the churches have passed by on the other side, as did the
priest and the Levite with the hurting and forsaken traveller
in the Parable of the Good Samaritan.

Many Northerners have appeared to embrace Islam after
moving to the city, and yet, it is debatable whether the
memorizing of a few Arabic formulas and occasional participation in prayer ritual can satisfy the deep longings of man
for peace and fulfilment. Moreover, these Northerners live
on the doorsteps of a great many Christians -- Christians
who have difficulty speaking Northern languages and integrating Northerners into their congregations. These Christians
find it hard to understand Northern customs, and it is not
easy for them to cast aside prejudices that Northerners are
intentionally and hopelessly backward. How important it is
for Christians in this kind of situation to remind themselves
that Northern Ghanaians are also Christ's redeemed, and that
as His ambassadors they have a word of peace to speak to them
from Him. The problem of where they are categorized is not
their problem; it's ours and calls for repentance on our part.
Perhaps then the fog will lift from our eyes and we will see
them as God sees them.

Over against the Northerners who fall somewhere between
Muslim and animist, there are the people who are truly Muslims. They, like Alihu and the Ahmadis (and sometimes
Muhammadu), take their Islam very seriously. Their faith
grows out of the teachings of the Quran and the interpreta-

tions given to it by the *Umma* and the *Hadith*. We meet them
at a different level altogether than the two groups referred
to above, still, our relationships with them are grounded in
the same principles by which God has dealt with us; kindness,
love, understanding, honesty, sincerity, faithfulness. It was
by His initiative that we came to experience these things.
He now expects us to exercise the initiative He gives in
sharing these with others.

One of our primary difficulties in relating to any of
these people is that the fog is very heavy and it's very
treacherous. This is because it's part of Satan's arsenal
of weapons to deceive us. By it, he causes all kinds of
interference to come between ourselves and God, and ourselves
and our fellow man. As with the rest of his deceits, however, this too, is vaporous, i.e., this fog erects barriers
out of nothing. It stands between us and others so that we
see them differently than they really are, and they, in turn,
see us differently than we really are. It is because of
this fog that we have difficulties speaking clearly to each
other and being understood.

Being vaporous doesn't mean that it is any less powerful
than if it were something tangible which we could see and
touch. In fact, it is no doubt more powerful a weapon in
that we cannot put our fingers upon it. We reach out to
grasp a problem whether in communication, improving relationships, or whatever, and the difficulty eludes us. It is
so hard to put our fingers upon the real problem because
when we clasp our hands together, there is nothing there.
In our frustration, the word of Peter assuring us of support
in our battles with an elusive Satan comes through the fog
to give us new strength and courage (I Pet. 5:5-11). Or as
Paul wrote, "We walk by faith, not by sight (2 Cor. 5:7).

There is a power encounter involved whenever we seek to
be obedient to the Word and zealous to live and communicate
its message to others.[98] Our enemy seems to be Islam, or
Catholicism, or Protestantism, or our neighbour. Our enemy,
rather,is Satan who is working effectively in the fog to dis-
tort our very apprehension of reality. Somehow he seems to
deceive many by the simple tactic of substituting "religion"
for the truth of the Gospel. It may be Protestant "religion"
or Catholic "religion" or Pentecostal "religion" or Islamic
"religion." All tend to substitute for the way of repentance
and faith a concept of "works," of "legalism," of salvation
through self-effort of one sort or another.

Christians have spoken of "the Muslim menace" (Cooksey 1931:148) and "the menace of Islam" (Idowu 1968:432). Muslims have retaliated by speaking of the "organized onslaught of Christianity" (Qureshi 1964:viii) and the "traditionally unhealthy Christian religious rivalry and spirit of bigotry" (Brelvi 1964:344). These are all fighting words which only help to perpetuate the fog. No one of us meets Islam or Christianity head on. The whole sum of human relationships breaks down to the fact that we come face-to-face in our neighbourhoods. The fog may never lift in the higher echelons of organized religion. It can at the local level when neighbour meets neighbour.

When the fog lifts, we see people as they really are, not as we imagined them to be. We see our churches as they really are -- not as we thought they were. We see ourselves as we really are, not as we had presumed we were. But, all this takes a miracle -- a miracle of God's overwhelming grace. New life for all is His offer to us. When it is accepted, the fog begins to lift.

NEW LIFE FOR ALL

When the fog lifts we see ourselves as we really are -- imperfections, possibilities and all. We see ourselves as part of the history of man as God Himself has entered into history and is bringing it to a conclusion. The story unfolds in this way:

> God gave life to man.
> Man rejected life.
> God has provided new life in Jesus.
> Man must accept new life in Jesus.
> New life is seen in man's behaviour.
> New life seeks to bring new life to others.[99]

This summary of what happens when God brings His grace to bear upon the human situation gives the background for the radical changes which are possible in the Christian life. These radical changes, causing us to see ourselves and our neighbours in a different light, are prompted because life is looked at in totally new perspectives. We see people hungering and thirsting for God's righteousness in a multitude of different ways, not even recognizing the reason why they feel at unrest and insecure.[100]

Not only do we find people caught up in uncertainty and baffled by the mystery of life, we find that the "good

tidings" we have to offer are not openly and gladly received
as such. The barriers to communication, as we have seen,
are multiple. Sometimes they are wrapped up in ourselves
--our exclusiveness, our pride, our superiority standing as
obstacles between ourselves and others. We find difficulty
freely welcoming people into our churches whose lifestyles,
cultures, and languages are different from our own for fear
that their presence will drive away some of our own people.
A new life for all perspective radically alters this selfish withholding of the natural outburst of friendliness
which ought to freely flow from those whose life is in
Christ.[101]

This outburst of friendliness might, however, move in
quite a different direction than seeking to integrate such
people into our own congregations. Recognizing the socio-
cultural problems involved when people are alienated from
their own culture and society, the new life in Christ may
prompt some of us to make the sacrifice of endeavouring to
become bi-cultural in order that the Gospel might be heard
with the least amount of external friction as possible.
This sacrifice might mean learning another language altogether, learning to enjoy and appreciate different foods,
wearing different clothes, mingling with different circles
of companions. It might mean founding a new congregation
and worshipping in a strange language, strange to the ambassador for Christ, but the language in which those to whom
he has gone feel at home.[102] In practical terms, this
might mean founding a Hausa-speaking congregation in Accra,
or a Dagbani-speaking congregation in Tamale.

In some ways, this matter of language is crucial. So
far, few Christians have paid the price of struggling to
learn another language and become part of another culture
for the sake of the Gospel.[103] Who of us are ready to pay
the price of trying to learn Arabic in order to better understand the powerful attraction this language holds over
the minds of West African Muslims? Who of us in a country
like Ghana are willing to make efforts to join the select
few who are able to communicate the Gospel in the Hausa
language? As a Christian community, we still have a long
ways to go to build good bridges of communication across
the barriers of many languages. The sad story is that we
haven't even made a beginning with some languages.

Before we conclude, there are yet two important points
that need to be made. The first has to do with who is
qualified and capable of giving an effective Christian
witness. There are those who quite honestly feel entirely

inadequate when it comes to speaking about their faith to
Muslims. They know so little about Islam and they can
only awkwardly, or not at all, handle any of the languages
spoken by Muslims. They may even feel incapable of beginning to express the meaning of their faith to another
Christian.

What we have had to say about study and preparation for
witness doesn't mean that when the Lord opens a door to
witness we should hesitate to step in because we feel in-
adequately prepared. Nowhere do we have any indication
that the Lord expects us to be specialists before we speak
a word of peace in Christ to our neighbours. Besides, we
have an exciting promise from the Lord -- spoken in regard
to another type of situation, but certainly applicable also
in this: "Do not be anxious beforehand what you are to
say; but say whatever is given you in that hour, for it is
not you who speak, but the Holy Spirit" (Mark 13:11). It
would be fitting, too, for us to learn from our Muslim
friends. So much of the spread of Islam south of the Sahara
has had the character of a lay missionary movement. How
far we, by comparison, have yet to go in applying the doctrine of the Universal Priesthood of All Believers! This
doctrine resurfaced so powerfully during the time of the
Reformation, and yet how little we have implemented its
revolutionary potential in the structures and the mission
of the church![104]

The second and final point has to do with sustaining new
life, a work of nurture and nourishment which is accomplished
through Word and Sacrament. The Word has been much emphasized on the African scene; strangely, the Sacraments have
not taken their rightful place of importance. On the one
hand, they have been presented as essential for strengthening the Body of Christ for its task; on the other, a reluc-
tance to ordain laymen with the authority to administer the
Sacraments has, because of a shortage of clergy, led to the
existence of a Sacrament-starved church. In recent years,
many voices have been calling for a reexamination and cor-
rection of this lamentable situation.[105]

One whose voice has come forward loud and clear is that
of John Mbiti, the East African theologian. Mbiti sees a
close connexion between the Sacraments and the proclamation
of the Gospel. In his estimation, they are at the very
centre of the life of the Church, and the Church ought to
be the very "centre of existence from which African peoples
may derive the fulfilment of their life's aspiration whether

in time of need or in time of feasting." It is in the
Church that they can experience "a communal life which has
a vaster scope and meaning than tribal life without Christ
could ever provide."[106]

This is indeed good news! The "good tidings" are for
all men! Moreover, the joy of sharing them with others is
ours as we await our Lord Jesus who promised, "I am coming
soon" (Rev. 3:11). In anticipation of this event and with
positive Christ-like attitudes and a warm spirit, approaching our Muslim neighbours in the Name and the love of
Christ can be a joyful adventure both for them and for us.
This is what a *Christian* approach to Muslims is all about.

> Now to Him who by the power at work within us
> is able to do far more abundantly than all
> that we ask or think, to Him be glory in the
> Church and in Christ Jesus to all generations,
> for ever and ever. Amen! (Eph. 3:20f).

Appendices

Appendix A
The Same God

Whenever it is postulated that Christians and Muslims worship the same God, there are some -- both Christians and Muslims -- who say this is simply untrue. Those who raise objections generally agree that Christians and Muslims worship one God, but will not accept the statement that they worship the same God. Admittedly, this problem is probably more of a Christian problem than it is a Muslim problem. Once a Muslim is ready to acknowledge that God can be known by a name other than *Allah* (i.e., God. *Onyame*, etc.), he will generally agree that Christians and Muslims worship "the same God." At the same time, he will insist, however, that Christians err in "associating" (*shirk*) others with God. This conclusion grows out of the common misunderstanding among Muslims, based partially on the Quran (5:119), that Christians worship a Trinity of Father, Mother, and Son.

The problem as it confronts Christians is another kind of a problem altogether. It is a question of whether you can say you are worshipping the same God when you have such different understandings of the nature of God. Those who are troubled by this concern say that although Christians and Muslims use the same name for God and many of the same words to describe Him, they are *not* talking about the same God because Christians are talking about the Triune God, Father, Son and Holy Spirit. They say that to conceive of God in any other way is not to talk of the true God. The

same rule of thumb is applied to "pagans" in Africa, the
followers of traditional African religion. Since African
"high Gods" are not understood as being the Holy Trinity,
the conclusion is that each African "high God" or "supreme
Being" is a false god.

While many Christians have been swift to pass this kind
of judgment upon the supreme God of African animists and
Allah of the Muslims, they have been less ready to level
such a judgment upon the God of the Jews. This inconsistency has, perhaps, never occurred to many of the same
Christians who so readily defend a policy of debunking the
"high God" of Africans and the Muslims' Allah.

The background reasons for this inconsistency are not
difficult to locate. The Bible speaks of the God of the
Jews and the God of the Christians as being not only One,
but the same. This conclusion is expressed in different
contexts, and in contexts which have, in reality, a wider
applicability than to just the relationship between the
God of the Jews and the God of the Christians. "There is
no distinction between Jew and Greek," says Paul, "the
same Lord is Lord of all and bestows His riches upon all
who call upon Him" (Rom. 10:12). In another place, Paul
asks, "Is God the God of Jews only? Is He not the God of
Gentiles also? Yes, of Gentiles also, since God is One"
(Rom. 3:29f).

At the time Paul wrote those words, the doctrine of the
Holy Trinity had not been formulated as we now know it, and
it seems convincingly evident that the question hadn't even
arisen as to whether the "Christian" God was different from
the God of the Jews. The problem as Paul analyzed the situation was not one of worshipping different Gods, but rather
of how to approach the one God. Did man approach Him, the
Creator and Life-Giver, by works, or by faith? Herein was
man's central problem -- not a question of different Gods.
Did man approach God on man's terms, or on God's terms?

Thus, when Paul approached the Athenians, he avoided the
insinuation that he was proclaiming to them someone with
whom they were totally unfamiliar. He commended them for
being "very religious," supporting his statement with the
observation that he had observed their "objects of worship,"
including an altar with the inscription, "To an unknown
god" (Acts 17:22f).

It is possible now to make similar inferences as to
whether or not, Christians and Muslims worship the same

God. If God is only recognizable as the Trinity, then we
would have to conclude that Christians and Muslims worship
a different God. We need to ask, however, whether the manifestations of God are limited to this particular manifestation. Does God only manifest Himself as Trinity? Does
He not manifest Himself in His creation? Does He not manifest Himself in "His eternal power and deity" (Rom. 1:20)?
Does He not manifest Himself in His "decree that those who
do such things (all manner of wickedness, evil, coveteous-
ness, malice, etc.) deserve to die" (Rom. 1:32)? Is He
not "the God of Abraham, the God of Isaac, and the God of
Jacob" (Matt. 22:32)?

It is the latter question which more than any other
forces us to take a second look at any quick judgment that
Christians and Muslims worship a different God. God iden-
tified Himself to Moses as "the God of Abraham, the God of
Isaac, and the God of Jacob" (Ex. 3:6), and this was how
Moses was to identify Him to the Israelites (Ex. 3:15).
This is how Peter identified the One who glorified Jesus
(Acts 3:13), and this is how the Quran identifies Him who
has given to man the religion of "surrender" (Q. 2:132f).

In addition to all these scriptural proofs that Christians and Muslims worship not only one God, but the same
God, there is another which can hardly be challenged --
the personal testimony of the Christians who were formerly
Muslims. As J.N.D. Anderson writes (relating what has also
been the experience of the author), "I have never met a
Muslim convert who regards the God he previously sought to
worship as a wholly false God; instead, he is filled with
wonder and gratitude that he has now been brought to know
that God as he really is, in Jesus Christ our Lord (1970:110).
In a very special way God has revealed Himself to men
in Jesus Christ (John 1:18; 12:45; 14:9; Col. 1:15-20;
Heb. 1:1-3). Paul talks of this special revelation as the
"mystery of Christ which was not made known to the sons of
men in other generations as it has now been revealed to
His holy apostles and prophets by the Spirit" (Eph. 3:4ff).
As Paul says again, "All the promises of God find their Yes
in Him" (2 Cor. 1:20). Thus, there is a totally new dimension to our understanding of God which comes with Jesus
Christ. This has been called by some the "saving knowledge"
of God (Mueller 1934:146).

All men "are without excuse, for although they knew God
they did not honour Him as God or give thanks to Him"
(Rom. 1:20f). That honour and thanks is more than mere lip

service (Is. 29:13; Amos 5:21-24; Matt. 7:21-23; 15:1-9)
and it is connected to trusting in God's promise and sub-
mitting to "God's righteousness" rather than relying upon
our own (Rom. 10:2f, Heb. 4). When the miracle of rebirth
which comes by way of faith in Christ happens, a new relationship with God begins. "Now that you have come to know
God, or *rather to be known by God*" (Gal. 4:9) is how Paul
describes the significance of this miracle. Those who accept God's free invitation of mercy in Christ (Is. 55:1;
Matt. 11:28; 2 Cor. 5:20; Rev. 3:20; 22:17) not only come to
know and experience God in a new way, but are known by God.
As Jesus said, "I know My own and My own know Me ... My
sheep hear My voice ... and no one shall snatch them out of
My hand" (John 10:14, 27f). It is that invitation to be
known and recognized by God which is our gift as Christians
to the Muslim world.

When we witness as Christians, our emphasis is misplaced
if the stress is upon the more perfect knowledge of God
which we have to offer, or worse yet, if we insist that we
know the true God when no one else does. The proper emphasis
is rather as John stated when summing up the purpose for
writing his Gospel, "That you may believe that Jesus is the
Christ, the Son of God, and that believing you may have life
in His name" (John 20:31). In another place John put it
this way: "If any one does sin, we have an advocate with
the Father, Jesus Christ the righteous" (I John 2:1). All
men know God, but Jesus alone brings us into a right relationship of fellowship with Him. Through Jesus we are "no
longer strangers and sojourners, but ... fellow citizens
with the saints and members of the household of God" (Eph.
2:19).

For background discussion on this subject, see Abbott
(1966:663), G. Allen (1943:41-51), Basetti-Sani (1967:130f),
Bavinck (1948:99; 1968:125), Danquah (1968:10-17), Estes
(1971:13), Glasser (1971), Idowu (1969), King (1971:104f),
Kraemer (1956:101-141), Kraft (1973:239ff), Neill (1971:77),
Newbigin (1969:59), Nicholson (1914:87f), Pieper (1950:372-
381), Reyburn (1967:26-30), Setiloane (1969:205ff) Taylor
(1963:83-92), and Wolf (1964:152f). For a sampling of African proverbs, many of which speak of God, see Rattray (1969:
254-278) and Danquah (1968:188-197).

Appendix B
The Name Isa

The Christian missionary's work among a heathen nation
may most briefly be designated to be the making known of the
name of Jesus, a name which God has given Him, and which is
above every name, "that at the name of Jesus every knee
should bow, of things in heaven, and things in earth, and
things under the earth"; that men might have their sins re-
mitted, be justified, and obtain life through this name;
that this name should be believed on, invoked, obeyed, confessed, held fast, trusted in, revered, honoured, magnified,
glorified; that in this name prayer and thanksgiving should
be offered, and that as in ancient times miracles were
wrought in this name, so now every thing should be done in
this name. In other words, the setting forth of the person
of Jesus of Nazareth forms the burden of the missionary's
preaching. All missionaries agree that the name of this
Person should be set forth and taught properly. When the
missionary comes to a people who have never in any way heard
of this Person, one should think, the missionary would be
glad to have an opportunity of retaining, in his preaching
and writing, the name of the Saviour, as it has been delivered to us in the Greek Scriptures. Practically, however, from the very nature of language, the missionary finds
this impossible ...

When the missionary comes among the Mohammedans, he finds
that the person of Jesus is by no means unknown among them,
but that their sacred book, the Koran, and their entire
literature, from the Arabic downwards, is pervaded by copious
allusions to the great prophet of the Christians. On close
investigation he finds that many of their notions concerning
Him are extremely correct. What they believe concerning Him
is this, that John the Baptist was sent to proclaim the coming of the Word, which they know to mean Jesus; for they
find in the Koran that it was announced to the Virgin Mary
by angelic agency, "Oh, Mary, God announces to thee the
Word, which comes from Him, and His name shall be Masih Isa
Ibnu Mariam, honourable, honourable in this world and the
world to come." The Koran then goes on to intimate that He
is to be born by the direct agency of God. They know, moreover, that He was born at Bethlehem, of no human father,
that He had the power of performing miracles, that He was
specially endowed with the Holy Spirit, that the miracles
for which His life was most remarkable were those of healing

and that He even raised the dead to life again; that He was
rejected by the Jews, that He ascended to heaven, and that
He will come a second time to destroy His great opponent ...
Indeed, the allusions to Jesus, in Mohammedan literature,
especially to His unlimited beneficence, to His kindness,
His meekness, His virtues, and His miraculous powers, origin,
and departure, are so copious ...

It would appear ... at first sight, that the missionary
would be glad to find the Mussulman acquainted with so much
of the sacred history; there is, at least, some point of
contact, of common standing ground between him and his opponents; they believe certain facts as well as we to be
indisputable history; the missionary might take advantage
of this to demonstrate and explain important truths, and
proceed eventually from these truths, to correct the mis-
apprehensions, misconception, and faulty and defective notions in the opponent's mind, and thus perhaps be able ultimately to show the incorrectness of certain statements in
his sacred books. For it may be considered as established
by this time, that it is erroneous to suppose that a creed
which is not wholly false, must be first entirely destroyed
and uprooted before the truth can be successfully applied.
Where there are even mere germs of truth, they sometimes
need only the right culture to awaken them to vitality, and
where there are but faint remains of the truth, let the
superincumbent mass of rubbish and debris but be carefully,
no matter how toilsomely, removed, and long-hidden foundations will be brought to light after centuries of conceal-
ment, and testify too strongly to the truth for the latter
than to be so easily rejected. Missionaries, I say, might
be supposed to be glad to find so much vantage-ground of
which they might avail themselves in their great struggle
for the truth. And such has been the course of most missionaries who have had to do with Mohammedans in various
countries.

In India, however, there have been some who are ready to
give up this apparent advantage, and who would prefer to
bring before the Mohammedans an entirely new personage by
the name of Yusua, of whom neither they, nor their father,
nor anybody else has ever heard before. They would abandon
all advantage, as they do in fact, from an unwillingness to
use the name by which the Mohammedans know our Saviour,
namely, Isa.

It has already been shown that on linguistic grounds the
Arabs, and any nation after them, have a full right to use

this or any other name to designate Jesus of Nazareth. Many objections, however, have been urged to the continued use of this name among missionaries, but they may conveniently, as to their main purport, be reduced under two heads.

The first is that the Isa of the Mohammedans is not the Jesus Whom we adore. They believe of Him many miracles which are not recorded in Scripture, and they have removed the two great pillars of the Christian system by denying His death, and His divinity.

To this objection it may be answered, in the first place, that these defects would continue to exist in the Musselman's creed, even if we *were* able, in some way, to change the name Isa into Yusua in their entire literature, sacred and profane, as well as in the minds of the whole Musselman world; a change of a name could not alter their doctrine. When a Mohammedan should hear a missionary pronounce the name of Him whom the Musselman knows beforehand to be the subject of the missionary's preaching -- if he should hear him pronounce Isa, Yusua, he would only put it down as one of the many odd pronunciations of these Feringhis, though he might think it particularly odd that they should thus mispronounce the name of their own prophet.

But, in fact, this objection is of far too wide a sweep to be forcible at all, when applied to the name of our Saviour alone. A missionary might well wish to alter the entire language of those among whom he labours, if he would eradicate at one pull the false and soul-destroying notions that attach to almost all the specific terms the missionary is using in his preaching and in his teaching. It is not the person and the work of our Saviour alone as to which the false religionist is in such grievous error, but sin, righteousness, justice, mercy, heaven, hell, forgiveness, faith, prayer, all these terms have been perverted from the truth, and none of them suggests to the Moslem and to the idolater what they suggest to those who are taught by the Bible. But we cannot think of discarding the terms themselves; we take those in the actual languages that had originally the true meaning, or such as have now a meaning in some measure approaching the truth, and use them in order to teach the whole, full, pure, truth. Whenever the missionary, in his preaching to a promiscuous assembly, uses words for the ideas mentioned or similar ones, he is conscious that at least half his audience, who may not be used to missionary preaching, attach wrong conceptions to them, and yet he can only explain partially, only correct some misconception, only teach a few men; he cannot think of introducing entirely new terms.

Nay, even the designation of that one great centre towards
which, after all, every religion pretends to aspire, and the
aspiration after which forms the one unfailing connecting
link between the Christian missionary and all heathens of
every name, namely GOD, with how many false notions is it
even encumbered in the Mohammedan's mind; how utterly different a being is He in his mind from what He is in the mind
of the Christian; the just Judge lost in the Sovereign, the
Father lost in the King, the prayer-hearing Parent lost in
a dread *ANANGKE*, the Person lost in a grand pantheistic
Negation, the ever-present One in a universal Nothing. All
these fearful misconceptions must be corrected, but we cannot change the name by which He is known. Were we to change
the name of our Lord, and the Mohammedan should ask us --
and the question *has* been put frequently -- whether Yusua
and Isa were two different persons, we could not say Yes,
for he holds too much of the truth concerning Jesus of
Nazareth. What he holds concerning Him is almost altogether
true, he only does not hold the whole truth. Were he to
ask further, Why, then, do you alter the name by which *we*
know Him? Some missionaries are inclined to answer, Because
Isa is not the name given Him by the angel, as we are informed in the Gospel of Matthew.

This, indeed, forms the second, and perhaps the princi-
pal, objection to the use of the name Isa. The allegation
is, that the original name has been *corrupted*, some say, by
accident, others, designedly, though some of the latter again
ascribe the "corruption" to the malignity of the Jews, whilst
others say that Mohammed purposely changed the collocation
of the letters of the name, in order to obscure its signifi-
cation ...

Nearly twenty years ago, the Rev. Joseph Jowett, then one
of the secretaries of the British and Foreign Bible Society,
in a letter to the Calcutta Auxiliary Bible Society, in
which he wisely deprecates the excessive zeal manifested by
the two parties for and against the retention of the name
Isa, as if the progress of the Gospel *depended* upon the form
of a name, suggests that the change may have been accidental.
True philology was comparatively young in those days, but
even then an accurate student of languages would have hesitated to ascribe any linguistic change to accident. There
is a reason and a law for all such changes; a language may
sometimes be found to be wanton in the mutations in which it
seems to delight, but there will be found to be method and
causality even in its wantonness; *lusus naturae*, monsters,
and accidents are as exceptional in the genesis of words, as

they are in that of men, animals, and vegetables. It will
be seen presently that the form Isa is not due to an accident ...

There is, then, no corruption in the name Isa that the
missionary should therefore be loth to adopt it. There is
less change in it than there is in the very Greek name, which
alone the Holy Spirit has seen good to reveal to mankind.
There is less change in it than this very Greek name has
undergone in its passage into other languages. In their
first pronounciamento on the subject, the Calcutta Auxiliary
Bible Society spoke of *"the name of Jesus"* as "the bond of
Christian brotherhood throughout the world!" This is a vast
and strange delusion. The very English name retains nothing
of the Greek but the unessential termination, changing every
sound in it, even so much that a vowel becomes a consonant;
and let the reader try how little this English name is like
the Saviour's name as pronounced in German, French, Russian,
Polish, Sirenian, Karelian, Italian, Spanish, Portuguese,
etc., and how widely these again differ among themselves.

Let the missionary moreover consider that the attempt to
crowd out the name Isa will and must ever prove futile. Even
granting that he may ultimately be able to render the Koran
obsolete, there are remaining vast literatures which contain
that name thousands of times, and which, as to its classical
portion, only Vandal hands would ever dare, and no hands will
ever be able, to displace. As Homer the Greek and Cicero the
Roman are still the foundation of our Christian humanities,
so Hariri the Arab and Hafiz the Persian may yet form the
standing vernacular models for an Asiatic Christian literature.

Our Lord, in condescending to become man, has accepted all
the conditions of our common humanity; not only was He hungry,
thirsty, weary, grieved, afflicted, and smitten, but He submits also to have His earthly name undergo all the changes
and mutilations to which every thing earthly is subject. To
the Christian of every nation and every tongue, His name is
sweet and euphonious, not intrinsically, but on account of
all the blessings of which it is the emblem and the earnest.

If we inquire what these missionaries intend to substitute for the well-known name of Isa, they say, *Yusua*, itself
an imperfect imitation of what is conjectured by fallible men
to have been the Hebrew equivalent of the true name revealed
in Scripture. Verily a circuitous route and a large demand
on our unquestioning submissiveness!

Even granting that the angel spoke to Joseph in Hebrew or Aramaic, the very fact of the name being recorded in Greek only is an intimation that every language has a right to call the name in accordance with its own laws ...

It may be observed, in conclusion, that this paper confines itself almost wholly to the name of Jesus in reference to its use among Mohammedans, because the writer's labours lie entirely among a Mohammedan people; but it may be remarked, at the same time, that in versions or books intended for a mixed population of Mohammedans and Hindus, those who *have* a knowledge of Jesus should be considered before those that have not; and moreover, that as in India Mohammedans are everywhere found intermingled with Hindus, it is best, for the sake of uniformity, to use the name Isa only, wherever it is at all feasible. It has been said that in preaching Jesus to a Hindu, the name Isa finds his mind preoccupied by the notion which he has obtained from the Mohammedans, that Isa is a mere prophet, somewhat inferior to Mohammed, whilst another name avoids this difficulty. This is a poor device, at the very best. For supposing even that in teaching a Hindu the truth concerning our Saviour, the name *Yusua* finds his mind less prejudiced than the name Isa would have done; if the Hindu is at all awakened by the truth thus newly brought before him, it will not be long before his neighbours, the Mohammedans -- who, like the true proselytisers that they are, are well known immediately to seize upon anyone that shows the slightest inclination to abandon his idolatry -- will tell him that Yusua and Isa are one and the same person; and nothing whatever will have been gained by the introduction of the new name, whilst there might be the additional risk of raising suspicions in the mind of the inquirer, that the missionary had attempted to trick him; and the reaction then ensuing in such a mind would destroy all the good effects supposed to be obtained by the use of the new name.

September, 1860   I. Loewenthal

Reprinted from *The Muslim World* (July, 1911) by permission from an Investigation by the Rev. Isidor Loewenthal, Missionary to the Afghans, September, 1860.

Notes

CHAPTER 1: AKWABA -- MEET ME AND MY NEIGHBOURS

1. *Akwaba* ("welcome") is a common Akan greeting. Akan is spoken by about half the people in Ghana, Fanti and Twi belonging to this language family.

2. Names are very significant in African society, communicating information like day of birth, circumstances surrounding birth, place in the family line of descent, etc. Kwesi e.g., is a male born on Sunday; Ama, his wife, a female born on Saturday. In addition, Christians are usually given biblical names, as is the case with Matthew, Jonathan, and James, or a name from a denominational heritage, like Pius. Most of the Muslim names in Ghana have come from Arabic by way of the Hausa language. This gives them a distinctive form as is indicated by the following sampling:

Arabic	*Hausa*	*English*
'Abdallāh	Abdullāhi	"Slave of God"
'Abd al-Malik	Abdulmalik	"Slave of the king"
Ādam	Adamu	Adam
Ibrāhīm	Ibrahima	Abraham
Sulaymān	Sulaimānu (Sule)	Solomon
Ya'qūb	Yākubū	Jacob, James
'Uthmān	Usumānu (Usman)	Uthman

For a more complete list of Arabic names and their Hausa equivalents, see Paden (1973:429-431). The Naming Ceremony, ordinarily falling on the eighth day after birth, is an important occasion among all Africans. Trimingham goes into some detail as to what this involves among Muslims (1959:154-158).

3. Malam is a West African corruption of the Arabic *mu'allim* (teacher). See Trimingham (1968:59ff) for useful insights into the role of "clergy" in Islam.

4. Because of inadequate police protection, most firms and many private homes employ guards who patrol the premises at nighttime. In Ghana, most of these positions are filled by Northerners, many of them Muslim. Nightwatch is, of course, short for nightwatchman.

5. Abdullahi's becoming a Muslim is typical of what is happening to many migrants as they move from villages in the North into cities. On arrival in the city, the Northerner naturally identifies culturally with whatever Northern element is already there and which, for the most part, has probably become Muslim prior to his arrival. Since very few urban churches are prepared to wholeheartedly welcome Northerners into their fellowship (being comprised almost totally of Southerners), the Northern migrant (even those whose home villages are not islamized) goes one more step in his identification with the Northern urban community with which he associates. He becomes Muslim. Population statistics give striking evidence to the kind of progress Islam is making in taking urban migrants into its bosom (1960 Population Census of Ghana 1964: LXXXiv).

6. For much of its recent history, the Muslim community in Ghana has been divided into three main groups: 1) The Ghana Muslim Community, 2) The Ghana Muslim Mission, and 3) the Ahmadiyya. The Muslim Community, which was by far the largest prior to the Alien Quit Order of Dec., 1969, comprises primarily Muslims of Hausa, Yoruba, and Wangara descent. The Ghana Muslim Mission was organized in 1957, and draws its membership mainly from people indigenous to Ghana. Both groups are orthodox (Sunni) Muslims of the Maliki rite, as opposed to the Ahmadiyya. The Ahmadiyya claim a much larger membership in Ghana than they actually have. Except for a strong following among the Fantis around Saltpond, and for a sizable group in Wa, they are not large. The Ahmadiyya do, however, have a larger voice than their size would indicate. Having taken the lead in Muslim educational work, and now becoming involved in medical work, they are making some obvious and worthwhile contributions to the national life of Ghana. For a history and description of the Ahmadiyya movement in West Africa, including Ghana, see Fisher (1963). For an assessment of the relationships between each of these groups, consult Dretke (1968:92-101, 116-120).

7. The kind of church Kwesi and Ama attends goes under various names in Ghana: "Spiritual church," "independent church," "indigenous church." While "spiritual churches" have been springing up all over the South of Ghana, it is difficult to assess their real numerical strength since many people like Kwesi and Ama still look upon themselves as Presbyterian, Methodist, or whatever while worshipping regularly in a "spiritual church." The monumental work on this subject is Barrett (1968), but also useful are Baeta (1961, 1962), Turner (1967), Welbourn (1966). Muslim separatism has quite different characteristics although Fisher says that, like Christian separatism, it "is an attempt to maintain a balanced relationship between the faith and the practical circumstances in which the faith exists" (1969:139).

8. Alhaji (Alhaja for a female) is the honourary title given to a Muslim who has completed the pilgrimage to Mecca. Ghanaians widely believe that Alhajis have special "power" on their return, and that many become wealthy by selling this "power."

9. Trimingham helps us understand the varying stages through which people pass in moving from an animist orientation to becoming Muslim (1959:21-24, 1968:34-52). His analysis indicates that Islam slowly infiltrates a society without immediately challenging all its beliefs and practices. Gradually animistic traits and components are replaced by Islamic traits and components. Ideally, the *Shar'ia* should eventually dominate all aspects of life in a given society, but what happens in much of West African Islam is that Muslim thought and practice continue to have an animistic base. One can hardly make a careful study of Islam in West Africa without giving careful attention to the resultant syncretism, and its manifestation at many different levels. See also Rouch (1954:59-64).

10. The realities, problems and challenges of religious pluralism have captured the attentions and energies of many writers, each of whom in his own way has contributed something unique and yet complementary to the others in the search for where the Christian man of faith fits into the complicated picture of today. With almost yearly precision, exciting books have been coming off the press. Among these have been: Kraemer (1938), Toynbee (1956, 1957), Neill (1961), W.C. Smith (1964), J.V. Taylor (1963), Van Leeuwen (1964), Cragg (1968), Newbigin (1969), Watt (1969), J.N.D. Anderson (1970).

11. *Zongos* from the Hausa *Zongo* are a unique feature of the Muslim communities in Ghana, where Islam has not yet infiltrated society to a point of domination. *Zongo* was originally a "camping ground," a place outside a town where Muslim traders stayed while carrying on their trade. Gradually, traders settled in these areas, and the settlements grew. For dietary reasons and others, Muslims continued to maintain their separate quarters. The *Zongos* have served to isolate Muslims from the rest of the populace, giving them a posture of foreignness and, at the same time, mystery. It is this kind of separation which has helped create the problem we are facing in this book -- that of opening a new door to dialogue between Christians and Muslims. As is, there is a great ignorance of each other among both Christians and Muslims.

CHAPTER 2: THE PROBLEM OF WHERE TO BEGIN

12. The O'Neills discuss "duologue" as opposed to "dialogue" in their discussion of "Open Listening" as it relates to marriage. What they say is equally applicable to communication between Christians and Muslims (1972:121f).

13. Wilson (1959:26) and von Grunebaum (1953:19) call attention to the prominence of the Day of Judgment in Muslim thought.

14. For a comprehensive treatment of the conflict between Christian and Muslim, see N.A. Daniel (1960) and von Grunebaum (1953:31-62). Concerning the conflict between the North African Church and Islam, Trimingham concludes, "The North African Church died rather than was eliminated by Islam, since it had never rooted itself in the life of the country" (1926b:17).

15. The terms secularism and secularization speak of something that is of increasingly greater significance on the religious scene in Africa. The very fact that sacred and secular are distinguished at all is something new on the African scene where "'secular,' 'socialist,' 'communist' and 'capitalist' elements were all harmoniously joined together into a religious whole" (Mbiti 1970:348). For useful discussions on this phenomenon and its problem and challenge for Islam and Christianity see Cragg (1968:173), Hogg (1952:249), King (1971:106f), Kraemer (1938:7-17), Neill (1970:154), Newbigen (1969:29f,63), Newport (1971:93), Nolin (1967:222), Rahman (1968:272-276), Smith (1964:113f), Trimingham (1968:123ff), van Leeuwen (1964:333f, 354f, 414f), and Winter (1970a:39).

16. I know of no one who has written more forcefully, imaginatively, and convincingly on the place of "creativity" in the life of the Christian and the Church than Nicolas Berdyaev. Many of the ideas he "prophetically" puts forward have much to say when considering a Christian approach to Muslims. Taking Berdyaev seriously we can live and work in the full expectation of something totally new and creative emerging at the same time heeding his word, "We rightly criticize that theory of progress in which may be seen a false religion seeking to substitute itself for Christianity")1935:303). Another who writes vividly on the "new creation" and various aspects of it is P. Verghese of the Syrian Orthodox Church in South India (1965:25-29). See also Nissiotis (1965:3,43) and Strachan (1935:112-115).

17. Stephen Neill points out that "it takes two to make dialogue: the most disappointing factor in the present situation is the almost total failure so far of the Muslim scholar to approach Christianity with that reverence and openmindedness which he rightly demands of the Christian scholar in his approach to Islam ... We are still a very long way from the possibility of dialogue" (1970:61f). Perry reminds us that dispute can be a healthy initiator of productive dialogue (1958:225).

CHAPTER 3: SAME WORDS -- DIFFERENT MEANINGS

18. Parrinder (1965) examines all the quranic passages which speak of Jesus. Besides the "orthodox" understanding of Jesus' ministry of teaching and healing as rehearsed by Alihu, many tales of the unique accomplishments of Jesus circulate on a popular level in West Africa (See Trimingham, 1959:67). The same author also informs us that "village clerics ... recount weird tales about the life of Muhammad" (49). In fact, there is evidence to indicate that in many areas where accessibility to the Quran is limited (because of language and literacy difficulties), various of the miraculous works of Jesus are attri-

buted to Muhammad in popular thought. As King says, "The prophet did not claim to his followers to be what Jesus was to his, yet his being, his power, his character and relationship with God and man, remain central ... To a believer Muhammad is a person who goes through life with one, accompanying and showing the way, encouraging, exhorting, rebuking, and ultimately rewarding" (1971:25).

19. For hadith related to fasting, see Ali, M. (N.d.:222-231).

20. A Muslim with a teakettle (carrying water for ablutions) and a sheepskin (for kneeling upon during prayer) is a familiar scene in West Africa. The mosque which Alihu attended would be a building, or a simple enclosure marked off by stones, sticks or cement blocks, depending on how old, wealthy, or well-established that particular Hausa worshipping community was. The mosque situation for the whole of the Sudan belt is summed up by Trimingham (1968:129f). In another place, Trimingham comments, "A characteristic of Islam is its mobility. The mosque is only exceptionally a building" (1959:70). This idea of "mobility" is well worth pondering from a Christian missionary perspective. Cragg helps us make the necessary distinction between Muslim prayer and Christian prayer (1964:106). It can readily be seen that Muslim *salat* has much in common with liturgical worship as practised in many Christian churches. See also Cragg (1969:57-63) and Brelvi (1965:282-284). Brelvi includes photographs of the proper movements and a transcription of the proper Arabic formulas.

21. See W.C. Smith (1959) for a good introduction to the problems raised by a common vocabulary.

22. Many Christians falsely assume that Muslims "worship Muhammad." There is a similar problem here to that faced in trying to accurately describe African "ancestor worship." The thin line that goes between practices connected to the reverence and veneration of the ancestors and worship is often extremely difficult to draw. The same uncertainty prevails in certain areas of Africa as regards whether the Prophet and various Muslim saints are being venerated or worshipped in popular Muslim thought and practice. See Barrett (1968:119ff), Mbiti (1970:11f) and Taylor (1963:103-107).

23. A few years back Muslims in West Africa spoke of Allah as being different from the God worshipped by Christians and pagans. In keeping with this opinion, they were consistent in always using the name Allah. Whatever influences have come to bear upon the situation since that time, it is quite common now to hear Muslims following the general practice of Christians and using the name of God according to the language they are speaking. See Appendix A for a full discussion on the question of "the same God."

24. A perceptive, well-reasoned defence for the retention and use of the name Isa in witnessing to our risen Lord among Muslims is that written by the Rev. Isidor Loewenthal in 1860. Because what Loewenthal has to say is of substantive value not only for our discussion of this topic, but also for the whole problem of language as relates to com-

munication between Christians and Muslims, we have included a generous portion of his paper as Appendix B. L. Bevan Jones summarized the contents of Loewenthal's paper in the *Bible Translator*, ending his article as follows: "The conclusion to be drawn is clearly this -- that we should gratefully receive, and without hesitation use the name for Jesus which Muslims offer us and fill it, *for their sakes, and with a new content*" (1953:86). D.A. Chowhury (1953:26f) strongly opposes the use of Isa, while W.J. Bradnock (1953:103) suggests a combination of Christian and Muslim names, e.g. *Yesu* (Christian) *Almasih* (Muslim, i.e. Arabic: "the Messiah"). Horovitz traces the transliteration of a varied sampling of names from the O.T. into Arabic usage, including "Moshe" into "Musa" and "Yeshua" into "Isa" (1964).

25. Abd Al-Karim Al-Khatib, an Egyptian Muslim author, describes his relationship with Jesus in these terms: "As a Muslim I am required by my religion to believe in the Christ and in a Scripture revealed to him. I have no doubt that I am one of the followers of the Christ, just as I am one of Muhammad's followers ... You are a Christian who loves the Christ and wants to exalt him, and I am a Muslim whose love and esteem for the Christ is in no way less than yours. Then why should not the Christ unite us on the path together, at the point of our love for him and our desire to honor him? ... Thus in order for me to be a Muslim in truth -- or even a Christian in truth -- I must love the Christ, exalt him, honor and believe in him as a messenger of God, and in his Injil as a sacred book. And yet, despite this, there is still a difference in the way each of us approaches the Christ, in the ways we love, exalt and believe in him" (1971:95,97).

26. According to Manners and Kaplan, "observation is always selective and requires some interest, some point of view, or some theoretical framework if it is to be meaningful" (1968:5). The theoretical assumption underlying this study is that Muslims have "never met the real Jesus," and that were they to meet Him, many would accept Him as their Lord and Saviour. What we have attempted to observe and describe, therefore, are those factors which have hidden the real Jesus from the Muslim's eye of faith and what efforts in witness will help the Muslim to meet Him face-to-face.

27. In this book we only touch briefly upon the offence of the "Son of God" title to Muslims. Taylor's tracing of the Scriptural usage of this terminology is a reminder that the Christian cannot altogether avoid this offence in his witness (1962:52-65).

CHAPTER 4: GETTING TO THE HEART OF THINGS

28. A plea for intercommunion has come surprisingly from J.K. Amissah, the Roman Catholic Archbishop of Ghana (All Africa Conference of Churches 1969:79).

29. Wearing apparel has been a seriously debated topic in the African churches. In many areas women have traditionally kept their legs covered; hence, the big turmoil over mini-skirts. Some African countries have even banned the wearing of mini-skirts. The incident referred to in the text is not an isolated incident. Young men have

also been kept away from communion for not wearing suitcoats. See
Debrunner (1967:256-260) on the topic of "excluded Christians."

30. The picture of the balance on which man's good deeds will be
weighed over against his evil deeds is common in Muslim thought, being
drawn from the Quran (Q. 101:6-11). Cragg helps us put the whole matter of Muslim ritual and works into perspective with Christian ritual
and works (1964:16f). See also Wilson (1959:26).

31. The "Do this, avoid that" rule of thumb is very much a feature of West African Islam. *Fikh Akbar I*, one of the early creeds of
Islam, has as its second of ten Articles: "We enjoin what is just
and prohibit what is evil" (Wensinck 1965:103). As Trimingham says,
"The duties incumbent upon the (Muslim) community are summarized in
the maxim, 'to command right and forbid wrong.'" (1968:68). Trimingham
also traces the clash between Islamic law and customary law with an
interesting aside as to Islam's accomodation to animism and a demon-
strable conclusion regarding the spread of Islam under colonialism
(1952:274).

32. Wensinck (1965:26ff) and Williams (1971:225-303) discuss *jihad*.
For a modern-day interpretation of the concept, see Muhammad Ali (1950:
545-598) and Abd Ar-Rahman Azzam (1964:132-174).

33. According to W.C. Smith, "Islam is obedience or commitment,
the willingness to take on oneself the responsibility of living hence-
forth according to God's proclaimed purpose; and submission, the recognition not in theory but in overpowering act of one's littleness
and worthlessness before the awe and majesty of God (1964:103).

34. See Daniel (1960:109-114) for insights into the mentality behind the Crusades, and Neill (1964:113-116).

35. Nasr has a different comparison: "The Quran is to Christ as
the Prophet is to Mary" (1966:43f).

36. For a helpful treatment of the Talmud, see Epstein (1962:
511-151).

37. A.H. is "After the Hegira," the flight of Muhammad and his
followers from Mecca to Medina in 622 A.D. Muslim history usually
takes its beginning from this date.

On the development of the *hadith*, see Rahman (1968:43-47).
For selections of, see Jeffery (1958; 1962:79-250) and Muhammad Ali
(N.d.).

38. It would be interesting to compare the Islamic idea of *abd*
with Paul's idea of *doulos* in Rom. 6:18,22, and I Cor. 7:22.

39. Luther and the Lutheran Confessions speak of the Law as having
three functions. According to the *Solid Declaration* of the *Formula of
Concord*, "The Law of God serves (1) not only to maintain external dis-

cipline and decency against dissolute and disobedient people, (2) and
to bring people to a knowledge of their sin through the Law, (3) but
those who have been born anew through the Holy Spirit, who have been
converted to the Lord and from whom the veil of Moses has been taken
away, learn from the Law to live and walk in the Law" (Tappert 1959:
563f).   Our discussion has dealt primarily with Luther's Second
Function of the Law. The *Solid Declaration* also points up the sharp
distinction between Law and Gospel (Tappert 1959:561), a key ingredient in Lutheran theology, preaching, and practice since the time of
the Reformation. Herein lies one of Lutheranism's greatest contributions to the Christian's understanding of the differences between
Christianity and other religions, in particular, Islam. A proper distinction between Law and Gospel accentuates the uniqueness of the
Christian faith and the precious message of reconciliation which God
has commissioned His people to proclaim. See Walther (1929) and Elert
(1967).

CHAPTER 5: YOU ARE MY WITNESSES

40.   The animosity Jonathan displays toward Roman Catholics is not
unusual on the part of "Evangelicals" in Africa. Unfortunately, many
Evangelicals have not been alert to the kind of changes sweeping through
Catholicism as is evidenced by writers like Hastings (1964, 1967, 1971)
and Sarpong (1973).

41.   "It is simple enough," R. Neibuhr says, "to be tolerant on issues which are not believed to be vital. The real test of toleration
is our attitude towards people who oppose truths which seem important
to us, and who challenge realms of life and meaning towards which we
have a responsible relation" (1941:238).

42.   "Moslems, Christians, and Jews of any level of spiritual and
intellectual attainment should by all indications be able to speak to
one another more easily and with more fecundity than with others. Are
they not all, in a special and sacred way, brothers? Is not Abraham
the father of them all?" So asks Kritzeck in a useful little book
which makes us wonder if we have exploited this natural door to communication for all it is worth (1965:74).

43.   Marty has beautifully tied together the subject of "Church
Unity and Church Mission" (1964). See also Cragg (1968:193-218).

44.   For Muslim contributions to Ghanaian society, see Hodgkin
(1966) and Wilks (1961, 1966).

45.   Many Christian scholars have explored the significance of the
Resurrection as the central message of the Gospel. See Barth (1936:
524f), Kunneth (1965:11,152,155,295), Moltmann (1970:25,34-38), and
Tenney (1963:47).

46.   "The Christian must ... continually remind himself that no man
is 'saved' by Christianity as a religion, but only by the gospel as
such (i.e. the saving action of God as recorded and interpreted in

the N.T.). This is different in kind not only from the non-Christian
religious systems, but also from Christianity itself, viewed as a
system. Man-in-Christianity lies under the judgment of God in the
same way, and for the same reasons, as man-in-paganism" (Anderson
1970:11). See also Neill (1970:207-234). "The call to 'be converted'
needs to be heard as loudly and as often within the realm of Christianity as in those of the 'other' religions, because 'being converted'
means not 'being converted' to Christianity but to Jesus Christ"
(Kraemer 1965:96).

CHAPTER 6:   TRUTH AND FREEDOM

47. The Muslim understanding that the quranic text circulating
among men is an exact reproduction of the original copy in heaven
puts the Quran into quite a different position among Muslims from
that which the Bible occupies among Christians. Various efforts have
been made to define and clarify that position, among them Asad (1964),
Cragg (1971, 1973), Jeffery (1962:17-75), Nasr (1966:42-45), Schuon
(1963:43-86), and Watt (1969).

48. For the Muslim understanding, see Elder (1923:242-258) and
Parrinder (1965:105-121). For an Ahmadiyya interpretation, see Ahmad
(1947:581-584). A serious and thought-provoking attempt on the part
of a Muslim to understand the crucifixion is that by Hussein, who in-
terprets it from a standpoint of mankind being on trial. In his concluding remarks he says, "In the events of Good Friday all the factors
in evil and sin were present. Every day of life its tragedy is repeated (1959:210).

49. The tendency to formalize practices and procedures and its
accompanying difficulties are well illustrated in recent controversies and crises in the Lutheran Church - Missouri Synod. Not only
have congregations and individuals in the U.S. been affected, but efforts have been made to control and standardize the doctrine taught
and practised by overseas "daughter churches." On legalism and "the
tendency to bury God under the Law" see Bavinck (1960:261-266).

50. See Note 16 above and Nolin (1967:221ff).

51. For useful exegetical treatment of the Hebrew and Greek words
used in this chapter, see Blackman (1950:269f) and Dodd (1953:139f,
170-178). A theme worth further exploring is that put forward by
Greeley, "Christians are faithful to one another in all their relationships because God's fidelity gives them the confidence that their
own fidelity requires and because they understand that their fidelity
is an exercise in their vocation of manifesting God's love to the
world" (1974:9).

52. Watson beautifully summarizes this love in his introduction
to Nygren (1953:viii-x).

CHAPTER 7: CONVERSION

53. On conversion, see Green (1951:16-42), Hoffman (1968:1-20),
Maurier (1968:225-268), Newbigin (1969:88-115), Tippett(1970:19-37),
and Wente (1947:168-187). Some, like Tillich, are very negative on
conversion: "Not conversion, but dialogue. It would be a tremendous step forward if Christianity were to accept this" (1963:95).
Curtain struggled with the question: "If Christianity required a
change of culture, which should come first, conversion or civilization" (1964:420).

        The question of conversion has far-reaching ramifications.
Perry asks, "What will Christianity displace in the cultures conceived and nurtured by these non-Christian faiths (Islam, Hinduism,
Buddhism)? What will happen to the Taj Mahal, to Hindu temples and
Buddha images, to the arts, the ethics, the ethos, and so on, which
each of these religions has inspired and fostered? Can Christianity
herself remain unchanged in this encounter which now involves her at
every point on the globe and at every point of human concern. Every
one of these questions is urgent both for every Christian nowadays
has to be a missionary Christian or no Christian at all and for the
non-Christian to whom we address the claims of the Gospel. Since
Christianity is always under the corrective judgment of the Gospel
which calls Christianity into being as a religion, we need continually
to ask ourselves, What is it we are carrying to men of these other
religions? In answering this question we are led to ask what in our
faith must be purged before we make our missionary approach to our
rival religions" (1958:214f)?

54. The statement that evangelism is not "a matter of tested
methods and proved patterns" does not exclude theory and research as
important elements of preparation for a faithful Christian witness.
See McGavran (1970:5f) and Myrdal (1957:164).

55. "The doctrine of Atonement is wholly opposed to reason"
(Ahmad 1947:cclvii). "Islam ... is founded upon rational principles.
Indeed, the revolution brought about by the Holy Prophet in the history of religious thought is that he won over converts not by means
of miracles, but by rational persuasion. Instead of paralysing the
intellect of people, the demand of the Holy Quran from man is to open
his eyes and exercise his rational faculty" (Bawany 1961:x). These
expressions are typical of Muslim writers who often try to prove the
"reasonableness" of the teachings of Islam over against those of
Christianity. Bishop (1965:346,356) tries to argue a case for "the
reasonableness of Christ," although his equivocation of "magnanimity"
with "reasonableness" seems to this author a weak kind of exegesis
which will hardly carry much weight with a Muslim. See also Levonian
who differentiates between Islam as mainly "a religion of dogmas about
God and man, angels and the Last Day; whereas Christianity ... is essentially a religion of spiritual experience of forgiveness, reconciliation and new life" (1940:134f). See also Kraemer, who seeks
"to show that Biblical thinking, the whole world of attitudes and decisions and modes of being implied in the Biblical revelation is a

type wholly *sui generis*, distant from religious thinking in the usual understanding of the word, and equally distant from philosophical thinking" (1956:449).

56. Other Christians may disagree with Lutherans who are very strong on insisting that man "cannot by his own reason or strength believe in the Lord, or come to Him." As Luther said: "We are people who have been born, not fashioned by men, but 'begotten.' This is not our work. As little as a child contributes to its being born, so little do we contribute to our being spiritually born"(Plass 1959:347).

57. For a short, but deep and penetrating insight into "what happened when the Church and the churches came to Africa," see Kretzmann (1965:35-41). His profound understanding of the nature of the Church is most helpful.

58. The "Bridge of God" concept has been fully developed by McGavran (1955).

59. See McGavran (1955:68-99; 1970:296-334), Shearer (1966:143-151), and Wold (1968:123-155; 205-212) on people movements. Pickett reminds us that: "Excessive individualism ... has fastened itself like a parasite upon the life of the church. Group conversions are rare in these tribal countries! They should be the normal way of accepting the Christian faith" (1963:119f). Mbiti, from observing traditional African religions, adds, "Traditional religions are not primarily for the individual, but for his community of which he is a part ... To be human is to belong to the whole community, and to do so involves participating in the beliefs, ceremonies, rituals and festivals of that community. A person cannot detach himself from the religion of his group, for to do so is to be severed from his roots, his foundation, his context of security, his kinships and the entire group of those who make him aware of his own existence. To be without one of these corporate elements of life is to be out of the whole picture (1970:3). For a firsthand account of a people movement in Ghana, see Krass (1973:154-159; 1969:244-247, 375f) and McGavran (1969:247-250). McGavran carefully analyzes significant features of this movement among the Chokosis and illuminates some of the causes underlying its momentum (1969:247-250).

Berdyaev looks into the nature of Protestantism with conclusions which have interesting bearing on the subject of people movements: "It must ... be noted that individualism is inherent not only in Protestantism, but in the whole of Western Christianity ... The spirit of *sobornost*, the idea of the collective character of the ways of salvation, is opposed to this sort of individualism. In the Church we are saved with our brethren, all together" (1935:355).

CHAPTER 8: DIALOGUE

60. How much dialogue has been a subject of prominent interest during the past several years is indicated by the abundance of articles and books which deal with it. Looking at dialogue from a Muslim point

of view is Al Faruqi (1968:45-77) and from a Christian perspective:
Anderson (1970:26-30), Basetti-Sani (1967:126-137, 186-196), Beaver
(1968:113-125), Bijlefeld (1967:171-177), Brown (1971:65-78), Copeland
(1971:53-64), Corbon(1965:68-74), Estes (1971:5-16), Gensichen (1971:
29-40), Habib (1969:111), Hallencreutz (1970), Kitagawa (1962),
Neill (1970), Nolin (1967:204-224), Rahbar (1965:353-359), Samartha
(1970:392-403), Smith (1959), Speight (1965), Trimingham (1955), Watt
(1967a:19-23), and the Zurich Consultation (1970:382-391). For a
fascinating discussion in dialogue, see Al-Khatib (1971:90-101) and
Nolin (1969:74-79).

An indication of how people of Muslim background may question
the Christian's intention and purpose in initiating dialogue is given
by S.J. Samartha, who relates how "Hasan Askara, a Muslim sociologist
from Hyderabad ... refers to the initiative taken by the Christians
in calling the Ajaltoun (Lebanon) meeting and raises the question why
people of other religions did not take such an initiative. He goes
on to ask: 'Are they self-sufficient? Are they incapable of using
dialogue for missionary purposes?' Both these questions imply extremely opposed possibilities. The first question suggests that the
Christians needed other faiths for their enrichment, as if they were
poorer if they did not enter into a dialogue. The second question
implies that there was no question of enrichment or consciousness of
inadequacy but a more sophisticated tool was being forged by the
Christians in the shape of dialogue to propagate Christianity" (1970:
394).

61. Reyburn questions the "catechism" approach used in many instances to teach converts, suggesting this approach grew out of a mentality which assumed that the religious mind of the convert was "an
empty basin to be filled for the first time in his life" (1967:30).
As Barrett says, "The eight hundred tribal societies of Africa were
far from being a *tabula rasa* when white contact began; they were rich,
complex and continuously evolving" (1971:3). H.R. Niebuhr analyzes
"five sorts of answers" of what happens when Christ enters any such
societies through the preaching of the Gospel (1951:40-45). Today
there is a new appreciation both for what Africans have developed in
their cultures to consecrate into the service of the Lord and what of
their cultures can be further developed to His glory. See Nketia
(1958), Weman (1960), and Sarpong (1973) for discussion on music and
worship.

62. According to Bavinck, "The only basis we can ground our message upon is the certainty that God was concerning Himself with these
Gentiles before we met them. God was occupying Himself with them before we came to them ... The preacher of the gospel ... does not open
the dialogue between God and his listeners: he merely opens a new
chapter. He has a point of contact, not a point of contact in human
reason or human virtue, but in God's work and God's mercifulness.
That is the beauty of the missionary tast" (1948:109f). The fact that
"God has been working" does not mean that when conversion comes, there
is not a decisive break. "Conversion," Maurier says, "does not con-
sist only in leaving a life which a man recognizes as inconsistent

with morality, for that is not enough to call a good man a "Christian"; the decisive element is acceptance of the salvific plan of God, which necessarily tears him away from exclusively human concerns" (1968: 226).

For a full treatment of the whole question as to how God has been working among non-Christians, see Gamaliel, whose "fundamental hypothesis" is, "that God works in the non-Christian religions through the Law and he works in the Church and the Kingdom through the Law and the Gospel. The Law is at work in non-Christian religions as conscience, as mores, orders of preservation, and as social, religious, and political institutions. The goodness of God manifest in creation and preservation has to be distinguished from the grace of God which is received through faith in Christ. The Law of God, which is in its perfect form in the decalogue, is present in an imperfect form in the human heart as natural law" (1974:13).

63. Nolin suggests that "Love may well mean no actual 'witness' at all, for a time, only a willingness to listen. No communication can ever be effective when unilateral; love recognizes this and modifies its expressions of incomparability for the sake of conversation. It senses that only in this way may friends be led into a deeper mutual discovering of this very incomparable Gospel" (1967:217f).

64. We have not made efforts to discover and describe the "light" which some have seen in Islam and other religious expressions. That light is essentially the light of the Law, and as such puts man under condemnation, revealing his guilt and the precarious nature of his position before God. The light of the Gospel comes to him through the Means of Grace -- the Word and the Sacraments. When the human predicament is understood in this way, arguments like those of Watt "towards one religion" appear weak and inconclusive (1963:160-175). Similarly with Hoffman's argument that "while we should strive to make Christians better Christians, we ought also to make Moslems better Moslems, Hindus better Hindus, and Jews better Jews ... sincerely like them to be better followers of their chosen religion and leave all matters to Almighty God" (Hoffman 1968:18f).

CHAPTER 9: ALL THINGS TO ALL MEN

65. Butchers are an important segment of the Muslim communities in Ghana. As this writer says elsewhere: "Their handling of meat distribution insures that a correct Muslim procedure will be followed in the slaughter of animals. It is not unusual for the Head Butcher to become a man of some considerable influence in a Muslim community" (Dretke 1968:166).

66. On the surface, an effort to empathize with Muslims during this sacred month by joining them in the fast is highly commendable. At the same time, there are hidden factors which need to be carefully explored, e.g., why are Muslims fasting? It is the month in which Muslims believe the Quran was revealed (Q. 2:185). It may be that the Christian feels uncomfortable about giving such a witness. Per-

haps a better alternative would be to fast during Lent which practice would serve two useful purposes: 1) It would enable Christians
to identify with a very healthy Muslim practice, while at the same
time, 2) giving Christians an opportunity to witness to Muslims
about certain key and significant events in their own life and
faith, the Suffering and Passion of our Lord.

CHAPTER 10: PAVING NEW GROUND

67. Properly: Al-Hajj Umar ibn Abi Bakr of Keti Krachi (c.A.D.
1850-1934). See Hodgkin (1966:453-456).

68. This Ghana Government Decree in December, 1969, initiated
one of the largest people movements in modern times. All persons
in Ghana without valid residence permits were forced to leave --
most of them Africans from neighbouring states (estimates vary between 50,000 and 2½ million). One of the ironies of the situation
was that many of the families affected had lived in Ghana for two
and three generations. They were however, still marked as foreigners
-- even though they had been given the right to vote by Kwame Nkrumah.
Under these circumstances it came as a great shock when a demand was
made for "valid residence permits." The Evangelical Lutheran Church
of Ghana lost approximately half its membership, but the hardest hit
of all was the Ghana Baptist Convention, which had 72 buildings
standing idle after this mass exodus. Until that time, the Baptist
Convention had been very largely a Yoruba church, and the 72 buildings simply represented Yorubas who had left.

The Muslim community was affected more than was the Christian community -- so much so that many Muslims suspected that the
order came as a "Christian" move to oust Muslims from the country.
The Prime Minister in power was Kofi Busia, a Methodist lay preacher.
Since the Muslim community in Ghana was so very largely made up of
foreign elements (the three major tribal groupings being Hausa,
Yoruba, and Wangara in that order), there was a strong feeling that
the "Alien Quit Order" had a religious motivation. This was hardly
the case, however, in that thousands and thousands of Christians
were affected as well, the motivation having its roots primarily in
the increasingly difficult economic situation of the country. During
and after the exodus of the aliens, much evidence supported the conclusion that the Muslim community was "stereotyped as a foreign element in Gold Coast society" (Dretke 1968:114). Muslims from the
North wearing Northern smocks were attacked by local citizens and
reminded that they had been ordered to leave the country. Letters
from Muslims appeared in daily newspapers reminding the populace of
Ghana that many native Ghanaians were Muslims. One side development
from this whole situation was that thousands of Muslims began to
wear "Western" clothes, rather than be marked as a distinct element
in society by way of robes and smocks. In the Arabic class of which
this author was a part (under the auspices of the Ghana Institute of
Languages), a real turnabout came after the "Quit Order." Prior to
that time more than ninety percent of the students were dressed in
"Muslim" garb; after that, the percentages were just reversed.

69. The official "Statement of the History and Aims of the Ghana Muslim Mission" states: "We are making efforts to work hand in hand with the Christian Council in respect of management of Mission Schools" (Dretke 1968:144).

70. Modern translators can well profit from Luther's insights into the work of translation. See Wentz (1953:27ff) and Luther (1960: 105-223).

71. Patai tries to describe what this means to Muslims and the Arab world, using a most appropriate chapter heading: "Under the Spell of Language" (1973:41-72). See also Nasr (1966:44f) and Cragg (1971:54-72).

72. For an excellent evaluation and interpretation of the impact of Westernization, with its accompanying secularism, upon the Muslim world and that world's feelings of frustration and helplessness in the face of that threat, see Patai (1967:364-406; 1973:268-313). See also Rahman (1968:261-289).

73. An unfortunate problem in Ghana, as in many other places in the world, is the gap which separates "conciliar" Christians from "evangelical" Christians. The generalizations which are made like that above -- are not only unfair, but simply untrue. The same evil torments Christian-Muslim relations the world over, as well as inter-tribal relationships.

74. Many Christians are puzzled as to why Muslims are not in Christian Councils, or engaged in "Church Union" talks. Even Cragg asks, "Are the instincts and goals of the ecumenical movement in any sense extendable beyond the borders of Christianity itself" (1973:194)? The number of those who are bewildered is simply another indicator of how crucial a study like this is to the stimulation of a faithful witness on the part of Christians among Muslims.

75. West African Muslims have taken very seriously the idea of an "Expected Deliverer" (*al-Mahdi*) appearing from time to time on the world scene, fulfilling some of the functions which Muhammad did -- cleansing and purifying the true religion of God. For a selection of Muslim writings on the subject of the *Mahdi*, see Williams (1971: 189-251).

76. The question of the boundaries between the *Dar al-Islam* and the *Dar al-Harb* became quite a burning issue in nineteenth century West Africa, leading to three *jihads* which played an important role in the implanting of Islam in certain areas. Short-lived, but important "theocratic" states emerged from two of them; out of the third came the Empire of Uthman Dan-Fodio (See Trimingham 1962b:177-186, 195-207) and M.G. Smith (1966:408-420). The correspondence between Uthman dan-Fodio and Al-Kanemi is extremely interesting (Hodgkin 1960:198-205). The news of distant *jihads* and the question of Muslims living under pagan rulers caused considerable consternation among Kumasi Muslims (Wilks 1966:324ff). Modern "orthodox" Muslims

have similar concerns, for "everywhere legislative power belongs to 'secular' governments" (Charney 1971:21).

77.   The "Black Muslims" are to Islam something like the Ahmadiyya -- a sect outside the fringes of orthodox Islam.   They are largely localized in the U.S., their emphasis on "blackness" distorting the universal brotherhood message of Sunni Islam.   For an introduction to this American phenomenon, see Lincoln (1961).   Malcolm X, one of their most famous spokesman, changed his "Black Muslim" attitudes towards race after visiting the Middle East and Egypt.   Unfortunately, he did not live long enough after that to seriously influence the movement, but his biography still lives on after him (Little 1965).   The last few years have seen many dramatic changes in the Black Muslim organization, including a change of name (World Community of Al-Islam in the West), a change of direction (away from black nationalism and anti-white teachings toward the mainstream of Islam), and a change in leadership (voluntary handing over of power from Wallace Deen Muhammad to a ruling Council).   See Drummond (1978:1,13).

78.   On Abrogation, see Jeffery (1958:66ff).

CHAPTER 11:   MUHAMMAD AND THE QURAN

79.   Muhammad has also been identified as Anti-christ on the basis of passages in the Book of Revelation (Charles   1931:18,24).

80.   Useful historical background to the life, work, and person of Muhammad, as well as the early development and spread of Islam, is found in Watt (1953, 1961a, 1961b, 1962a, 1962b), Andrae (1935), and Glubb (1970).

81.   Each chapter of the Quran is titled after some item -- not even necessarily significant -- mentioned in that particular *Sura*. Many Christian scholars have seen a clear reference to the Lord's Supper in Sura 5:115-118.   Many who try to read the Quran for the first time are puzzled by its lack of continuity and repetition.   Unlike the N.T. which is largely a book of letters, the Quran is more like a book of sermons.   The order of their appearance in the Quran is similar to the appearance of the Prophets in the Bible, the longer texts first.   In actual size, the Quran is somewhat shorter than the N.T. The argument as to whether Christians can in good conscience print and distribute the Quran and other books by Muslim writers goes back at least to Luther's time.   Through his urging, the Council of Basel authorized the printing of Bibliander's translation of the Quran and other materials (Kritzeck 1964:viif).   Cragg, in one of his latest books (1973), wrestles with the question of what relevance the Quran can have to those outside Islam.

82.   Attitude is extremely important.   Whether overt, or hidden, it influences our approach to others.   As Thomas says, "Different attitudes will follow from different interpretations of the significance of other religions.   If other religions are understood to be simply idolatry and the creation of human self-assertion, then one attitude

may be appropriate. If, however, other religions are seen to be honest human attempts to respond to the manifestation of God in nature
and conscience, then quite a different attitude will follow" (1969:
11). Peter the Venerable, one of the first Christians on record to
seriously study Islam, did not hesitate to pass judgment upon Muhammad
and Islam, yet admitted he did not quite know how to categorize
Muhammad and his followers -- whether as Christian heretics, or pagans
(Kritzeck 1964:143f). For those who are quick to pass judgment upon
Islam because of the quranic attacks upon Christianity, Watt argues
"that there is no primary attack on Christianity in the Quran," but
that the "apparent criticisms of Christianity to be found in the
Quran ... should ... be regarded as attacks on Christian heresies
which orthodox Christians would themselves criticize" (Watt 1967b:
197,201). "Right down to present time," Van Leeuwen says, "Islam has
invariably held a mirror up to Christianity" (1964:344).

We should make a distinction between judgments upon Muhammad
and judgments upon Islam. Bijlefeld (1959), who has brought a fresh
and exciting approach to Islam as Editor of the *Muslim World*, argues
very powerfully that we do not have enough information in hand to know
what Muhammad's actual position toward Christ was. Muhammad saw
Judaism and Christianity -- not from the Scriptures, but from Jews
and Christians he met, many of whom had fled for their lives from
both the centres of Judaism and Christianity. What he saw happening
in Christianity -- the rise of Mariolatry, the praying to saints, the
worshipping of their relics -- struck him as nothing less than gross
idolatry (See Note 75 above). Thus, what has happened in Islam theo-
logically may be quite different from what Muhammad envisioned. For a
sampling of Bijlefeld's insight, see *Muslim World* editorials from
1967 onwards, e.g. July, 1967.

Using I Cor. 13:4-7 as a starting point, Nolin also calls for
an abeyance of judgment and urges Christians to approach Muslims "not
to condemn ... not counting their trespasses against them ... not keeping accounts of wrong" (1967:217). Jesus' "judge not that you be not
judged" certainly cannot mean, however, that the Christian refrains
from speaking judgment. Whenever the Gospel is preached, judgment is
involved, for the invitation of the Gospel is received by people who
have been found wanting under the Law. Thus, at some point or another
in his witness, the Christian comes to speak of sin. According to
Jocz, "The awareness of sin dominates biblical man" (1968:95).

In struggling to understand the fact of man's inclination to
evil, Christians have generally concluded that since the fall of Adam
and Eve into sin, man's nature is basically sinful (Original Sin).
Muslims challenge this doctrine, insisting men are born with a clean
slate. They have control of their own destinies and the power to
choose good or evil. Faced with this denial, Christians often rush
to defend the doctrine of Original Sin at all costs. Unfortunately,
what is so easily lost sight of in the ensuing debate is that the
Christian faith does not stand or fall with this teaching. The doctrine of Original Sin is only an attempt to explain what Christians
-- on the basis of their experience and God's revelation -- see as an

important root cause of one of the most baffling mysteries of human existence, the problem of evil. No one denies that men inherit from their parents the colour of their skins, the size of their bodies, and the shape of their features. Is it really so preposterous, the Christian asks, to conclude that our human nature is also inherited from our parents? It is this nature which exhibits itself in our preoccupation with evil and our inclination towards evil rather than towards good. A typical Muslim point of view is that given by Jamali, "The individual in Islam is born pure and innocent, knowing nothing, and unable to distinguish between good and evil" (1965:71). See also Nasr (1966:24f). For valuable insight into the problem of talking about sin cross-culturally, see Smalley (1967:61-64).

83. Muslims commonly speak of the "Speech of God," which stands in a sort of contradistinction to the "Word of God." See al-Khatib (1971:93-98). It is the conviction of this author that we have not yet begun to explore the depths of meaning which come via this distinction. As Christians, our understanding of the Word is that it is "living and powerful" (Heb. 4:12), while for the Muslim it is a once-for-all-spoken Word, a command, a warning. See also Cragg (1956:64) and Schuon (1963:43-86). We should note, too, that as we dig deeper into the Bible in our search for "points of contact" with Muslims, we shall find our own faith deepening, and our admiration and awe for the Bible increasing. As Tippett testifies: "My contacts with Fijian and Indian brothers in Christ, whose value systems were different from mine, rather than syncretizing my religion, drove me deeper and deeper into the Scriptures, and opened to me non-Western perspectives that greatly blessed my soul. I discovered that the Bible was more than a Western book" (1972:131).

84. *Ajami*, more properly, *Aljami* -- the name given to the writing of the Hausa language in Arabic script. This was looked upon by many Muslims as a kind of corruption of the Arabic language, and actually means that in its original meaning. Since Arabic is a sacred language, any other language is a corruption. Since many Muslims in Ghana cannot understand Arabic, but can read the Arabic script, Ajami texts are much sought after in the Muslim communities. We have not yet begun to develop the communication potential of Ajami translations of the Scriptures.

85. See Wach (1968:85).

86. This idea of being one with God is very much a part of *Sufi* Islam. The *Sufis* are Muslim mystics, some of whose writings appear almost as Christian writings. A dominant theme in their literature is love. The Sufis have not had as wide and as deep an influence among West African Muslims as has been the case in parts of North Africa and East Africa. For useful background on the Sufis, see Nicholson (1914) and Shah (1971).

87. Because Christians have not always taken into consideration that God meets men where they are, many parts of Africa today live with the situation described by Idowu: "It was a serious mistake

that the Church took no account of the indigenous beliefs and customs
of Africa when she began her work of evangelization. It is now obvious that by a misguided purpose, a completely new God who had nothing to do with the past of Africa was introduced to her peoples. Thus,
there was no proper foundation laid for the Gospel message in the
hearts of the people and no bridge built between the old and the new;
the Church has in consequence been speaking to Africans in strange
tongues because there was no adequate communication" (1968:433).

CHAPTER 12: A DAY OF GOOD NEWS

88. This pattern of conversion comes from the real life experience of a personal friend of the author.

89. For reports and anlyses of the phenomenal church growth among
people of Muslim background in Indonesia, see McGavran (1969:256ff),
Simatupang (1969), and Thomson (1968).

90. Islam, too, uses "the Way" as an important concept. See p.
46f above.

91. Tracing the 1815 1914 "more extensive geographic spread than
ever before" of the Gospel, Latourette designates that period "the
Great Century" (1954;36-59). Winter describes 1945-1969 as "The
Twenty-Five Unbelievable Years" (1970a). Reflecting upon the vivid
evidences of God's working among and through his ambassadors during
those stirring times may stimulate us to be more faithfully obedient
to His "call to new adventure" (Neill 1964:574) in our own time,
actually praying for and expecting to see equally great demonstrations of response to the Gospel -- also from Muslims.

The "prayer and study cell" idea introduced by Yakubu and
Pius may work well on a community basis in their neighbourhood. In
other neighbourhoods such a pattern might function best along denominational lines. McGavran's contention is that God's obedient servant will make bold plans and only the testing of them will reveal
how workable they are (1970:360,368f). This buoyant way of looking
at the future in terms of an intensification of mission is quite different from that expressed by some writers, e.g. Watt, who calls for
a recognition of the "complementarity of the great religions," and
concludes that "missionary work as understood by European and American Christians in the nineteenth and early twentieth centuries is
no longer possible" (1969:117). Along a slightly different line,
but just as negative, Smith ventures, "I personally do not expect
many conversions from one tradition to another anywhere in the world
in the coming hundred years" (1963:12).

92. Barnett provides valuable insight into the whole process of
innovation. He notes that innovators "take, as their material, ideas
and ideas of ideas" from "the cultural inventory that is available"
to them (Barnett 1953:10,16). In practical terms, this means that
when a Muslim becomes a Christian, the cultural inventory from which
he draws his ideas is now both Muslim and Christian. Add to this

the influence of the Holy Spirit upon such an individual and the freedom he has in the Gospel and he becomes a potentially effective bridge
between the Gospel and his own people. Winter reminds us that Christianity "is by nature a faith that both welcomes and encourages cultural pluralism"(1973:258). Christianity will be enriched by what
Muslims can "baptize" from their cultures into the service of the
Lord Christ. Missiologists can profit immensely from studying Service's "Law of Evolutionary Potential" (1960:93-122; 1971:29-49). This
law states that "the more specialized and adapted a form in a given
evolutionary state, the smaller is its potential for passing to the
next stage." It operates alongside what Service calls "the principle
of Stabilization," which "occurs as an end product of adaptation."
Noting that "evolution means increasing adaptation to an environment,"
Service concludes that "it ultimately becomes nonprogressive."

     93. Still too often unheeded are Allen's pleas for recognizing
and working with the Spirit rather than controlling new church planting in such a way that the Holy Spirit's efforts are stifled. Allen's
works (1960, 1962a, 1962b) are worth reading and rereading. See also
McGavran (1955:134-136) as he deals with this question relative to
its importance for people movements.

     94. Tippett (1967:351f) and Pickett (1963:119) allude to the dif-
ficulties created for Christian witness by the problem of denominational jealousies. See also Marty (1964:41ff).

     95. For a full discussion of the "universal fog" which hinders a
proper assessment of whether churches are growing, or not, and why,
or why not, see McGavran (1970:67-82).

     96. Dretke (1968:79-83, 115), Levtzion (1968:xvi; 1969:309f), and
Rouch (1954:59-64) dispel the "fog" that the Northern Territories are
Muslim, while giving evidence that Northern migrants are becoming Muslim in the cities. Reeck's research among the Mende of Sierra Leone
calls into question the assertion "that major proportions of indigenous populations in forest areas in West Africa are in the process of
conversion from traditional religious practices and beliefs to Islam"
(1972:183). Even outside the forest areas, Islam has not swept all
before it, as is so often assumed (See Diamond 1967). What this means
for Christian missions is that many more people than a preliminary,
cursory, surface search might indicate are potentially open and re-
ceptive to the Gospel without the kind of communication difficulties
which would be involved were they to be Muslim. This does not mean
that there are no problems in communicating the Gospel to animists,
or to people who are partially islamized. It simply means that the
problems are of a different nature. A helpful concept in trying to
understand the degrees of Islam's penetration into various segments
of a given tribe, or area, is Steward's concept of levels of socio-
cultural integration (1955:43-77). Levtzion (1968) gives some excellent insight into the different levels of Islam which pertain among
the various tribes of the Middle Volta Basin, not only as to how Islam
affects each tribe as a whole, but also how it affects different families and communities within that tribe from the chief on down. The

fact that Islam is gaining adherents among Northerners in the South
continues to mark the various Muslim communities as immigrant, or
stranger, settlements. Cohen's study (1969) of Hausa migrants in
Ibadan pictures situations similar to those found in Ghana. Although
Ghana's North is far from being solidly Muslim, a similar situation
prevails as in the northern part of the Sudan where the strong Muslim
presence causes open criticism of Christian contributions toward meeting education and medical needs. As Daniel reports, "Both Catholics
and Protestants are suspected of exploiting education and hospital
services to influence the religious ideas of Moslems" (Daniel 1969:
210).

97. Greenway calls for "a constant reappraisal of missionary
strategy" in the light of the migration of the masses to the city.
"If the gears of missions are not shifted to keep up with social
change, God-given opportunities for discipling the nations will be
lost" (1972:227). Caldwell observed a "relatively large volume of
rural-urban migration" in Ghana (1969:206). This situation emphasizes the need for stronger mission efforts in the fast growing cities
but, as Tippett reminds us, this cannot be done at the expense of in-
tensive work at the village level (1967:352).

98. See Tippett (1967:100-118; 1972:125-143) and Wach (1968:152).
Much of what Tippett says relative to animism applies equally to
Islam. We have already noted that West African Islam has a strong
animistic base.

99. New Life For All, surfacing first in Northern Nigeria, is a
programme of congregational lay training and prayer which seeks to
equip the whole membership of the church for the task of evangelism.
Coleman's (1964) evangelism leadership training principles offer
promise of working well alongside NLFA principles. We have added a
sixth principle to those which are regularly given as the story of
new life for all.

100. The Reformation owes much of its initial impetus to Luther's
hunger and thirst for righteousness. When he discovered after anguished suffering and struggle (his *Anfechtung,* as he called it) that
God's righteousness is no longer a demand upon us, but a gift offered
freely to us, he actually became capable of pointing out to us the
essence of that Gospel which is now our privilege to share with our
Muslim friends. For a good exposition of Luther's concept of righteousness, see Arndt (1947).

101. According to Bishop, "What the world of Islam needs today
... is an explosion of friendliness -- the kind that was incontro-
vertible because of Jesus and those who spread discipleship around
the Mediterranean ... It was an untrammeled friendliness" (1965:356).
A young Kusasi pastor pointed out to the author the only two churches
in the South of Ghana in which he knew his people had a welcome were
the Presbyterian Church in Agogo and the Lutheran Church in Tema.
This is a sad commentary regarding the multitude of churches existing
in the South.

102. Welbourn and Ogot (1966) isolate this longing as one of the basic causes for the independent, spiritual church movement in Africa. A desire to serve that need deserves to fit into our church planting plans.

103. Bonhoeffer's "costly grace" concept (1973:45-60) and the total discipleship to which that grace calls and commits a person has practical repercussions in the kind of demands placed upon us when it comes to living our faith across cultural boundaries.

104. See Luther (1970:xvii, 309ff). Unfortunately, with all Luther's insight and writing, even the Lutheran churches have never fully freed themselves from the lingering clericalism that hangs as a pall over the spontaneous expansion of the church in so many areas of the world. Perhaps there is some hope for crawling out of this predicament. As Winter suggests, there is a "great amount of ferment ... today as every kind of organizational restructuring is under consideration in order to somehow free the sleeping giant of Christiandom for more effective mission" (1970b:33). See also Beyerhaus (1964: 119ff). Oosthuizen notes how Islam has been spread by laity without expensive organization (1968:19). Trimingham calls attention to how "the laicization of religious functions adds to its (Islam's) appeal" (1959:31).

105. Among those who have analyzed the lamentable situation which exists, coming forward with positive suggestions for improvement are Allen (1962a:105ff; 1962b:148f), Hastings (1967, 1971), and Sundkler (1960). See also Mbiti (1969:181-183).

106. For a helpful understanding of the Church and its mission in the light of the confusion regarding the "nature of the responsible Church in the mission field," see Beyerhaus (1964:107-134).

Glossary

NOTE ON BIBLE AND QURAN REFERENCES, ARABIC TRANSCRIPTION,

AND GLOSSARY OF TWI AND HAUSA WORDS

Bible passages are quoted from the Revised Standard Version, unless indicated otherwise. A few passages are quoted from the King James Version, New English Bible, Jerusalem Bible and Living Bible.

The quranic passages are taken from Arberry's *The Koran Interpreted* (1955), except for the passages in Chapter 6. These are taken from *The Holy Quran* translated by A. Yusuf Ali. The copious notes and commentary which accompany English translations of A. Yusuf Ali (1946), and that published by Mahmud Ahmad (1947) are extremely valuable for the student of Islam. A. Yusuf Ali and Asad represent Orthodox (Sunni) Islam, while Muhammad Ali and Mahmud Ahmad represent the Ahmadiyya.

Many Christians are puzzled by the spelling variations which appear in English texts: Mohammed vs. Muhammad, Moslem vs. Muslim, and Koran vs. Quran. The first word of each combination is perhaps more popular in common usage; the second represents an attempt at a more exact transliteration of the Arabic. The latter appears as standard in learned journals like *The Muslim World*, and we have chosen to follow that pattern in this book. Unlike practice in *The Muslim World*, however, diacritical marks have been omitted from the text since they are meaningless to English readers who have no background in Arabic. For those who benefit from such, the following list of words is included:

Arabic	*Meaning*
'Abd	slave
Ahmadiyya	followers of Ahmad
Allāh	God
Ayat	verse
Bismillāh	In the Name of God
Dār	country
Du'ā	intercessory prayer
Fātiha	opening

Arabic	*Meaning*
Fikh (or fiqh)	jurisprudence, law
Hadīth	tradition
Ḥajj	pilgrimage
Halāl	lawful
Ḥarām	forbidden
Ḥarb	war
'Ijmā'	concensus
Ijtihād	systematic original thinking
Imām	prayer leader
Injīl	Gospel
'Īsā	Jesus
'Islām	submission
Jihād	holy war
Kāfir	unbeliever
al-Kānamī	Nineteenth century king of Kanem-Bornu
Mahdī	deliverer
Muḥammad	Muhammad
Nabī	Prophet
Nisā'a	women
Qādī	judge
Qiyās	analogical reasoning
Qur'ān	Quran
Rahmān	merciful
Ramadān	month of fasting
Salāt	prayer
Ṣawm	fasting
Shahāda	confession of faith
Sharī'a	law
Sūfī	Muslim mystic
Sūra	chapter of the Quran
Tarīqa	history, Way
Ṭawrāt	Law of Moses
'Ulamā'	religious teachers
Umma	community of believers
Uthmān Ibn Fūdī	Uthman dan Fodio
Zakāt	alms

Akan	*Meaning*
Agoo!	May I enter?
Amee!	Come in.
Akwaba	Welcome
Ananse	Spider. Ananse is the hero and the villain in Akan folk tales.
Asempa	Good news
Asuafo	learner, disciple
Kente	a special woven cloth
Nyame, Onyame	God
Onyankopong	God

Hausa	*Meaning*
Duniya	World
Malam	Muslim teacher (a corruption of the Arabic *mu'allim*)
Riga	gown, robe
Sunana	my name
Zongo	Stranger's quarters. The word is *zango* in Nigerian Hausa. In Ghana the name is applied to sections of a town where Muslims live.

Bibliography

For useful bibliographies on Islam, Islam and Christianity in Africa, and Christian communication, interaction, and relationships with non-Christians, see G. Anderson (1961:315-336), Cragg (1956:359-367; 1959;155-160), Debrunner (1967:361-368), Gibb (1953:193-201), Guillaume (1954:203-206), King (1971:114-143), Levtzion (1968:204-215), Rahman (1968:323-326), and Vander Werff (351-366).

AHMAD, Mahmud
    1947   *The Holy Quran*, Vol. 1.   Qadian, India: Sadr Anjuman
           Ahmadiyya.
AL-FARUQI, Ismail Ragi A.
    1968   "Islam and Christianity: Diatribe or Dialogue," *Journal of*
           Ecumenical Studies, Vol. 5, No. 1, pp. 45-77.
ALI, A. Yusuf
    1946   *The Holy Quran*, Vol. 1, 2.   Cambridge, Massachusetts: Hafner.
ALI, Muhammad
    N.d.   *A Manual of Hadith*.   Lahore: M. Dost Mohammad, Ahmadiyya
           Building.
    1935   *The Holy Quran*.   Lahore: Ahmadiyya Anjuman-I-Ishaat-I-Islam.
    1950   *The Religion of Islam*.   Lahore: M. Dost Mohammad, Ahmadiyya
           Building (First printed, 1936).
AL-KHATIB, Abd Al-karim
    1971   "Christ in the Quran, the Taurat, and the Injil," *Muslim*
           World, Vol. LXI, No. 2, pp. 90-101.   Hartford.
ALL AFRICA CONFERENCE OF CHURCHES
    1969   *Engagement*   (Abidjan, 1969).   Nairobi: All Africa Confer-
           ence of Churches.
ALLEN, Geoffrey
    1943   *The Theology of Missions*.   London: SCM Press.
ALLEN, Roland
    1960   *The Ministry of the Spirit*.   Grand Rapids, Michigan: Eerdmans.
    1962a *Missionary Methods: St. Paul's or Ours?* Grand Rapids: Eerdmans.
    1962b *The Spontaneous Expansion of the Church*. Grand Rapids: Eerdmans.
ANDERSON, Gerald (ed)
    1961   *The Theology of the Christian Mission*. New York: McGraw-Hill.
ANDERSON, J.N.D.
    1970   *Christianity and Comparative Religion*.   London: Tyndale Press.

ANDRAE, Tor
    1935 *Mohammed, The Man and His Faith*   (Translated by Theophil
          Menzel). New York: Barnes and Noble, Inc.
ARBERRY, A.J.
    1955 *The Koran Interpreted.* New York: Macmillan.
    1964 *Aspects of Islamic Culture.* London: Allen and Unwin.
ARNDT, William
    1947 "The Doctrine of Justification" in Th. Laetsch (ed), Vol. 2.
ASAD, Muhammad
    1946 *The Message of the Quran.* Mecca: Muslim World League.
AZZAM, Abd Ar-Rahman
    1964 *The Eternal Message of Muhammad* (Translated by Caesar E.
          Farah). New York: Devin-Adair Co.
BAETA, C.G.
    1961 "Conflict in Mission: Historical and Separatist Churches" in
          Gerald Anderson (ed).
    1962 *Prophetism in Ghana: a Study of Some 'Spiritual' Churches.*
          London: Student Christian Movement Press.
BAETA, C.G. (ed)
    1968 *Christianity in Tropical Africa.* London: Oxford U. Press.
BARNETT, H.G.
    1953 *Innovation: The Basis of Cultural Change.* New York: McGraw-
          Hill.
BARRETT, David
    1968 *Schism and Renewal in Africa.* Nairobi: Oxford U. Press.
    1971 *African Initiatives in Religion.* Nairobi: East African
          Publishing House.
BARTH, Karl
    1936 *The Doctrine of the Word of God* (Translated by G.T. Thomson).
          Edinburgh: T. & T. Clark.
BASETTI-SANI, Giulio
    1967 "For a Dialogue Between Christians and Muslims," *Muslim World,*
          Vol. LVII, No. 2, pp. 126-137; No. 3, pp. 186-196, Hartford.
BAVINCK, J.H.
    1948 *The Impact of Christianity on the Non-Christian World.* Grand
          Rapids: Eerdmans.
    1960 *An Introduction to the Science of Mission* (Translated by David
          H. Freeman). Philadelphia: Presbyterian and Reformed Pub-
          lishing Co.
    1968 *The Church Between Temple and Mosque.* Grand Rapids: Eerdmans.
BAWANY, Ebrahim Ahmed
    1961 *Islam -- Our Choice.* Karachi, Pakistan: Begun Aisha Bawany
          Wakf.
BEAVER, R. Pierce
    1961 "The Apostolate of the Church" in Gerald Anderson (ed).
    1968 *The Missionary Between the Times.* Garden City, New York:
          Doubleday.
    1973 *The Gospel and Frontier Peoples.* South Pasadena: William
          Carey Library.
BERDYAEV, Nicolas
    1935 *Freedom and the Spirit.* New York: Chas. Scribner's Sons.
BEYERHAUS, Peter, and LEFEVER, Henry
    1964 *The Responsible Church and the Foreign Mission.* Grand Rapids:
          Eerdmans.

BIJLEFELD, Wm. A.
1959 *De Islam als na-christelijke religie.* The Hague.
1967 "The Danger of 'Christianizing' our Partners in the Dialogue," *Muslim World,* Vol. LVII, No. 3.
BISHOP, Eric F.F.
1965 "The Reasonableness of Christ," *Muslim World,* Vol. LV, pp. 346-356, Hartford.
BLACKMAN, E.C.
1950 "Truth," in Alan Richardson (ed).
BOMFORD, T.
1911 "The Right Angle of Approach," *Muslim World,* July, 1911. Hartford.
BONHOEFFER, Dietrich
1973 *The Cost of Discipleship.* New York: Macmillan.
BRADNOCK, Wilfred J.
1953 "On the Use of the Name 'Isa," *The Bible Translator,* Vol. 4, No. 1. London: United Bible Societies.
BRAIMAH, J.A., and GOODY, J.
1967 *Salaga, the Struggle for Power.* Oxford: University Press.
BRELVI, M.
1964 *Islam in Africa.* Lahore: Institute of Islamic Culture.
1965 *Islam and Its Contemporary Faiths.* Karachi: Technical Printers.
BRIGHT, John
1953 *The Kingdom of God.* New York: Abingdon Press.
BROWN, Ralph E.
1971 "How Dialogue Can be Used to Witness to Muslims," *Evangelical Missions Quarterly,* VII, No. 2, pp. 65-78.
BUTTRICK, George Arthur
1962 *The Interpreter's Dictionary of the Bible.* New York: Abingdon.
CALDWELL, J.
1969 *African Rural-Urban Migration.* London: C. Hurst.
CHARLES, R.H.
1913 *Studies in the Apocalypse.* Edinburgh: T. & T. Clark
CHARNEY, Jean-Paul
1971 *Islamic Culture and Socio-Economic Change.* Leiden: E.J. Brill.
CHOWDHURY, D.A.
1953 "Should We Use the Terms 'Isa' and 'Beta'?" *The Bible Translators,* Vol. 4, No. 1. London: United Bible Societies.
COHEN, Abner
1969 *Custom and Politics in Urban Africa.* Los Angeles, University of California Press.
COLEMAN, Robert E.
1964 *The Master Plan of Evangelism.* Old Tappan, New Jersey: Fleming H. Revell Co.
COOKSEY, J.J. and McLEISH, Alexander
1931 *Religion and Civilization in West Africa.* London: World Dominion Press.
COPELAND, E. Luther
1971 "Christian Dialogue With Major World Religions," *Review and Expositor,* Vol. LXVIII, No. 1, pp. 53-64.
CORBON, Jean
1965 "Islam and Christianity, Impasse or Hope of Dialogue?" *Student World,* Vol. 58, No. 1, pp. 68-74. Geneva: World Student Christian Federation.

CRAGG, Kenneth
  1956   *The Call of the Minaret.* London: Oxford U. Press.
  1959   *Sandals at the Mosque* New York: Oxford U. Press.
  1964   *The Dome and the Rock.* London: S.P.C.K.
  1965   "Ahmadiyya," *Counsels in Contemporary Islam*(Islamic Surveys,
         3), Edinburgh: University Press.
  1968   *Christianity in World Perspective.* New York: Oxford U. Press.
  1969   *The House of Islam.* Belmont, California: Dickenson Publish-
         ing Co.
  1971   *The Event of the Quran.* London: George Allen & Unwin.
  1973   *The Mind of the Quran.* London: George Allen & Unwin.
CURTIN, Phillip D.
  1964   *The Image of Africa.* Madison: University of Wisconsin Press.
DAMBORIENA, Prudencio
  1971   "Aspects of the Missionary Crisis in Roman Catholicism" in
         Wm. J. Danker and Wi Jo Kang (eds).
DANIEL, Norman
  1960   *Islam and the West.* Edinburgh: University Press.
  1969   "The Sudan," in James Kritzeck and Wm. H. Lewis (eds).
DANKER, Wm. J., and KANG, Wi Jo (eds)
  1971   *The Future of the Christian World Mission.* Grand Rapids:
         Eerdmans.
DANQUAH, J.B.
  1968   *The Akan Doctrine of God.* London: Frank Cass and Co.
DEBRUNNER, Hans W.
  1967   *A History of Christianity in Ghana.* Accra: Waterville
         Publishing House.
DIAMOND, Stanley
  1967   "The Anaguta of Nigeria: Suburban Primitives," in Julian H.
         Steward (ed).
DICKSON, Kwesi A. and ELLINGWORTH, Paul (eds)
  1969   *Biblical Revelation and African Beliefs.* London: Lutterworth.
DODD, C.H.
  1953   *The Interpretation of the Fourth Gospel.* Cambridge: Univer-
         sity Press.
DRETKE, James
  1968   "The Muslim Community in Accra, A Historical Survey," An un-
         published M.A. thesis, University of Ghana, Legon.
DRUMMOND, Bill
  1978   "Black Muslims' Leader Resigns," *Los Angeles Times,* Part I,
         Sept. 12, 1978, pp. 1,13.
ELDER, E.E.
  1923   "The Crucifixion in the Koran," *Muslim World,* Vol. III, July,
         1923, pp. 242-258. Hartford.
ELERT, Werner
  1967   *Law and Gospel* (Translated by Edward H. Shroeder). Philadel-
         phia: Fortress.
EPSTEIN, I.
  1962   "Talmud," in George A. Buttrick (ed).
ESTES, Joseph R.
  1971   "Jewish-Christian Dialogue as Mission," *Review and Expositor,*
         Vol. LXVIII. Louisville, Kentucky: So. Baptist Theological
         Seminary, pp. 5-16.

FARAH, Caesar E.
1968 *Islam*. New York: Woodbury.
FISHER, Humphrey J.
1963 *Ahmadiyyah*. Oxford: University Press.
1969 "Separatism in West Africa," in James Kritzeck and Wm. H. Lewis (eds).
GAMALIEL, James
1974 "The Evangelical Stance Toward Non-Christian Religions." An unpublished D. Miss. dissertation, Fuller Seminary, Pasadena, California.
GENSICHEN, Hans-Werner
1971 "Dialogue with Non-Christian Religions," in Wm. J. Danker and Wi Jo Kang (eds).
GHANA
1964 *1960 Population Census*, Vol. III, Special Report "E."
GIBB, H.A.R.
1953 *Muhammadanism*. London: Oxford University Press.
GLASSER, Arthur F.
1971 "Mission and Cultural Environment," *Towards A Theology for The Future*. Clark H. Pinnock and David F. Wells (eds). Carol Stream, Illinois: Creation House.
GLUBB, John Bagot
1970 *The Life and Times of Muhammad*. London: Hodder and Stoughton.
GREEN, Bryan
1951 *The Practice of Evangelism*. New York: Charles Scribner's.
GREELEY, Andrew
1974 "What It Means to be Faithful," *Faith at Work*, Vol. LXXXVII, No. 3, April, 1967. Colombia, Maryland: Word, Inc.
GREENWAY, Roger S.
1972 "Urbanization and Missions," in Donald McGavran (ed).
GUILLAUME, A.
1954 *Islam*. London: Penguin Books.
HABIB, Gabriel
1969 "Possibilities of Christian-Moslem Dialogue," *Christian Century*, January, 1969, p. 111.
HADDAD, Robert M.
1970 *Syrian Christians in Muslim Society*. Princeton: University Press.
HALLENCREUTZ, Carl F.
1970 *New Approaches to Men of Other Faiths*. World Council of Churches, Research Pamphlet, No. 18, Geneva: W.C.C.
HASTINGS, Adrian
1964 *The World Mission of the Church*. London: Darton, Longman & Todd.
1967 *Church and Mission in Modern Africa*. London: Burns & Oates.
1971 *Mission and Ministry*. London: Sheed & Ward.
HILLMAN, Eugene
1973 "Pluriformity in Ethics: A Modern Missionary Problem," in R. Pierce Beaver (ed).
HODGKIN, Thomas
1960 *Nigerian Perspectives*. London: Oxford University Press.
1966 "The Islamic Literary Tradition in Ghana," in I.M. Lewis (ed).

HOFFMAN, Ronan
    1968   "Conversion and the Mission of the Church," *Journal of
           Ecumenical Studies*, Vol. 5, pp. 1-20. Philadelphia: Temple
           University.
HOGG, Wm. Richey
    1952   *Ecumenical Foundations*. New York: Harper & Brothers.
HOLWAY, James D.
    1971   "Islam and Christianity in East Africa," in David B. Barrett
           (ed).
HOROVITZ, Joseph
    1964   *Jewish Proper Names and Derivatives in the Koran*. Hildesheim:
           Georg Olms.
HUSSEIN, M. Kamel
    1959   *City of Wrong*. London: Geoffrey Bles.
IDOWU, E. Bolaji
    1968   "The Predicament of the Church in Africa," in C.G. Baeta (ed).
    1969   "Introduction." "God," in Kwesi A. Dickson and Paul
           Ellingworth (eds).
JAMALI, Mohammad Fadhel
    1965   *Letters on Islam*. London: Oxford University Press.
JEFFERY, Arthur (ed)
    1958   *Islam, Muhammad and His Religion*. New York: The Liberal Arts
           Press.
    1962   *A Reader On Islam*. 'S-Gravenhage: Mouton & Co.
JOCZ, Jacob
    1968   *The Covenant*. Grand Rapids: Eerdmans.
JONES, L. Bevan
    1953   "On the Use of the Name 'Isa'," *The Bible Translator*, Vol. 4,
           No. 1, pp. 83-86. London: United Bible Societies.
KING, Noel Q.
    1971   *Christian and Muslim in Africa*. New York: Harper & Row.
KITIGAWA, Joseph M.
    1962   "Other Religions," in Ralph C. Raughley, Jr. (ed).
KRAEMER, Hendrik
    1938   *The Christian Message in a Non-Christian World*. New York:
           Harper & Brothers.
    1956   *Religion and the Christian Faith*. London: Lutterworth Press.
    1965   *Why Christianity of All Religions* (Translated by Hubert
           Hoskins). Philadelphia: Westminster Press.
KRAFT, Charles H.
    1973   "Church Planters and Ethnolinguistics," in A.R. Tippett (ed),
           God, Man and Church Growth. Grand Rapids: Eerdmans.
KRASS, Alfred C.
    1969   "A Case Study in Effective Evangelism in West Africa," Sept.
           1967, pp. 244-247. "More on the Chokosi People Movement,"
           July, 1969, pp. 375f. *Church Growth Bulletin*, Vol. I-V, Donald
           A. McGavran (ed). South Pasadena: William Carey Library.
    1973   "The Mission of the Evangelical Presbyterian Church of Ghana
           to the Chokosi People," in R. Pierce Beaver (ed).
KRETZMANN, Martin L.
    1965   "The Church in Africa and the African Churches" in *Addis
           Ababa* (The Third All-Africa Lutheran Conference). Geneva:
           Lutheran World Federation.

KRITZECK, James, and WINDER, R. Bayly (eds)
  1959 *The World of Islam.* New York: Macmillan.
KRITZECK, James
  1964 *Peter the Venerable and Islam.* Princeton: University Press.
  1965 *Sons of Abraham, Jews, Christians, and Moslems.* Baltimore:
    Helicon.
KRITZECK, James, and LEWIS, Wm. H. (eds)
  1969 *Islam in Africa.* New York: Van Nostrand-Reinhold Co.
KUNNETH, Walter
  1965 *The Theology of the Resurrection.* St. Louis: Concordia
    (First published in German, 1951).
LAETSCH, Theodore (ed)
  1947 *The Abiding Word,* Vol. 1-2. St. Louis: Concordia.
LATOURETTE, Kenneth Scott
  1954 *The Christian World Mission in Our Day.* New York: Harper &
    Brothers.
LEVONIAN, Lootfy
  1940 *Islam and Christianity.* London: George Allen & Unwin.
LEVTZION, Nehemia
  1968 *Muslims and Chiefs in West Africa.* London: Oxford U. Press.
  1969 "Coastal West Africa," in James Kritzeck and Wm. H. Lewis
    (eds).
LEWIS, T.M. (ed)
  1966 *Islam in Tropical Africa.* London: Oxford U. Press.
LEWIS, W.H.
  1969 "Nationalism and Modernism," in James Kritzeck and Wm. H.
    Lewis (eds).
LINCOLN, C. Eric
  1961 *The Black Muslims in America.* Boston: Beacon Press.
LITTLE, Malcolm
  1965 *The Autobiography of Malcolm X* (Assistance of Alex Harley).
    New York: Grove Press.
LOEWENTHAL, Isidor
  1911 "The Name 'Isa'," *Muslim World,* July, 1911, pp. 267-282.
    Hartford.
LUTHER, Martin
  1960 *Luther's Works.* American Edition. Vol. 35. E. Theodore
    Bachman (ed); Helmut T. Lehmann (Gen. ed). Philadelphia:
    Muhlenberg Press.
  1970 *Luther's Works.* Vol. 39. E.W. Gritsch (ed); Helmut T.
    Lehman (Gen. ed). Philadelphia: Fortress Press.
MANNERS, Robert A. & KAPLAN, David
  1968 *Theory in Anthropology.* Chicago: Aldine Publishing Co.
MARTY, Martin E.
  1964 *Church Unity and Church Mission.* Grand Rapids: Eerdmans.
MAURIER, Henri
  1968 *The Other Covenant, A Theology of Paganism* (Translated by
    Charles McGrath). New York: Newman Press.
MBITI, John S.
  1968 "The Ways and Means of Communicating the Gospel," in C.G.
    Baeta (ed).
  1969 "Eschatology," in Kwesi A. Dickson and Paul Ellingworth (eds).

1970 *African Religions and Philosophy.* Garden City, N.Y.: Double-
      day & Co. (Originally published in 1969 by Praeger Publishers).
1971 "New Testament Eschatology and the Akamba of Kenya" in David
      B. Barrett (ed).
1972 "Christianity and Traditional Religions in Africa," in Donald
      McGavran (ed).
McGAVRAN, Donald A.
1955 *The Bridges of God.* New York: Friendship Press.
1969 "Comment" (On the Chokosi People Movement, Sept., 1967: 247-
      250). *Church Growth Bulletin,* Vol. I-V. Donald McGavran (ed).
      South Pasadena: William Carey Library.
1970 *Understanding Church Growth.* Grand Rapids: Eerdmans.
1972 *Crucial Issues in Missions Tomorrow.* Chicago: Moody Press.
MOLTMANN, Jurgen
1970 "Theology as Eschatology." "Towards the Next Step in the
      Dialogue," in Frederick Herzog (ed), *The Future of Hope.*
      New York: Herder & Herder, Inc.
MUELLER, John Theodore
1934 *Christian Dogmatics.* St. Louis: Concordia.
MYRDAL, Gunnar
1957 *Rich Lands and Poor.* New York: Harper and Row.
NASR, Seyyed Hossein
1966 *Ideals and Realities of Islam.* London: George Allen & Unwin.
NEILL, Stephen
1964 *A History of Christian Missions.* Middlesex, England:
      Penguin Books, Ltd.
1970 *Christian Faith and Other Faiths.* London: Oxford Press.
1971 "Syncretism and Missionary Philosophy Today," *Review and
      Expositor,* Vol. LXVIII, No. 1, pp. 65-80. Louisville, Kentucky:
      Southern Baptist Theological Seminary.
NEWBIGIN, Leslie
1969 *The Finality of Christ.* Richmond, Virginia: John Knox Press.
NEWPORT, John P.
1971 "Secularization, Secularism, and Christianity," *Review and
      Expositor,* Vol. LXVIII, No. 1, pp. 81-93. Louisville, Kentucky:
      Southern Baptist Theological Seminary.
NICHOLSON, Reynold A.
1914 *The Mystics of Islam.* London: G. Bell and Sons.
NIEBUHR. H. Richard
1951 *Christ and Culture.* New York: Harper and Row.
NIEBUHR, Reinhold
1941 *The Nature and Destiny of Man.* New York: Scribner's Sons.
NILES, Daniel T.
1959 *The Preacher's Calling To Be Servant.* London: Lutterworth.
NISSIOTIS, Nikos A.
1965 "Our History: a Limitation or a Creative Power?" *Student
      World,* Vol. LVIII, pp. 33-43. Geneva: World Christian Stu-
      dent Federation.
NKETIA, J.H.
1958 "The Contribution of African Culture to Christian Worship,"
      The Church in Changing Africa. New York: International
      Missionary Council.

NOLIN, Kenneth
    1965 "Truth: Christian -- Muslim," *Muslim World*, Vol. LV, July
          1965, pp. 237-245. Hartford.
    1967 "A Theological Base for Dialogue with Muslims," in Herbert
          Jai Singh (ed), *Inter-Religious Dialogue*. Bangalore: Chris-
          tian Institute for the Study of Religion and Society.
    1969 "Al-Masih fi'l-Quran w'l-Tawrat w'l-Injil" (A Book Review),
          Muslim World, Vol. LIX, No. 1, 1969, pp. 74-79. Hartford.
NYGREN, Anders
    1953 *Agape and Eros* (Translated by Philip S. Watson). Philadelphia:
          Westminster Press.
O'NEILL, Nena and George
    1972 *Open Marriage*. New York: M. Evans and Co.
OOSTHUIZEN, G.C.
    1968 *Post-Christianity in Africa*. Grand Rapids: Eerdmans.
PADEN, John N.
    1973 *Religion and Political Culture in Kano*. Los Angeles: Univer-
          sity of California Press.
PALMER, H.H.
    1962 "Truth." *New Bible Dictionary*, J.D. Douglas (ed). Grand
          Rapids: Eerdmans.
PARRINDER, Geoffrey
    1965 *Jesus in the Quran*. London: Faber and Faber.
PATAI, Raphael
    1967 *Golden River to Golden Road*. Philadelphia: University of
          Pensylvania Press.
    1973 *The Arab Mind*. New York: Charles Scribner's Sons.
PERRY, Edmund
    1958 *The Gospel in Dispute*. Garden City, N.Y.: Doubleday.
PICKETT, J. Waskom
    1963 *The Dynamics of Church Growth*. New York: Abingdon Press.
PIEPER, Francis
    1950 *Christian Dogmatics*, Vol. 1-2. St. Louis: Concordia.
PLASS, Ewald M.
    1959 *What Luther Says*, Vol. 1. St. Louis: Concordia.
QURESHI, Ishtiaq Husain
    1964 "Introduction," in Mahmud Brelvi.
RAHBAR, Daud
    1965 "Christian Apologetic to Muslims," *International Review of
          Missions*, Vol. LIV, July, 1965, pp. 353-359. Geneva: W.C.C.
RAHMAN, Fazlur
    1968 *Islam*. New York: (Anchor) Doubleday (Originally published
          by Holt, Rinehart and Winston in 1966).
RATTRAY, R. Sutherland
    1969 *Hausa Folk-Lore, Customs, Proverbs, Etc.* Vol. II. New York:
          Negro Universities Press.
RAUGHLEY, Ralph C. Jr. (ed)
    1962 *New Frontiers of Christianity*. New York: Association Press.
REECK, Darrell L.
    1972 "Islam in a West African Chiefdom," *Muslim World*, Vol. LXII,
          No. 3, Hartford.
REYBURN, William D.
    1967 "The Transformation of God and the Conversion of Man," in
          Wm. A. Smalley (ed).

RICHARDSON, Alan (ed)
    1950 *A Theological Word Book of the Bible*. New York: MacMillan.
ROUCH, Jean
    1954 *Notes on Migrations into the Gold Coast* (Translated into
          English by P.E.O. and J.B. Heigham). Paris.
SAMARTHA, S.J.
    1970 "More Than an Encounter of Commitments," *International Review
          of Missions*, Vol. LIX, 236, pp. 392-403, Geneva: W.C.C.
SARPONG, Peter
    1973 "The Worship Life of the Church." Unpublished paper presented
          at "Conference on the Mission of the Church in Ghana Today,"
          Jan. 9-16, 1973, Kumasi, Ghana.
SCHILDKNECHT, Franz
    1969 "Tanzania," in James Kritzeck and Wm. H. Lewis (eds).
SCHUON, Frithjof
    1963 *Understanding Islam* (Translated by D.M. Matheson). New York:
          Roy Publishers.
    1970 *Dimensions of Islam* (Translated by P.N. Townsend). London:
          George Allen & Unwin.
SERVICE, Elman R., and SAHLINS, Marshall D. (eds)
    1960 *Evolution and Culture*. Ann Arbor: The University of Michigan
          Press.
SERVICE, Elman R.
    1971 *Cultural Evolutionism*. New York: Holt, Rinehart and Winston.
SETILOANE, G.M.
    1969 "I Am An African," *International Review of Missions*, Vol.
          LVIII, April 1969, pp. 204-207. Geneva: W.C.C.
SHAH, Idries
    1971 *The Sufis*. Garden City, New York: (Anchor) Doubleday.
SHEARER, Roy E.
    1966 *Wildfire: Church Growth in Korea*. Grand Rapids: Eerdmans.
SIMATUPANG, T.B.
    1969 "The Situation and Challenge of the Christian Mission in
          Indonesia Today," *South East Asia Journal of Theology*,
          Vol. 10, No. 4. Singapore.
SMALLEY, W.A. (ed)
    1967 *Readings in Missionary Anthropology*. Tarrytown, N.Y.:
          Practical Anthropology.
SMITH, M.G.
    1966 "The Jihad of Shehu Dan Fodio: Some Problems," in I.M.
          Lewis (ed).
SMITH, Wilfred Cantwell
    1959 "Comparative Religion: Whither and Why," in Mircea Eliade
          and Joseph M. Kitagawa (eds), *The History of Religions*.
          Chicago: University of Chicago Press.
    1960 "Some Similarities and Differences Between Christianity and
          Islam: An Essay in Comparative Religion," in James Kritzeck
          and R. Bayly Winder (eds).
    1963 *The Faith of Other Men*. New York: New American Library.
    1964 *The Meaning and End of Religion*. New York: (Mentor) The New
          American Library (First published in 1962).

SPEIGHT, R. Marston
  1965 "Some Bases for a Christian Apologetic to Islam," *International Review of Missions,* Vol. LIV, April, 1965, pp. 193-205. Geneva: W.C.C.
STEWARD, Julian H.
  1950 *Area Research.* New York: Social Science Research Council, Bulletin 63.
  1955 *Theory of Culture Change.* Urbana: University of Illinois.
  1967 *Contemporary Change in Traditional Societies,* Vol. 1. Urbana: University of Illinois Press.
STRACHAN, R.H.
  1935 *The Second Epistle of Paul to the Corinthians.* London: Hodder and Stoughton.
SUNDKLER, Bengt
  1960 *The Christian Ministry in Africa.* London: S.C.M. Press Ltd.
TAPPERT, Theodore
  1959 *The Book of Concord.* Philadelphia: Muhlenberg Press.
TAYLOR, John V.
  1963 *The Primal Vision.* London: S.C.M. Press.
TAYLOR, Vincent
  1962 *The Names of Jesus.* London: MacMillan.
TENNEY, Merrill C.
  1963 *The Reality of the Resurrection.* New York: Harper & Row.
THOMAS, Owen C., (ed)
  1969 *Attitudes Toward Other Religions.* New York: Harper & Row.
THOMSON, Alan
  1968 "The Churches of Java in the Aftermath of the Thirtieth of September Movement," *South East Asia Journal of Theology,* Vol. 9, No. 3. Singapore.
TILLICH, Paul
  1963 *Christianity and the Encounter of the World Religions.* New York: Columbia University Press.
TIPPETT, Alan R.
  1967 *Solomon Islands Christianity.* London: Lutterworth Press.
  1969 "Vatican II and Church Growth," *Church Growth Bulletin,* Vols. I-V, pp. 219-221. South Pasadena: William Carey Library.
  1970 *Church Growth and the Word of God.* Grand Rapids: Eerdmans.
  1972 "Possessing the Philosophy of Animism for Christ," in Donald McGavran (ed).
TOYNBEE, Arnold Joseph
  1956 *An Historian's Approach to Religion.* New York: Oxford U. Press.
  1957 *Christianity Among the Religions of the World.* New York: Scribner's.
TRIMINGHAM, J. Spencer
  1952 *Islam in Ethiopia.* London: Oxford U. Press.
  1955 *The Christian Church and Islam in West Africa.* I.M.C. Research Pamphlet No. 3, London: S.C.M. Press.
  1959 *Islam in West Africa.* Oxford: Clarendon Press.
  1962a *Islam in East Africa.* I.M.C. Research Pamphlet, No. 9. Edinburgh: Edinburgh House Press.
  1962b *A History of Islam in West Africa.* London: Oxford U. Press.
  1968 *The Influence of Islam Upon Africa.* New York: Frederick A. Praeger.

TURNER, H.W.
  1967 *African Independent Church*. London: Oxford U. Press.
VAN LEEUWEN, Arend Th.
  1964 *Christianity in World History*. New York: Scribner's.
VANDER WERFF, Lyle L.
  1977 *Christian Mission to Muslims*. South Pasadena: William
        Carey Library.
VERGHESE, P.
  1965 "The Newness of Our Christian Faith," *Student World*, Vol.
        LVIII, pp. 23-32. Geneva: World Student Christian Federation.
VON GRUNEBAUM, Gustave E.
  1953 *Medieval Islam*. Chicago: University of Chicago Press.
WACH, Joachim
  1968 *Understanding and Believing*. Kitagawa, Joseph M. (ed).
        New York: Harper and Row.
WALTHER, C.F.W.
  1929 *The Proper Distinction Between Law and Gospel*. Reproduced
        from the German edition of 1897 by W.H.T. Dau. St. Louis:
        Concordia.
WATT, W. Montgomery
  1953 *Muhammad at Mecca*. Oxford: Clarendon Press.
  1961a *Islam and the Integration of Society*. Evanston, Illinois:
        Northwestern University Press.
  1961b *Muhammad Prophet and Statesman*. London: Oxford U. Press.
  1962a *Islamic Philosophy and Theology*. Edinburgh: University Press.
  1962b *Muhammad at Medina*. Oxford: Clarendon Press.
  1963 *Truth in the Religions*. Edinburgh: University Press.
  1967a "Thoughts on Muslim-Christian Dialogue," *Muslim World*, Vol.
        LVII, No. I, pp. 19-23. Hartford.
  1967b "The Christianity Criticized in the Quran," *Muslim World*,
        Vol. LVII, No. 2, pp. 197-201. Hartford.
  1968 *What Is Islam*. London: Longmans, Green & Co.
  1969 *Islamic Revelation in the Modern World*. Edinburgh: Univer-
        sity Press.
WELBOURN, F.B. and OGOT, B.A.
  1966 *A Place to Feel At Home*. London: Oxford.
WEMAN, Henry
  1960 *African Music and the Church in Africa*. Uppsala: Uppsala
        Universitets Arrskrift 1960: 3, ab Lundequistska Bokhandeln.
WENSINCK, A.J.
  1965 *The Muslim Creed*. London: Frank Cass & Co.
WENTE, W.H.
  1947 "Conversion," in Th. Laetsch (ed), Vol. 1.
WENTZ, Abdel Ross
  1953 "Luther and His Methods of Translating," *The Bible Transla-
        tor*, Vol. 4, No. 1. London: United Bible Societies.
WILKS, Ivor
  1961 *The Northern Factor in Ashanti*. Legon, Ghana: University of
        Ghana.
  1966 "The Position of Muslims in Metropolitan Ashanti," in I.M.
        Lewis (ed).
WILLIAMS, John Alden, (ed)
  1971 *Themes of Islamic Civilization*. Berkeley: University of Cali-
        fornia Press.

WILSON, J. Christy
    1959 *Introducing Islam.* New York: Friendship Press.
WINTER, Ralph D.
    1970a *The Twenty-Five Unbelievable Years.* South Pasadena:
        William Carey Library.
    1973 "Christian History in Cross Cultural Perspective," in A.R.
        Tippett (ed), *God, Man and Church Growth.* Grand Rapids:
        Eerdmans.
WINTER, Ralph D., and BEAVER, R. Pierce
    1970b *The Warp and the Woof.* South Pasadena: William Carey Library.
WOLD, Joseph Conrad
    1968 *God's Impatience in Liberia.* Grand Rapids: Eerdmans.
WOLF, Eric R.
    1964 "Santa Claus: Notes on a Collective Representation," in
        Robert A. Manners (ed), *Process and Pattern in Culture.*
        Chicago: Aldine.
ZURICH Consultation
    1970 "Christians in Dialogue With Men of Other Faiths,"
        International Review of Missions, LIX, 236, pp. 282-391.
        Geneva: W.C.C.
ZWEMER, S.M.
    1911 "The Name Isa," *Muslim World,* July, 1911, pp. 265f. Hartford.

Index to Biblical
and
Quranic References

QURANIC REFERENCES

General Index

259

Dr. James P. Dretke is General Adviser of the Islam-in-Africa Project, headquartered in Nairobi, Kenya. From 1957 to 1977 he worked in Nigeria and Ghana, first with the Evangelical Lutheran Church of Nigeria, later on, with a sister Church in Ghana. From 1969 to 1977 he served as IAP Ghana Area Adviser, with the added responsibility of being IAP West Africa Regional Coordinator from 1975 to 1977.

Mr. Dretke is a graduate of Concordia Seminary, St. Louis. He has done graduate work at the Kennedy School of Missions (Hartford), the University of Ghana, Southern Methodist University, the University of California at Los Angeles, and Fuller Seminary. In addition, he has studied Arabic and French at the Institute of Ghana Languages, and German at the Goethe Institute, Accra.

Dr. Dretke, a native of Manawa, Wisconsin, is married to Barbara Biar of Dallas, Texas. They are the parents of five children.

Books by the William Carey Library

GENERAL

American Missions in Bicentennial Perspective edited by R. Pierce Beaver, $8.95 paper, 448 pp.

The Birth of Missions in America by Charles L. Chaney, $7.95 paper, 352 pp.

Education of Missionaries' Children: The Neglected Dimension of World Mission by D. Bruce Lockerbie, $1.95 paper, 76 pp.

Evangelicals Face the Future edited by Donald E. Hoke, $6.95 paper, 184 pp.

The Holdeman People: The Church in Christ, Mennonite, 1859-1969 by Clarence Hiebert, $17.95 cloth, 688 pp.

Manual for Accepted Missionary Candidates by Marjorie A. Collins, $4.45 paper, 144 pp.

Manual for Missionaries on Furlough by Marjorie A. Collins, $4.45 paper, 160 pp.

The Ministry of Development in Evangelical Perspective edited by Robert L. Hancock, $4.95 paper, 128 pp.

On the Move with the Master: A Daily Devotional Guide on World Mission by Duain W. Vierow, $4.95 paper, 176 pp.

The Radical Nature of Christianity: Church Growth Eyes Look at the Supernatural Mission of the Christian and the Church by Waldo J. Werning (Mandate Press), $5.85 paper, 224 pp.

Social Action Vs. Evangelism: An Essay on the Contemporary Crisis by William J. Richardson, $1.95x paper, 64 pp.

STRATEGY OF MISSION

Church Growth and Christian Mission edited by Donald McGavran, $4.95x paper, 256 pp.

Church Growth and Group Conversion by Donald McGavran et al., $2.45 paper, 128 pp.

Committed Communities: Fresh Streams for World Missions by Charles J. Mellis, $3.95 paper, 160 pp.

The Conciliar-Evangelical Debate: The Crucial Documents, 1964-1976 edited by Donald McGavran, $8.95 paper, 400 pp.

Crucial Dimensions in World Evangelization edited by Arthur F. Glasser et al., $7.95x paper, 512 pp.

Evangelical Missions Tomorrow edited by Wade T. Coggins and Edwin L. Frizen, Jr., $5.95 paper, 208 pp.

Everything You Need to Know to Grow a Messianic Synagogue by Phillip E. Goble, $2.45 paper, 176 pp.

Here's How: Health Education by Extension by Ronald and Edith Seaton, $3.45 paper, 144 pp.

The Indigenous Church and the Missionary by Melvin L. Hodges, $2.95 paper, 108 pp.

Literacy, Bible Reading, and Church Growth Through the Ages by Morris G. Watkins, $4.95 paper, 240 pp.

A Manual for Church Growth Surveys by Ebbie C. Smith, $3.95 paper, 144 pp.

Mission: A Practical Approach to Church-Sponsored Mission Work by Daniel C. Hardin, $4.95x paper, 264 pp.

Readings in Third World Missions edited by Marlin L. Nelson, $6.95x paper, 304 pp.

AREA AND CASE STUDIES

Aspects of Pacific Ethnohistory by Alan R. Tippett, $3.95 paper, 216 pp.

A Century of Growth: The Kachin Baptist Church of Burma by Herman Tegenfeldt, $9.95 cloth, 540 pp.

Christian Mission to Muslims – The Record: Anglican and Reformed Approaches in India and the Near East, 1800–1938 by Lyle L. Vander Werff, $8.95 paper, 384 pp.

The Church in Africa, 1977 edited by Charles R. Taber, $6.95 paper, 224 pp.

Church Growth in Burundi by Donald Hohensee, $4.95 paper, 160 pp.

Church Growth in Japan by Tetsunao Yamamori, $4.95 paper, 184 pp.

The Church in Africa, 1977 edited by Charles R. Taber, $6.95 paper, 224 pp.

Church Planting in Uganda: A Comparative Study by Gailyn Van Rheenen, $4.95 paper, 192 pp.

Circle of Harmony: A Case Study in Popular Japanese Buddhism by Kenneth J. Dale, $4.95 paper, 238 pp.

The Deep-Sea Canoe: The Story of Third World Missionaries in the South Pacific by Alan R. Tippett, $3.45x paper, 144 pp.

Ethnic Realities and the Church: Lessons from India by Donald A. McGavran, $8.95 paper, 272 pp.

The Growth Crisis in the American Church: A Presbyterian Case Study by Foster H. Shannon, $4.95 paper, 176 pp.

The Growth of Japanese Churches in Brazil by John Mizuki, $8.95 paper, 240 pp.

The How and Why of Third World Missions: An Asian Case Study by Marlin L. Nelson, $6.95 paper, 256 pp.

I Will Build My Church: Ten Case Studies of Church Growth in Taiwan edited by Allen J. Swanson, $4.95 paper, 177 pp.

Indonesian Revival: Why Two Million Came to Christ by Avery T. Willis, Jr., $5.95 paper, 288 pp.

Industrialization: Brazil's Catalyst for Church Growth by C.W. Gates, $1.95 paper, 96 pp.

The Navajos are Coming to Jesus by Thomas Dolaghan and David Scates, $4.95 paper, 192 pp.

New Move Forward in Europe: Growth Patterns of German-Speaking Baptists by William L. Wagner, $8.95 paper, 368 pp.

People Movements in the Punjab by Frederick and Margaret Stock, $8.95 paper, 388 pp.

Profile for Victory: New Proposals for Missions in Zambia by Max Ward Randall, $3.95 cloth, 224 pp.

The Protestant Movement in Bolivia by C. Peter Wagner, $3.95 paper, 264 pp.

Protestants in Modern Spain: The Struggle for Religious Pluralism
by Dale G. Vought, $3.45 paper, 168 pp.

The Religious Dimension in Hispanic Los Angeles by Clifton L.
Holland, $9.95 paper, 550 pp.

The Role of the Faith Mission: A Brazilian Case Study by Fred
Edwards, $3.45 paper, 176 pp.

Solomon Islands Christianity: A Study in Growth and Obstruction
by Alan R. Tippett, $5.95x paper, 432 pp.

Taiwan: Mainline Vs. Independent Church Growth by Allen J.
Swanson, $3.95 paper, 300 pp.

Tonga Christianity by Stanford Shewmaker, $3.45 paper, 164 pp.

*Toward Continuous Mission: Strategizing for the Evangelization
of Bolivia* by W. Douglas Smith, Jr., $4.95 paper, 208 pp.

*Treasure Island: Church Growth Among Taiwan's Urban Minnan
Chinese* by Robert J. Bolton, $6.95 paper, 416 pp.

Understanding Latin Americans by Eugene Nida, $3.94 paper,
176 pp.

The Unresponsive: Resistant or Neglected? by David C.E. Liao,
$5.95 paper, 168 pp.

An Urban Strategy for Africa by Timothy Monsma, $6.95 paper,
192 pp.

*Worldview and the Communication of the Gospel: A Nigerian Case
Study* by Marguerite G. Kraft, $7.95 paper, 240 pp.

*A Yankee Reformer in Chile: The Life and Works of David Trum-
bull* by Irven Paul, $3.95 paper, 172 pp.

APPLIED ANTHROPOLOGY

Becoming Bilingual: A Guide to Language Learning by Donald
Larson and William Smalley, $5.95x paper, 426 pp.

Christopaganism or Indigenous Christianity? edited by Tetsunao
Yamamori and Charles R. Taber, $5.95 paper, 242 pp.

*The Church and Cultures: Applied Anthropology for the Religious
Worker* by Louis J. Luzbetak, $5.95x paper, 448 pp.

*Culture and Human Values: Christian Intervention in Anthropo-
logical Perspective* (writings of Jacob Loewen) edited by
William A. Smalley, $5.95x paper, 466 pp.

Customs and Cultures: Anthropology for Christian Missions by
Eugene A. Nida, $3.95 paper, 322 pp.

Manual of Articulatory Phonetics by William A. Smalley, $5.95x
paper, 522 pp.

Message and Mission: The Communication of the Christian Faith
by Eugene A. Nida, $3.95x paper, 254 pp.

Readings in Missionary Anthropology II edited by William A. Smalley, $9.95x paper, 912 pp.

Religion Across Cultures by Eugene A. Nida, $3.95x paper, 128 pp.

Tips on Taping: Language Recording in the Social Sciences by
Wayne and Lonna Dickerson, $4.95x paper, 208 pp.

THEOLOGICAL EDUCATION BY EXTENSION

*The Extension Movement in Theological Education: A Call to the
Renewal of the Ministry* by F. Ross Kinsler, $6.95 paper,
304 pp.

The World Directory of Theological Education by Extension by
Wayne C. Weld, $5.95x paper, 416 pp., *1976 Supplement only,*
$1.95x, 64 pp. booklet
Writing for Theological Education by Extension by Lois McKinney,
$1.45x paper, 64 pp.

REFERENCE

*An American Directory of Schools and Colleges Offering Mission-
ary Courses* edited by Glenn Schwartz, $5.95x paper, 266 pp.
*Church Growth Bulletin, Second Consolidated Volume (Sept. 1969-
July 1975)* edited by Donald McGavran, $7.95x paper, 512 pp.
Evangelical Missions Quarterly, Vols. 7-9, $8.95x cloth, 830 pp.
Evangelical Missions Quarterly, Vols. 10-12, $15.95 cloth, 960 pp.
*The Means of World Evangelization: Missiological Education at the
Fuller School of World Mission* edited by Alvin Martin, $9.95
paper, 544 pp.
Protestantism in Latin America: A Bibliographical Guide edited by
John H. Sinclair, $8.95x paper, 448 pp.
Word Study Concordance and New Testament edited by Ralph and
Roberta Winter, $29.95 cloth, 2-volume set.
The World Directory of Mission-Related Educational Institutions
edited by Ted Ward and Raymond Buker, Sr., $19.95x cloth, 906 pp.

POPULARIZING MISSION

Defeat of the Bird God by C. Peter Wagner, $4.95 paper, 256 pp.
The Night Cometh: Two Wealthy Evangelicals Face the Nation by
Rebecca J. Winter, $2.95 paper, 96 pp.
The Task Before Us (audiovisual) by the Navigators, $29.95,
137 slides.
The 25 Unbelievable Years: 1945-1969 by Ralph D. Winter, $2.95
paper, 128 pp.
*The Word-Carrying Giant: The Growth of the American Bible
Society* by Creighton Lacy, $5.95 paper, 320 pp.

BOOKLETS

The Grounds for a New Thrust in World Mission by Ralph D. Win-
ter, $.75 booklet, 32 pp.
1980 and That Certain Elite by Ralph D. Winter, $.35x booklet, 16 pp.
The New Macedonia: A Revolutionary New Era in Missions Begins
(Lausanne paper and address) by Ralph D. Winter, $.75 book-
let, 32 pp.
Penetrating the Last Frontiers by Ralph D. Winter, $1.00 book-
let, 32 pp.
Seeing the Task Graphically by Ralph D. Winter, $.50 booklet, 16 pp.
The Two Structures of God's Redemptive Mission by Ralph D.
Winter, $.35 booklet, 16 pp.
The World Christian Movement: 1950-1975 by Ralph D. Winter,
$.75 booklet, 32 pp.

HOW TO ORDER

Send orders to William Carey Library, 1705 N. Sierra Bonita
Avenue, Pasadena, California 91104 (USA). Please allow four to
six weeks for delivery in the U.S.